COPÁN: THE RISE AND FALL OF AN ANCIENT MAYA KINGDOM

DAVID WEBSTER

The Pennsylvania State University

ANNCORINNE FRETER

Ohio University

NANCY GONLIN

Bellevue Community College

HARCOURT COLLEGE PUBLISHERS

Fort Worth Philadelphia San Diego New York Orlando Austin San Antonio
Toronto Montreal London Sydney Tokyo

Publisher	Earl McPeek
Executive Editor	Lin Marshall
Developmental Editor	Sarah Davis-Packard
Project Editor	Claudia Gravier
Art Director	David A. Day
Production Manager	Andrea Archer

ISBN: 0-15-505808-8

Library of Congress Catalog Card Number: 99-62187

Copyright © 2000 by Harcourt Brace & Company

Address for Domestic Orders
Harcourt Inc., 6277 Sea Harbor Drive, Orlando, FL 32887-6777
800-782-4479

Address for International Orders
International Customer Service
Harcourt Inc., 6277 Sea Harbor Drive, Orlando, FL 32887-6777
407-345-3800
(fax) 407-345-4060
(e-mail) hbintl@harcourtbrace.com

Address for Editorial Correspondence
Harcourt College Publishers, 301 Commerce Street, Suite 3700,
Fort Worth, TX 76102

Web Site Address
http://www.harcourtcollege.com

Harcourt College Publishers will provide complimentary supplements or supplement packages to those adopters qualified under our adoption policy. Please contact your sales representative to learn how you qualify. If as an adopter or potential user you receive supplements you do not need, please return them to your sales representative or send them to: Attn: Returns Department, Troy Warehouse, 465 South Lincoln Drive, Troy, MO 63379.

Printed in the United States of America

9 0 1 2 3 4 5 6 7 8 751 9 8 7 6 5 4 3 2 1

Harcourt College Publishers

To Gordon R. Willey, Claude F. Baudez, and William T. Sanders, pioneers of a new generation of research at Copán, to the hundreds of skilled Honduran field-workers and staff instrumental in making this research a reality, and to all the Copán scholars yet to come.

ABOUT THE SERIES

These case studies in archaeology are designed to bring students, in beginning and intermediate courses in archaeology, anthropology, history, and related disciplines, insights into the theory, practice, and results of archaeological investigations. They are written by scholars who have had direct experience in archaeological research, whether in the field, laboratory, or library. The authors are also teachers, and in writing their books they have kept the students who will read them foremost in their minds. These books are intended to present a wide range of archaeological topics as case studies in a form and manner that will be more accessible than writings found in articles or books intended for professional audiences, yet at the same time preserve and present the significance of archaeological investigations for all.

ABOUT THE AUTHORS

David Webster is Professor of Anthropology at the Pennsylvania State University, where he has taught since 1972. His general research interests include the cultural ecology and cultural evolution of complex societies, ancient warfare and political economy, settlement and household archaeology, and demographic reconstruction. Between 1980 and 1997 he conducted many seasons of fieldwork at Copán, Honduras, and is currently involved in landscape and settlement archaeology in the Piedras Negras region of northwestern Guatemala.

Nancy Gonlin grew up on the East coast of the USA where her parents took her to numerous historical and natural sights of the region, from which she developed an abiding interest in the past. After completing her undergraduate work in anthropology at Juniata College, she went on to complete her M.A. and Ph.D. at Penn State University. It was here that she had the wonderful opportunity to study the Classic Maya first-hand with her co-authors. Webster, Freter, and Gonlin formed a successful research team and worked together for three field seasons at Copán. Gonlin has also had the opportunity to do archaeological research in the central highlands of Mexico, surveying and testing Formative to Postclassic sites of the region. Gonlin has taught at numerous institutions, including Penn State, Kennesaw State University, and The University of Georgia. She is presently teaching at Bellevue Community College in the state of Washington, amidst the backdrop of the beautiful landscape of the Pacific Northwest.

AnnCorinne Freter got her B.A. from the University of San Diego in 1978, her M.A. from the University of Houston in 1981, and her Ph.D. from the Pennsylvania State University in 1988. She is currently an Associate Professor and assistant dean at Ohio University where she has taught since 1986.

ABOUT THIS CASE STUDY

Classic Maya culture is not the oldest civilization of Ancient America. It was not the most geographically widespread. It was not the most urbanized nor did it field the most powerful armies of its day. Its kings and aristocracy squabbled for prestige and power while they degraded their natural environment. Nevertheless, of all of the cultures of the Pre-Columbian world the Maya have most held the imagination of modern people ever since their gorgeous temples and magnificent art became known to the reading public in the mid-nineteenth century. Excitement about the Maya is even reflected in this series, as it is the only ancient culture represented by more than one Case Study, at present.

Much of the public fascination with the Maya comes from their use of art styles which appeal to modern sensibilities. Chiseled in stone or delicately painted on ceramic vessels, the Maya portrayed themselves and their gods in representational styles which allow the viewer to identify personages interacting with one another. But while we could grasp at an understanding of what was being portrayed, clear knowledge of what was depicted eluded scholars for decades because the glyphic writing system included in the art could not be read. While it frustrated some scholars, this only added to the romanticism of the Maya for the general public.

It is now well known that in the last two decades great advances in the decipherment of Maya writing has pushed these ancients from prehistory into history. We can now read the life histories of monarchs, learn of their successes and failures, of the religious beliefs they held and rituals they performed, and build detailed political histories of the rise and fall of dynasties and kingdoms. This has led to an interesting situation in which there is sometimes a certain amount of tension between "dirt" archaeologists and epigraphers who study glyphs. The situation is not unlike that described by James Deetz for the sometimes testy relations between historians and historical archaeologists in the United States. Each camp thinks that what the other is doing is either redundant or irrelevant to the "true" investigation of the past, or, at least, there is a reluctance on each side to address common issues and questions. The truth is, however, that a richer, more robust interpretation of the past comes from the interplay between different modes of investigation in which each spurs scholars working in the other field to look at their data in new ways.

The authors of this book are engaged in just this kind of interplay. Their research methodology and interests are in the tradition of field archaeology but this work is done in the context of the knowledge of the other kinds of information being produced by a host of scholars in the multi-institution and international research programs which have been carried out at Copán in the last 25 years. Reflecting the tenor of the times, the interpretations offered here on the rise and fall of the Copán polity are not necessarily viewed the same way by other researchers at the site and in the region. The project described in this book nevertheless has been carried out in the great tradition of regional settlement surveys and in the context of subsequent stages of investigation.

Rather than a final word on the topic, this book is contributing to an important, long term conversation not only on the specifics of the rise and fall of Copán but also on how we understand the past. In this sense, in particular, it makes a welcome addition to the Case Studies in Archaeology series. In clear language and ordered presentation, the authors lay out the reasons why they conducted their research the way they did, the information they gathered, and the way they interpreted it. Students will learn much from this work as well as gain a fascinating glimpse into another aspect of that perennial favorite, the ancient Maya.

Jeffrey Quilter
Garrett Park, Maryland

PREFACE

The "products" of archaeology, in the imaginations of students and the public, are typically spectacular finds such as the "Iceman" discovered in the Italian Alps in 1991, or descriptions of sites of particular significance, such as Pompeii, or the great Mesoamerican city of Teotihuacan. Many books deal with archaeology on these levels because accounts of single finds or sites are easy to package in brief, compelling ways. Some of the other titles in the Case Studies in Archaeology Series, such as Payson Sheets's book on Ceren, deal very effectively with this kind of subject.

Far less common are accessible books or texts that explore another sort of archaeological endeavor—projects that attempt to reconstruct and evaluate whole sociopolitical systems and regional culture histories, and in some sense to explain how ancient social systems developed and declined through time. Research programs of this kind require years of varied field and laboratory efforts by many independent scholars and specialists and have become extremely important since the 1950s. They represent a whole new dimension of archaeological research that has contributed immensely to our understanding of the past. Unfortunately, such projects remain comparatively little-known in detail to nonprofessionals, in part because they are more challenging to write about and to publish in accessible ways.

We believe that the Case Studies in Archaeology series provides an ideal opportunity for such a regional overview. In this volume we describe a long tradition of archaeological research at Copán, Honduras, and review what we have learned from it. Copán is a world-famous Classic Maya center in the highlands of western Honduras whose great temples, palaces, carved monuments and inscriptions have been investigated since the 1830s. Since 1975 a series of projects has focused not only on the royal center of Copán itself, but on reconstructing the whole Copán kingdom. One goal of these projects has been to develop a detailed culture history of the region from the time of the earliest farmers through the heyday of the kingdom between about A.D. 400 and 800, and its eventual collapse. More generally, the issues are the adaptation of an ancient Maya population to a particular tropical environment, and how we explain the changes we detect in the archaeological record. Thousands of people now visit Copán each year, where they view reconstructed buildings, monuments, and museum displays. These only tell part of the story, however, and here we try to fill in many of the details and present information on many still unresolved issues.

Collectively, these interrelated Copán projects were carried out at a very crucial time in the history of Maya archaeology. Earlier pioneering efforts of similar scale were carried out elsewhere, such as the University of Pennsylvania research at Tikal, Guatemala. By the 1970s and 1980s not only were more powerful archaeological methods and techniques available, but great break-throughs had been made in understanding Classic Maya inscriptions and iconography. Together with unprecedented levels of funding, these developments produced at Copán the most ambitious and varied set of long-term projects ever carried out in the Maya Lowlands.

All of the authors are veterans of Copán field and laboratory research. In this volume we balance the facts and interpretations of archaeology with detailed considerations of the methods used to reconstruct what happened at Copán. Our intent is to make clear what we have found out about Copán, but also how research has been designed to answer specific questions. Methods considered include excavations, large-scale regional settlement surveys, paleoenvironmental and ecological analyses, innovative chronological assessments, skeletal analysis, experimental archaeology, and interpretations from art and inscriptions. This is a lot to package in a single overview volume, but we believe the following chapters provide a comprehensive overview of a long tradition of research and what it tells us about the rise and fall of a major Maya kingdom.

While any number of projects and cultures could provide the focus of a volume such as this, Copán has several distinct advantages. The Classic Maya are arguably the most widely-known and high-profile of the great Precolumbian cultures of the New World. Most people know something about them and want to know more. Because the Maya had writing and calendars, actual people and dated events are part of the story. More specifically, Copán is a world-famous site, the destination of thousands of tourists each year, and featured in many popular films and books—most recently the widely broadcast television series *Out of the Past* produced by the Annenberg CPB Project (Webster was co-director of this series). Viewers of this out of the past can see many of the excavations and laboratory studies we review in the following chapters actually being carried out. Both the Classic Maya in general and Copán in particular are thus already in the public eye and have a natural constituency among the public.

The Copán polity has enjoyed the longest history of research of any major Maya kingdom. Some years ago Gordon Willey remarked that Copán has assumed the traditional importance of Tikal as a window into the Maya past because of the richness and variety of research conducted there. Much information on Copán has been available in scholarly and popular publications, but the last book-length presentation that summarizes research both from the perspective of the center of Copán (i.e., the royal household and the political/ritual core of the kingdom) and that of the larger region (i.e., the whole polity) is almost a decade old (Fash, 1991). Each of the authors has extensive research experience at Copán and is well-prepared to contribute to a new synthesis.

Our book, as already noted, emphasizes two main themes: 1) the research projects and methods that the authors, along with many other colleagues, have used to reconstruct the growth and decline of a major Maya polity, and 2) the specific reconstructed events and processes that derive from this research. More specifically, the themes are the reconstruction of Copán's political, agricultural, and demographic histories, the means by which we comprehend these, the ways they relate to one another, and the evolutionary lessons we derive from them. Our aim is to tell a story both about what we know, and why we think we know it.

Much of the published synthetic material on Copán deals specifically with the royal center itself—the temples, monuments, and palaces of the Copán rulers and their families and retainers. Excavations over the last decade by William Fash, Barbara Fash, Robert Sharer, Ricardo Agurcia, E. Wyllys Andrews V, and many others have produced the best available architectural sequence for a royal Maya center. Epigraphers and iconographers such as David Stuart, Linda Schele, and Karl Taube have enlightened us about the associated inscriptions and art. While highly detailed and innovative, such presentations continue a long re-search tradition that heavily emphasizes Maya centers. Our own interests and re-search experience, by contrast, concentrate much more heavily on regional synthesis, and this is our main thrust. The archaeology and history of the Copán Main Group is reviewed, but we consider it within a broader regional perspective that is heavily focused on settlement survey, demographic reconstructions, re-constructions of diet and agriculture, household archaeology, domestic and polit-ical economy, and sub-royal elites. Our book thus nicely complements William Fash's *Scribes, Warriors, and Kings* (Thames and Hudson 1991), which mainly concerns the royal center and dynastic history.

Research at Copán is ongoing, and much of the information we present here is relatively new, some of it in fact never published before. Much of it is also highly innovative and unique, and hopefully of particular interest not only to Mayanists and Mesoamerican archaeologists, but also anyone interested in ar-chaeological research design. Our presentation of both methods, data, and inter-pretation obviously emphasizes our own work and conclusions, but we also acknowledge and review the contributions of others, as well as interpretations that are different from our own. This is important because of the many indepen-dent projects that are working, or have worked, to reconstruct this great ancient kingdom of the Classic Maya and explain its ultimate demise.

Generous support from many institutions has contributed to the work of the authors and their colleagues since 1980. These include the Instituto Hondureño de Antropología e Historia, the National Science Foundation, the National En-dowment for the Humanities, the Wenner-Gren Foundation, the Foundation for the Advancement of Mesoamerican Studies Inc., the Annenberg/CPB Project, the Pennsylvania State University, Ohio University, the National Oceanic and Atmospheric Administration, and Earthwatch.

Essential to the field and laboratory research carried out during our own PAC II and related projects were the efforts of many people, including Elliot Abrams, Eloisa Aguilar, Ricardo Agurcia, Charles Cheek, Michael Davis, Melissa Diamanti, Susan Evans, William Fash, Barbara Fash, Valerie Gates, An-drea Gerstle, Joseph Guilano, James Hatch, Julia Hendon, Amy Kovak, John Mal-lory III, Patricia Miller, Guillermo Murcia, Carson Murdy, Richard Paine, David Reed, Berthold Riese, David Rue, John Seldomridge, James Sheey, Mary Spink, Saul Murillo, Phillip Starr, Glenn Storey, Rebecca Storey, Thomas Sussenbach, Alfred Traverse, Peter van Rossum, Rene Viel, Stephen Whittington, Randolph

Widmer, John Wingard, Scott Zeleznik, and the late Daniel Wolfman. Many more individuals of course contributed to non-Penn State projects.

Although our conclusions are our own, we have benefited greatly from suggestions, information, and sometimes criticism and animated debate provided by all of the above, and in addition from E. Wyllys Andrews V, Wendy Ashmore, Marilyn Beaudry-Corbett, Michael Glascock, Peter Gould, Elizabeth Graham, Kenneth Hirth, Joseph Michels, Hector Neff, David Pendergast, Gary Peterson, Robert Sharer, Don Rice, Prudence Rice, Linda Schele, Payson Sheets, David Stuart, and Stephen Houston.

The combined skills and artistic talents of the Ohio University Graphics and Media Department have graced this book with many line drawings prepared by Peggy Sattler and Sam Girton, and several photographs were processed and enhanced by Lars Lutton.

Jeffery Quilter, general editor of the Case Studies series, motivated us to begin our Copán book. The editorial staff at Harcourt College Publishers greatly facilitated the production of the book and made the process as painless as possible, especially Lin Marshall, executive editor; Sarah Davis-Packard, developmental editor; Claudia Gravier, project editor; Andrea Archer, production manager; and David A. Day, art director.

As always, the authors bear sole responsibility for all errors of fact, logic, and/or interpretation.

DAVID WEBSTER
ANNCORINNE FRETER
NANCY GONLIN

CONTENTS

CHAPTER I

Copán: A Classic Maya Polity and Its Environment

INTRODUCTION

Shortly after A.D. 400, a dynasty of Maya kings established itself in a small, verdant, river valley in the tropical highlands of what is now western Honduras. Over the next four centuries 16 successive rulers carved out a regional polity of several hundred square kilometers, populated by thousands of subjects, from great lords to common farmers. Royal power and authority emanated from an impressive regal-ritual center where kings built elaborate palaces, temples, and ball courts, and were themselves buried. Art and hieroglyphic inscriptions on buildings, altars, and stelae celebrated royal rituals, ancestors, and important events in the lives of kings and nobles.

Archaeologists call this capital Copán, and the larger polity the Copán kingdom. The ancient name used by the Classic Maya was apparently written several different ways, and is rendered phonetically *Xukpi* by some epigraphers (Schele & Mathews, 1998, pp. 133, 345). Although its exact meaning is unclear, *Xukpi* probably refers to the location of Copán on the southeastern periphery of the Maya Lowlands of Mesoamerica. Another possible ancient name for Copán was *Ox Witik* (Stuart, 1992, p. 171). Throughout this book we will simply use the conventional label Copán.

The kingdom prospered for 400 years, but by the end of the 8th century the last Copán rulers were beset by severe political and economic crises. Twenty years later royal construction projects stopped and no more inscriptions were made, marking the abrupt collapse of the dynasty. A handful of noble families survived for a century or two longer, but the sustaining population declined gradually after about A.D. 850. A few farmers continued to cultivate the landscape at least until about A.D. 1400, but after that time the valley seems to have been deserted.

Copán was one of many great regional polities in the Maya Lowlands, an enormous region of about 250,000 sq km in southern Mexico and northern Central America (Figure 1-1). During the Classic Period (A.D. 250–900) scores of other Maya kingdoms flourished here, all participants in the flowering of what we call Classic Maya civilization. Archaeological research shows that many of them had histories similar to Copán's, but nowhere else in the Maya Lowlands, and in fact for few ancient societies anywhere in the world,

FIGURE 1-1   MAP OF THE MAYA REGION OF MESOAMERICA SHOWING COPÁN AND OTHER SITES MENTIONED IN THE TEXT.

can we piece together such a detailed and dramatic story of the rise and fall of an ancient kingdom.

What we know about Copán, and how we have come to know it, are the themes of this book. Part of the story is that archaeologists have been steadily working at Copán since the 1880s, amassing a huge amount of evidence. More important, since the mid-1970s, multiple archaeological projects have carried out many different kinds of innovative research at Copán, both at the royal capital itself and in its surrounding territory. Each project has only investigated a piece of the ancient puzzle (see Fash 1991 and Webster 1999 for recent overviews). Our goal in this book is to provide the "big picture" of Copán's cultural and political history, the evolution and decline of the polity, and how its population adapted, or failed to adapt, to the distinctive tropical environment of the region. We must begin, however, where archaeological work started more than a century ago—with the regal-ritual center of Copán itself.

THE COPÁN MAIN GROUP
AND THE URBAN CORE

As Maya centers go, Copán is rather small compared to other Classic period giants such as Tikal, Calakmul, or Caracol, each of which are several sq km in area. Copán's central temples, courtyards, and palaces, collectively comprising the Main Group, today extend over about 12 ha, or 0.12 sq km (Figure 1-2). Earthquakes and river erosion long ago destroyed eastern sections of the site, creating the celebrated Corte, a vast vertical slice through centuries of superimposed architecture (Sharer, Traxler & Miller, 1991). Prior to this damage the Main Group was larger than it is today—probably around 15–20 ha.

What first attracted archaeologists to the Main Group was not its scale, however, but rather the wealth of its sculpture and inscriptions. Stelae depicting royal personages in ritual garb, often paired with carved altars, are concentrated in the vast courtyards that dominate the northern sections of the site (Figure 1-3 & Plate 1-1). These open spaces are big enough to have accommodated the whole population of the kingdom. Here too are the great ball court, one of Copán's oldest buildings, and the Temple of the Hieroglyphic Stairway (Structure 26), which displays the longest known Classic Maya text (Fash et al., 1992). Its summit temple was dedicated to the founder of the dynasty, and inscriptions and statues on the west-facing stairway itself celebrated his successors, particularly in their roles as warriors. Deep within it are elaborate burials of kings and nobles.

The imposing Structure 11, with a summit temple facing both north and south, unites the northern courtyards with a more private, elevated zone of architecture called the Acropolis (G. Stuart, 1997). This immense mass of architecture contains well over 200,000 cu m of construction fill. Acropolis buildings are arranged around the East and West Courts. On the north side of the East Court is the temple/residence Structure 22, built to metaphorically represent a sacred mountain and with façade sculpture that symbolizes the Maya cosmos. Immediately to the west is an apparent *Popol Nah,* or council house, where kings met with other notables (Stomper, 1996). Beneath Temple 18, located on the south side of the court, is a huge vaulted burial chamber, unfortunately looted long ago, that was probably constructed as the tomb of the last ruler.

The West Court is dominated by Temple 16, its sculptural themes redolent of war, death, and sacrifice. Deep within it is a long sequence of beautifully preserved earlier buildings that commemorate the first king. Burials associated with the first constructions date back to the 5th century, and may be those of the dynastic founder and his queen (G. Stuart, 1997). At the foot of Structure 16's

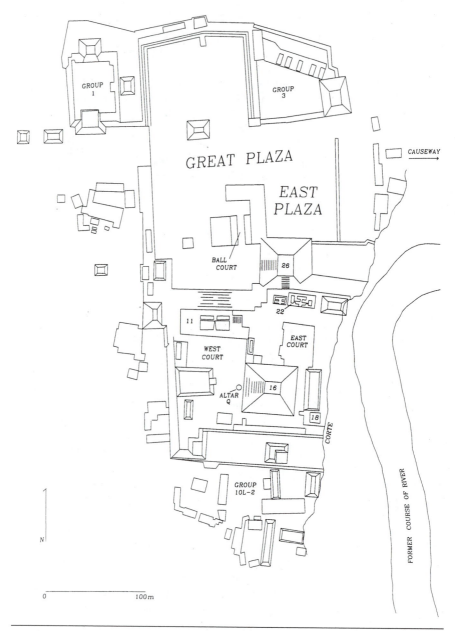

FIGURE 1-2   PLAN OF THE COPÁN MAIN GROUP AND THE ROYAL COMPOUND 10L-2; NUMBERS INDICATE BUILDINGS DISCUSSED IN TEXT.

FIGURE 1-3   ALTAR AND STELA IN COPÁN'S GREAT PLAZA, AS SHOWN IN A
LITHOGRAPH MADE FROM AN 1839 DRAWING BY FREDERICK CATHERWOOD.

PLATE 1-1   TWO STELAE IN THE GREAT PLAZA DEPICTING COPÁN'S 13TH RULER, 18 RABBIT.

stairway is Altar Q (Plate 1-2). Long thought to represent a "congress of astronomers," we now know that this monument was commissioned by the 16th and last king, *Yax Pasah,* to metaphorically affirm his dynastic connections to fifteen preceding sovereigns, who are shown and named in order around its sides.

Attached to the southern section of the Acropolis is the imposing Group 10L-2, recently excavated by E. Wyllys Andrews V of Tulane University and his students (Andrews & Fash, 1992). After about A.D. 600 it apparently functioned as the royal residential enclave where rulers, their close relatives, and retainers, all actually lived most of the time.

The huge architectural complexes visible today in the Main Group were mostly built after A.D. 700 or 750. They represent only the last construction phases of a Maya royal center that gradually assumed its final form over more than 400 years. The first buildings of the Main Group, which date to the 5th

PLATE I-2   ALTAR Q IS LOCATED AT THE FOOT OF THE WEST STAIRCASE OF STRUCTURE 16. THE TWO CENTRAL FIGURES ON ITS WEST FACE SHOW COPÁN'S DYNASTIC FOUNDER (LEFT) PRESENTING A BATON OR SCEPTER TO THE 16TH AND LAST KING (RIGHT), WHO COMMISSIONED THE CARVING OF THIS MONUMENT.

century or perhaps even earlier, were simply constructed of adobe and river cobbles rather than the fine cut stone of later times. A vast system of tunnels, now totaling more than 2.4 km in length, has revealed many details of architectural stratigraphy, as well as buried monuments, that can be linked to the dynastic and population history of the kingdom.

Extending to the northeast and southwest of the Main Group are two concentrations of dense settlement called the El Bosque and Las Sepulturas enclaves, the latter linked by a raised causeway to the royal establishment (Figure 1-4). Along with the Main Group itself, these two enclaves, which have over 1000 mapped structures, form the Copán *urban core*. Before parts of Las Sepulturas were washed away by the river or buried under eroded soil from the hills, there were probably 1,400–1,800 buildings in an area of about 1 sq km—a density of residential structures higher than that found at any other Classic Maya center. Nor were these all small buildings. Many of them represent the remains of multi-courtyard elite households, with fine cut-stone buildings, some as much as 10 m in height, and heavily embellished with sculpture. Many great nobles of the kingdom clearly chose to live in the urban core within 800 m of the Main Group. Part of their motivation to do so was its proximity to good alluvial soils, but they also desired to be near the royal court, the political heart of the kingdom. Some of these elite compounds were built as late as the 8th century, while others had been at least intermittently occupied for well over 1,000 years.

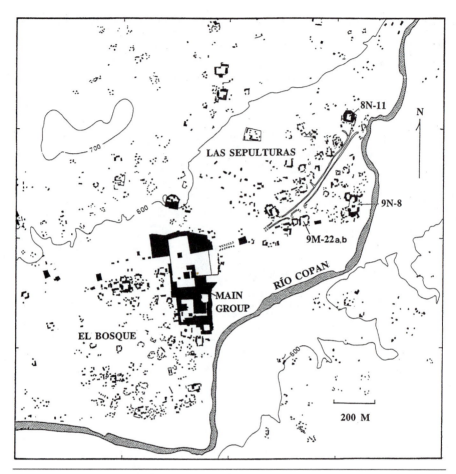

FIGURE 1-4   PLAN OF COPÁN'S URBAN CORE SHOWING THE EL BOSQUE AND LAS SEPULTURAS URBAN ENCLAVES FLANKING THE MAIN GROUP, AND LOCATIONS OF SEVERAL EXCAVATED ELITE RESIDENCES.

Buildings and monuments in the Main Group, the urban core, and the out-lying countryside had not only political, religious, and residential functions, but were also sometimes placed to commemorate various astronomical events of sig-nificance to the Classic Maya (e.g., see Aveni 1977, Vogrin 1979, and Bricker & Bricker 1999).

SETTLEMENT AND HOUSEHOLD ARCHAEOLOGY

Thousands of people now visit the Copán Main Group and the urban core each year, marveling at the reconstructed temples and palaces. Such fascination with

Maya central places, however, is hardly new. In the early 16th century, Spanish explorers were astonished by the first Maya towns they sighted along the east coast of Yucatán, likening them to Cairo and Seville, great cities they had visited in the Old World. A little later Diego de Landa, the first Bishop of Yucatán, remarked that no other part of the New World boasted such a wealth of large architecture. Landa correctly assumed that the great abandoned ruins so conspicuous on the landscape were built by the ancestors of the living Maya he knew.

For over a century, archaeologists have traditionally devoted most of their efforts to investigating the architecture, monuments, and tombs at major centers of the kind that so impressed Landa—including Copán. Such center-oriented research was attractive because sponsors of field projects placed a high priority on acquiring objects of aesthetic value for museums and on reconstructing impressive temples and palaces to attract tourists and glorify the ancient cultures of the Maya world. From a strictly archaeological perspective, work in monumental site cores was logistically simple, and provided the complex architectural stratigraphy useful in determining chronological changes. Art and inscriptions were heavily concentrated around major architectural complexes, and eventually yielded symbolic information concerning not only chronology, but the identities, actions and world views of kings and other Maya elite people.

Research focused on Maya central places, including Copán, remains today an essential and productive strategy, particularly because iconographers and epigraphers can now interpret art and hieroglyphic inscriptions in considerable detail. These, in turn, are keys to how the Maya thought about the world and to the central sociopolitical institutions of Maya societies, which, due to these new data, are now understood in more sophisticated ways than ever before.

As long ago as the 1940s, however, the limitations of center-oriented research, and our conceptions of the Classic Maya derived from it, were becoming evident, in part because of what the centers themselves began to yield. Murals found at Bonampak depicting warriors and battles undermined the cherished idea that the Classic Maya were a uniquely peaceful civilization. Royal burials unearthed at centers such as Palenque showed that Maya centers were ruled by kings, rather than priestly intellectuals, as many had earlier believed. Breakthroughs in understanding Maya hieroglyphs confirmed the existence of royal dynasties. Pioneering investigations of the peripheries of large centers revealed many more household remains, and by inference more people, than expected.

All these discoveries caused Mayanists to ask new questions. What was the territorial extent of ancient Maya polities? How were they organized politically and socially? How did kingdoms interact with each other? How many people supported places like Copán, where did they live, and how did they wrest a living from their tropical environments? How did rulers and nobles relate to the commoners who built the palaces and temples? Despite the efforts of a few scholars to broaden research perspectives, little was known that could help resolve these issues. In the 1960s, accordingly, archaeologists began to retool their research with just such questions in mind. At the heart of these efforts were *regional settlement archaeology* and *household archaeology*.

Settlement Archaeology

Settlement archaeology seeks to document as much ancient human activity as possible over large regions, not just at impressive central places. Chief among the tools of settlement archaeology is surface survey, in which teams of archaeologists, usually aided by maps, aerial photographs, or other remote sensing images and devices, walk systematically across a landscape and search for any surviving archaeological traces of where people lived, hunted, farmed, buried their dead, carried out rituals, or extracted resources. Sites encountered are mapped and collections of surface artifacts are recovered if possible. Surveys are site-oriented, but they usually also include the collection of information about soils, vegetation, water sources, and other features of site locales. Although many ancient sites have been destroyed, buried, or are otherwise not visible, surface surveys yield quick and spatially extensive insights about how people distributed themselves on ancient landscapes, how they used resources, and how they related to one another because many sites have survived and can be identified from surface remains. A useful overview of settlement research in Mesoamerica can be found in Nichols (1996).

Not all of the sites found on settlement survey are of course contemporary with each other, nor is it always obvious what kinds of activities occurred at them just from their surface traces. For these reasons, surveys are often followed up by test excavations to acquire artifacts that are both chronologically sensitive and that reveal site functions. This kind of work is especially important in regions where vegetation inhibits the collection of artifact samples from the surface. When large numbers of roughly contemporary sites and their functions can be determined, whole settlement systems may be analyzed to reconstruct both how people lived at particular times, and what kinds of changes occurred through time. Most important, archaeologists can reconstruct ancient demographic and land-use histories.

An emerging complementary research approach, *landscape archaeology,* investigates environmental features not tied directly to archaeological sites. The intent is to describe and evaluate environmental factors of significance to ancient people, to reconstruct how ancient environments differed from modern ones, and to resolve issues of how people interacted with specific parts of the landscape. Whole landscapes are often examined by geologists, botanists, hydrologists and other specialists working in tandem with archaeologists. Incorporation of ethnographic surveys is also desirable where possible, because the way modern people use landscapes provides clues about ancient behavior.

Landscapes, of course, had ideological and ritual as well as material significance. Mesoamerican peoples in a sense envisioned landscapes as living, divine bodies, and features such as mountains, streams, springs, caves, and trees could hold great religious or spiritual importance. Although not an explicit part of Copán research, we will see later that such ideological concerns have implications for the collapse of the Copán polity.

Archaeologists today often routinely incorporate the capabilities of Geographic Positioning Systems (GPS) into their settlement or landscape research.

Such technology greatly facilitates the precise location of sites or landscape features, especially where conventional mapping is rendered difficult by vegetation, topography, or the sheer scale of the region being investigated. In addition, GPS spatial information, along with much other relevant data, can easily be inserted into a Geographical Information System (GIS). Such computer based systems have the capability to display and interpolate both spatial and non-spatial information in sophisticated ways, but more important can be used as analytical tools to explore many dimensions of complex data sets and generate new predictive models. GIS and GPS technologies were not commonly available when the basic settlement research central to our concerns was done at Copán between 1975 and 1984. Ours is thus probably one of the last "old-fashioned" settlement projects in this respect, although we hope to adapt many of the Copán data to GIS use in the future.

Household Archaeology

The archaeological sites most often encountered when doing regional surface surveys are (generally) the remains of human settlements. In the Maya Lowlands, such sites are usually the remains of households—residential places where people lived together and cooperated with one another to achieve a variety of essential goals, including the production, sharing, and consumption of resources, reproduction, enculturation of children, and maintainance of effective relationships with their neighbors and the outside world. As the basic institutional building blocks of all societies, households offer extremely rich insights into ancient behavior of all kinds. Ethnographic accounts of traditional Chorti Maya living in the vicinity of Copán provide useful models for reconstructing ancient households (Wisdom, 1940).

In many parts of the world, unfortunately, surface surveys cannot recover remains of individual households. For example, in the Basin of Mexico, far to the northwest of the Maya Lowlands, surveys can often identify only large surface scatters of artifacts that mark the remains of whole communities composed of eroded adobe (mud) buildings. Extensive excavation is required to reveal the detailed household structure of such settlements. Among the Classic Maya, by contrast, people tended to live in dispersed, or at least reasonably discrete, clusters of buildings that had basal platforms, and sometimes superstructures, of durable stone and earth. Although finding such sites on landscapes densely overgrown with tropical vegetation is often a real challenge, Maya archaeologists routinely document the distribution and character of ancient residences from surface remains. Subsequent test excavations and horizontal stripping can confirm the residential functions of such sites, reveal the variety of domestic arrangements, and document histories of occupation.

Household research stimulates and provides necessary data for other specialized ancillary studies. For example, the Maya habitually buried their dead in and around their residences. Analysis of skeletal material from household excavations can provide important paleodemographic and paleopathological inferences, and bone chemistry can tell us much about ancient diets. Similarly, examination of organic remains from soil samples recovered in and around residential structures allows reconstruction of the range of wild and domestic plant resources used by the Maya. Models of construction costs for excavated household structures help us to understand differences in wealth and status, as well as the scale of labor demands imposed by the political economy. We shall later review the results and implications of several ancillary studies of this kind.

Household archaeology has become a powerful tool at Copán and throughout the Maya Lowlands. In egalitarian societies households tend to resemble one another. There were striking differences in social rank and wealth in ancient Maya communities, however, and one measure of such differentiation is variation in household arrangements. In fact, it is useful to think of ancient Maya polities as hierarchies of households, from the palaces of kings to the small, dispersed homes of common, rural farmers. Variation among households can thus tell us much about the basic social units that lived and worked together in particular places. Just as important, many things that archaeologists most want to know about, including kingship, the political authority of lesser nobles, rituals, specialized economic activity, trade and exchange, and production of subsistence goods, all are strongly tethered to households in one way or another. In short, Maya households served not only the interests of their occupants, but also much wider functions that in other societies may be spatially separated from household locales. Epigraphic and iconographic evidence increasingly suggests that such house-centered perspectives are not just imposed by archaeological observers, but were part of the world-view of the Classic Maya themselves. House metaphors and symbols are associated with buildings of all kinds, including the grandest temples (Houston, 1998).

Since 1975 archaeologists from many institutions have carried out regional settlement surveys, test-pitting, and extensive excavations over much of the Copán Valley. How this research has been structured, and the interpretations derived from it, are the main concerns of this book. We particularly emphasize the methods and results of settlement and household archaeology done by Pennsylvania State University archaeologists, including all of the authors, since 1980. Such research at Copán is very much an ongoing process, however, and our story will by no means be the last word on the ancient Copán kingdom.

LANDSCAPE, ENVIRONMENT, AND AGRICULTURE

The historical demographer Massimo Livi-Bacci recently imagined an ideal set of circumstances for examining the long-term, adaptive relationships between people and their agricultural resources:

> Consider an agricultural population isolated in a deep valley. The difference between births and deaths results in slow growth, so that the population doubles every two centuries. Initially the more fertile, easily irrigated, and accessible lands are cultivated—those in the plain along the river. As population grows, and so the need for food, all the best land will be used, until it becomes necessary to cultivate more distant plots on the slopes of the valley, difficult to irrigate and less fertile than the others. Continued growth will require the planting of still less productive lands,

higher up the sides of the valley and more exposed to erosion. When all the land has been used up, further increase of production can still be obtained by more intensive cultivation, but these gains too are limited, as the point will eventually be reached when additional inputs of labor will no longer effectively increase production. In this way demographic growth in a fixed environment (and, it must be added, given a fixed level of technology) leads to the cultivation of progressively less fertile lands with ever greater inputs of labor, while returns per unit of land or labor eventually diminish (Livi-Bacci, 1997, pp. 80–81).

As we shall see in this section, Livi-Bacci might well have been describing Copán. From the archaeological perspective, landscapes are both settings for ancient human activity and artifacts in their own right, in the sense that they were altered by the ancient people who lived on and utilized them. Ancient human populations and their environments were both dynamic, and a major task of regional research is to determine how each affected the other. To accomplish this, archaeologists must reconstruct what past environments were like. The starting point is obviously the modern environment, and we are fortunate that geographers, geologists, botanists, and other scientists associated with various archaeological projects have investigated Copán's features, and how it was used, in considerable detail (Olson, 1975; I. Baudez, 1983; Turner et al., 1983; Wingard, 1992, 1996). In this section the Copán regional environment as it exists today is described, in part based on their investigations. Long ago, however, some of its ancient features were quite different, as we shall see in due course.

PLATE 1-3   VIEW OF THE COPÁN POCKET LOOKING WEST. THE MAIN GROUP IS IN THE DARK BAND OF VEGETATION IN THE CENTER OF THE PHOTO, AND THE MOUNTAINS ON THE FAR HORIZON ARE IN GUATEMALA.

The Copán region is transitional in elevation and topography between the Maya Lowlands and the highlands of Guatemala and El Salvador. If one were to fly over the Honduran part of the Copán Valley today, the general impression would be of a few small islands of flat land in a vast sea of rugged mountains. These little islands are strung out along the Río Copán, which has its headwaters about 30 km to the northeast of the Main Group (Figure 1-5). In five places the floor of the river valley widens out to form areas of deep alluvial soil, locally called *bolsas,* or pockets. Encroaching mountains and foothills elsewhere severely constrict the width of the valley, sometimes to no more than a few hundred meters.

The Copán pocket is about 12.5 km long and up to 4 km wide. A cross-section of it would reveal several closely juxtaposed ecological zones defined by soil and slope (Figure 1-6). On the floor of the valley are the bottomlands, composed either of active alluvium or older, higher terraces. These together are called *vega* lands, and form the prime agricultural soils. Immediately adjacent to the *vega* are gently sloping piedmont zones and low foothills. Behind the piedmont rises the much higher, steep, mountainouous country, composed of locally variable bedrock, that dominates the Copán drainage. This pattern is duplicated on a smaller scale in the other four pockets and in places along the major tributary streams, but always in locally distinct ways. In many places

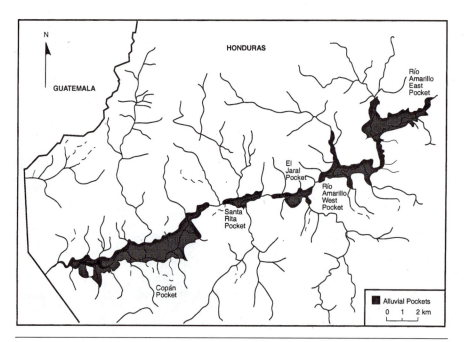

FIGURE 1-5   MAP OF THE COPÁN DRAINAGE IN HONDURAS, SHOWING THE LOCATION OF THE LARGEST ALLUVIAL POCKETS ALONG THE MAIN STREAM. THE MAIN GROUP LIES IN THE CENTER OF THE COPÁN POCKET.

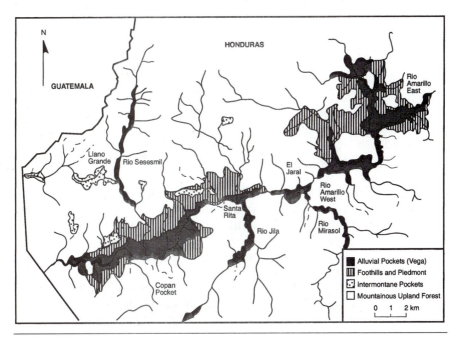

FIGURE I-6   MAJOR TOPOGRAPHIC ZONES OF THE COPÁN VALLEY.

there is no appreciable *vega* land, and foothills rise abruptly from the valley floors. In some places there are broad intermontane basins. Altitude and slope partly determine temperature and rainfall, and it is useful to think of the Copán Valley as a "patchy" environment in terms of the distribution and variable extent of those features most important to humans.

The Copán pocket has by far the largest expanse of bottom land—about 1,200 ha of active alluvium and slightly higher, older alluvial terraces. Here, about 12 km upstream from what is now the Guatemalan border, the ancient kings established the Main Group. While the Copán pocket floor is about 600 m above sea level (asl), adjacent peaks rise to nearly 1,400 m asl. The other alluvial pockets are smaller, and otherwise less agriculturally attractive. The Río Amarillo valley floor, for example, is extensive, but is poorly drained and has much sandy soil. Most important, alluvial soils everywhere are very limited in contrast to the uplands. Lumped together, all the pockets combined have only about 2,500 ha of level bottom land that was preferred by farmers and that thus forms the agricultural core of the polity. Most people today live on these alluvial pockets or on the sloping piedmont zone or foothills adjacent to them, as did the ancient inhabitants of the valley.

The Río Copán originates in the Sierra Gallinero divide about 36 km northeast of the Guatemalan border. Because the gradient of the river is so steep (falling from about 1,100 m asl at its headwaters to 550 m asl at the border) the river is not navigable, but its main and tributary valleys nevertheless form major routes of communication. The main stream flows southwest into Guatemala, where it is known as the Río Camotán, eventually joining the much larger Río Motagua that continues northeast into the Gulf of Honduras. The upper Motagua Valley in turn provides a route to the southwest into the Guatemalan highlands.

Along the major northern tributary, the Río Sesesmil, lie other small alluvial pockets. This stream leads over a high pass directly to the lower Motagua Valley, and is the most direct route to southern Belize and the Petén heartland of Classic Maya civilization. Quiriguá, the nearest major Classic Maya center, is about 50 km north of Copán (though much farther by foot) and is reached via the Sesesmil Valley. In its upstream direction the Río Copán provides access to the Chamelecón Valley to the east, and ultimately to the major drainages of central Honduras.

The main modern towns in the Honduran segment of the Copán Valley are located where major tributaries flow into the Río Copán—Copán Ruinas at the mouth of the Río Sesesmil, and Santa Rita at the mouth of the Río Jila. Both settlements have developed on, and unfortuately destroyed, impressive ancient archaeological sites. The other two major tributaries are the Río Mirasol in El Jaral, and the Río Blanco in Río Amarillo.

That section of the Copán drainage in Honduran territory undoubtedly constituted the core of the ancient polity, and it is important to emphasize just how small this region is. Any adult in good condition could walk from the Copán Main Group to the most distant part of the Río Amarillo East pocket in a day. A day and a half would certainly suffice to walk up the entire Sesesmil drainage. Most of the population, as we shall see later in Chapter 11, lived within a two to three hour walk of the royal establishment. Both geographically and socially, the core kingdom was very concentrated.

Although there were no other large Maya centers closer than a three to four day walk, Copán was effectively linked by its rivers to the Maya world to the west and northwest, and the non-Maya peoples to the east and southeast. Despite its overtly Lowland Maya traditions of architecture, art, and epigraphy, Copán had strong cultural, economic, and political affinities with the populations of central Honduras and the Maya highlands of Guatemala and El Salvador, most clearly reflected in its ceramic traditions, which resemble those of the latter regions more than the Maya Lowlands proper.

Like the Maya Lowlands in general, the Copán region has a strong wet season/dry season climate (tropical wet-dry, or Aw, in the Köppen climatic classification). Most rain falls between mid-May and January, and the driest month has less than 60 mm. Rainfall is heaviest in the upper sections of the valley and at the highest elevations, where about 2,000 mm fall annually. Only about 1,000 mm fall at the Guatemalan border, and almost desert-like conditions prevail in the Motagua Valley.

Average monthly temperature is 18°C, so despite its upland setting the Copán region is well suited to cultivation of traditional Lowland Maya subsistence staples such as maize and beans, as well as commercial crops such as tobacco and cacao. Many people in the valley today still practice extensive swidden cultivation in the uplands, using only hand tools. This practice was much more widespread a generation or two ago when population density was lower. Double cropping based on rainfall is possible at high elevations and in the uppermost reaches of the valley, although winter or dry season crops are frequently lost. Irrigation is necessary during the dry season to cultivate the valley floor. Since many small tributaries of the Río Copán dry up after the rainy season, gravity irrigation is restricted to those sections of bottom land near the mouths of permanent streams. Of these, the most important is the Sesesmil, which is used to irrigate much of the western Copán pocket near both the Main Group and the modern town of Copán Ruinas. Ownership of alluvial land, and especially irrigable fields, is concentrated in the hands of a few families today. This might also have been the Classic Maya pattern, but there is no direct evidence for such an inference.

Throughout the Maya Lowlands proper, soils almost everywhere develop on limestone bedrock of fairly recent geological origin. Although such soils are thin, they are often highly fertile. Upland hills and ridges were preferred for cultivation. Low-lying land tends to be poorly drained and to have heavy clay soils difficult to exploit with the wood and stone tools available to ancient farmers, unless special, labor-intensive techniques were used.

In the Copán Valley this situation is reversed. Bottom lands are much preferred, both today and in the past. Upland agriculture is less attractive because of the nature of the soils and steep slopes. Bedrock in much of western Honduras consists of ancient igneous and sedimentary deposits, such as rhyolitic ash-flow tuffs, biotic tuffs, basalts, and limestones, which have been heavily affected by Cretaceous volcanic activity. These generally weather into the low fertility soils that cover an estimated 84% of recently mapped uplands (Wingard, 1992, 1996). Limestone parent material is present in scattered patches, and better soils develop on it. Soils of high fertility (entisols and mollisols) cover only about 15% of the landscape and are heavily concentrated on the valley floors and the low foothills immediately adjacent to them. About 75% of the Copán landscape has slopes in excess of 8%, and 40% has slopes in excess of 16%. Erosion is thus a severe problem wherever agricultural activity causes deforestation in mountains and foothills. Bottomlands, though restricted in extent, are and were unquestionably the most productive, stable, and low-risk agricultural zones except where they are poorly drained, as in much of Río Amarillo.

Copán's geological deposits did contribute important non-agricultural resources to the ancient Maya. Clays for ceramic production are available, and pottery is still made by traditional methods in the Sesesmil foothills. Basalts and rhyolites were used to make *manos* and *metates,* the grinding stones necessary for every household. Soft volcanic tuffs could easily be quarried with stone and wood tools to construct public buildings, elite houses, sculptured stelae and altars. Local cherts, however, were of poor quality for making cutting tools, and from very early on the Copán Maya imported obsidian for this purpose from the distant mountains of Guatemala. Jade was also imported from very early times, probably from both the Motagua Valley and Costa Rica.

Before being disturbed by humans, the deep soils of the alluvial pockets supported a dense, mixed forest of mesic, semideciduous, broad-leaf tropical tree species that included mahogany, cedar, and ceiba. Fingers of such forest extended up into the hills along the moist soils of tributary streams, and also covered the smaller alluvial tributary pockets. Elsewhere, upland vegetation is dominated by oak and especially pine, particularly on the poorer soils. Travelers' accounts from the mid-19th century indicate much the same distribution in the then sparsely populated Copán Valley.

Plant and animal communities include many species useful to humans, and we review these in some detail in Chapters 8–9. As in many tropical forest environments, however, the biomass of large wild animals was low and could provide only limited food supplements for dense agricultural populations. Fish may be obtained from the rivers, but they are neither large nor numerous. The environment in early times thus had only a limited capacity to support foraging populations. In other parts of the Maya Lowlands, such as Belize, large rivers and marine ecosystems provided a rich array of natural dietary resources. High in their land-locked valley, Copán's inhabitants overwhelmingly consumed terrestrial plant or animal foods, and a fairly limited range of them, as we shall see in Chapter 9.

To summarize, climatic conditions are generally good for traditional pre-columbian agricultural crops, but the landscape is highly variable in its productivity and long-term stability. While attractive to farmers, most parts of the valley are also prone to destructive anthropogenic changes if populations are too dense, and if uplands are cultivated too intensively. Today deforestation and erosion are widespread and pose serious problems to farmers, albeit in a socio-economic milieu very different from that of the ancient Maya. More so than in other Maya regions, the patchy distribution of land of different kinds, and the very restricted amounts of high quality land, are both highly conducive to the emergence and maintenance of striking asymmetries in wealth and political power under conditions of high population density.

Like all pre-columbian Mesoamerican peoples, ancient Copañecos used hand tools of wood, stone, bone, and fiber. They lacked large domestic animals that could be used for agricultural tasks, such as plowing, or as beasts of burden. Most tasks had to be accomplished by human muscles, unaided by labor-saving devices such as wheels or metal cutting tools. Two consequences of this system are of utmost importance. First, the ability of individual farmers to generate agricultural surpluses was very limited. Second, cheap, bulk resources such as maize or beans could not have been efficiently transported over very great distances, because they had to move on human backs. In terms of its subsistence economy, the source of the food energy that powered the whole system, the Copán Valley was in ancient times very self-contained.

In some parts of the Maya Lowlands, such as the northern Petén region of Guatemala, the landscape was densely packed with large Classic Maya centers. Sometimes these were so close to one another that from the major temples of one center it must have been possible to glimpse those of one or more of its neighbors. Certainly any able-bodied person could have walked from one center to another in a day or two. Such packing created a very complex and fluid political landscape. Archaeologists are still trying to figure out if closely juxtaposed large centers were politically autonomous, or instead were integrated into hierarchies in which one capital dominated other centers. Epigraphic evidence suggests that many centers experienced cycles of independence and subordination as their political and military fortunes waxed and waned. Kent Flannery (1998) thinks that this pattern is widely associated with early states.

Such historical geopolitical processes are of interest to us at this point only because Copán's comparative isolation makes it an exception to such historical vicissitudes. Quiriguá, Copán's nearest large neighbor, is a stiff two to three day walk over rugged country and was the capital of a much smaller, weaker polity. Whatever the nature of its "foreign" interactions or relationships, Copán throughout its long history seems never to have been politically subordinated to any other center even after, as we shall see in Chapter 2, its dynasty experienced severe political reverses.

It should now be apparent that Copán presents us with an almost perfect self-contained laboratory, as envisioned by Livi-Bacci, for investigating how agrarian people adapted to their natural and social environments. Livi-Bacci's scenario raises questions fundamental to much recent Copán regional research. How did the history of regional demographic growth and decline relate to land use? How did ecological interactions between the Copán Maya and their regional environment influence Copán's political history and institutions, and contribute to the prosperity and eventual collapse of the polity? These are big questions, and they form the most basic themes of this book.

CHAPTER 2
Regional and Dynastic History

INTRODUCTION

As at other Classic Maya centers, the most secure dates at Copán derive from monument inscriptions. These provide a detailed dynastic history for the polity between about A.D. 400 and 822 (Fash & Stuart, 1991; Stuart, 1993). People inhabited the valley before and after this time, however, so the dynastic interval is encapsulated within a much longer regional ceramic sequence devised by René Viel (1983, 1993a, b), building on earlier work of John Longyear (1952). This sequence is shown in simplified form in Table 2-1.

As we shall see later, there is considerable controversy about the post-A.D. 800 chronology. For the present we are concerned only with the earlier parts of this sequence, that encompass the origins and maturation of the Copán polity.

TABLE 2-I
COPÁN CERAMIC SEQUENCE

General Mesoamerican Periods	Copan Ceramic Phases	Calendar Dates of Phases
Postclassic	Ejar 2 Phase	A.D. 950–1000
Epiclassic	Coner/Ejar 1 Phases	A.D. 800–950
Late Classic/Epiclassic	Coner	A.D. 600–800
Middle Classic	Acbi Phase	A.D. 400–600
Early Classic	Bijac Phase	A.D. 100–400
Late Preclassic	Chabij Phase	300 B.C.–A.D. 100
Middle Preclassic	Uir Phase (with Gordon funerary subphase)	900–300 B.C.
Early Preclassic	Rayo Phase	1400–900 B.C.

THE PREDYNASTIC COPÁN MAYA

Very little is known about the earliest inhabitants of the Copán Valley. If early foraging people lived there we have no clear traces of them. The first suggestive evidence of human activity comes from a well-dated sediment core recovered from a bog in the Copán pocket in 1989. We review the data from this core in detail in Chapter 8, but for now its main implication is that humans were burning off vegetation in the valley at least as early as 3600 B.C., and growing corn at least as early as 2000 B.C.

Not until about 1400 B.C. do we find direct archaeological evidence for the presence of early farmers in the form of Rayo phase ceramics, which are confined to the floor of the Copán pocket. Middle Preclassic pottery is found in the same locale, where distinctive funerary vessels have been recovered from cemeteries buried deep beneath alluvial deposits in the Las Sepulturas urban enclave. Funerary vessels of this date have also been found in burial caves in the Sesesmil tributary valley to the north of the Main Group (Rue et al., 1989). Early and Middle Preclassic settlements must lie nearby, and early farmers probably preferred the deep, fertile soils of the valley bottoms, with their permanent streams or other water sources, for their houses and crops. Rock outcrops carved with concentric circles and other geometric forms in the Sesesmil Valley might be of Early to Middle Preclassic origin, but are difficult to date.

During Late Preclassic times there was an explosion of population in many parts of the Maya Lowlands. Finds of this period are unexpectedly very rare at Copán, and are found both in the urban core and in scattered sites throughout the rest of the valley. We are not sure what this means. Either the Copán region did not participate in this general demographic expansion, or else the biggest Late Preclassic settlements are deeply buried by sediments and later buildings, particularly on the floor of the Copán pocket. Current deep testing is beginning to show that the latter is the more likely of the two possibilities. Given the difficulty of detecting such remains we might not ever be able to reconstruct the numbers of Late Preclassic people present, but our educated guess would put the whole Late Preclassic population of the valley at 1,000 people or fewer.

Needless to say, there are no Preclassic stelae with dates in the Long Count calendar, but a quasi-historical restrospective date on a much later altar raised by the 12th ruler refers back to some Preclassic event in 321 B.C. (Stuart 1992, p. 171).

Throughout the long Preclassic period the ceramics of Copán, and especially those in domestic assemblages, show strong relationships to the pottery of neighboring peoples in central Honduras and western El Salvador. More significant is that there are few connections with ceramic traditions of the Maya Lowlands to the northwest. Nevertheless, the presence of imported jade and Olmec-like motifs on Middle Preclassic vessels shows that Copán was far from isolated, and concentrations of costly materials in a few burials suggest that some social ranking was already present by Middle Preclassic times (Fash, 1991, pp. 66–71).

New pottery styles with strong affiliations with the highlands of Guatemala mark the beginning of the Early Classic period. Building projects at Group 9 (now buried under the modern town of Copán Ruinas), in the Copán Main Group, and at Cerro de las Mesas, Los Achiotes, and smaller sites in the Sesesmil and Río Amarillo valleys were begun at this time. Although little is known about Early Classic settlements or political organization, later monuments retrospectively commemorate named and titled people, who lived around A.D. 159–160, possibly including an early ruler called *Mah Kina Foliated Ahaw* (Schele & Freidel, 1990, p. 309; Schele & Mathews, 1998, p. 139). These individuals were important enough to have been remembered, but we do not know whether they were rulers of an early Copán dynastic line, venerated ancestors, or even if they actually lived in the Copán Valley. Judging from the restricted numbers and distributions of Early Classic artifacts, population was still sparse—probably in the range of a few thousand people.

Despite our inadequate knowledge of the early part of the regional sequence, several important things are clear. First, even though the valley was colonized by farmers very early, population growth was quite slow up until about A.D. 600. Second, although non-egalitarian social and political ranking might have emerged during the Middle Preclassic, it is not until A.D. 100–400 that we have indications of any sort of complex political organization. Finally, there is nothing particularly "Lowland Maya" about the archaeological record before A.D. 400.

Without inscriptions we cannot know whether Copán's early inhabitants spoke Mayan or some other non-Mayan language. As we shall see in Chapter 9, preliminary analyses suggest that Copan's ancient population was genetically dissimilar from modern Maya populations in northern Yucatán. Whatever the case, Copán's people had not yet participated in any meaningful way in the much earlier crystallization of Maya civilization evident at great centers such as Nakbe, Mirador, Cerros, and Tikal, far away to the north and west. All this was shortly to dramatically change.

THE COPÁN DYNASTIC SEQUENCE

About A.D. 400 many of the markers of Classic Maya elite culture suddenly appeared at Copán. An individual named *K'inich Yax K'uk Mo'* makes his appearance and is much celebrated on the monuments of his successors as the founder of the Copán dynasty (Table 2-2). Inscriptions pinpoint the founding event involving *K'inich Yax K'uk Mo'* at 8.19.10.11.0 8 Ahaw 18 Yax'kin, a date in the Maya Long Count calendar that correlates to September 9, A.D. 426 (Schele and Mathews 1998, p. 134).

The reign of *K'inich Yax K'uk Mo'* initiated the erection of monumental stelae and altars with hieroglyphic inscriptions and Long Count calendar dates, a distinctively Classic Maya iconographic style, and monumental architectural construction at the Main Group, which was the seat of the fledgling royal household. Copán began to use its own distinctive emblem glyph portraying a leaf-nosed bat (the name of the kingdom, *Xukpi*, was reconstructed from phonetic elements in this glyph). Eventually the polity and its rulers became identified with a set of patron deities named *Kan-Te-Ahaw* and *Bolon-K'awil*. Such patron gods, along with a central line of rulers and a well established central place, seem to be the essential elements in political and ethnic identity in the Classic Maya Lowlands.

For many years archaeologists have debated exactly what happened to cause all these changes. One possibility is that a sizable group of migrants from some distant Lowland Maya region entered the valley, quickly made themselves politically dominant, and introduced the trappings of Classic kingship and elite culture. This reconstruction accords with Stephen Houston's conception of "stranger kings"—dynasts who traveled far from their places of origins to establish new ruling lines. Such kings ruled polities with much less time depth than great ancient centers such as Tikal. Alternatively, trade, intermarriage between local prominent people and outsiders, or some other less dramatic processes might have promoted more gradual adoption of Maya ways.

Present evidence favors the "stranger king" hypothesis. We have little evidence of any kind of violent, warlike intrusion, conquest, or mass influx of foreign populations, although a recently discovered male skeleton that is probably that of the first ruler has a badly injured right arm, consistent with some kind of violence (G. Stuart, 1997). Isotopic studies of bone from this individual suggest that he is a foreigner (Traxler, 1998).

Ongoing excavations in the Copán Main Group are turning up indications of Preclassic occupation, and it seems increasingly likely that there were local notables already in the valley with whom *K'inich Yax K'uk Mo'* and his companions had to reach some sort of political accomodation.

Recent studies by Loa Traxler (1998) indicate that the palace of the founder is probably represented by a small patio group buried deeply beneath the East Court of the Acropolis. Most of these buildings were puddled adobe platforms with perishable, wattle and daub superstructures. The eastern one, named Hunal, had masonry construction and polychrome paint on its plastered surfaces. It was in this structure that the apparent founder's burial was located. A rich female burial from the building immediately overlying Hunal is interpreted as that of the spouse of *K'inich Yax K'uk Mo'*, and isotopic studies of her bones suggest she is of local origin. If these skeletal data are correctly interpreted, a foreign king seems to have married a locally prominent Copán woman at the very beginning of the dynasty. Four patio groups with adobe architecture to the northeast of the founder's compound are probably the residences of members of the fledgling Copán court, and even at this early date architecture begins to delineate the Great Plaza.

Influences from the great Classic metropolis of Teotihuacan in the Basin of Mexico are seen in burial pottery and the presence of imported green obsidian, and Hunal has Teotihuacan-related *talud-tablero* architectural elements. Depictions of *K'inich Yax K'uk Mo'* on the monuments of later kings show him wearing Teotihuacan elements on his costume. Teotihuacan was called *Puh*, or "Place of Cattail Reeds" by the Classic Maya (Schele & Mathews, 1998,

p. 134). Conceivably *K'inich Yax K'uk Mo'* tried to bolster his authority by asserting connections with this great metropolis, or even claiming descent from Teotihuacan lords.

Other symbolic and stylistic clues link Copán with the older and larger Maya center of Tikal in the northeastern Petén region of Guatemala, and with Kaminaljuyu in highland Guatemala, itself heavily influenced by Teotihuacan (Schele & Mathews, 1998, pp. 134, 344). Tikal had strong contacts with Teotihuacan. David Stuart (1998), on the basis of recent epigraphic work, believes that there was decisive interference by Teotihuacan in Tikal's dynastic succession about A.D. 378, and that a ruler with direct Teotihuacan connections was possibly installed on the throne there. How this might relate to Copán is still unclear, but foreign intervention at Tikal might well have set in motion processes of elite dislocation that eventually resulted in the founding of new "stranger king" centers, and Copán's dynastic history begins only a generation after these Tikal events.

However they came to power, both *K'inich Yax K'uk Mo* and his consort, as previously noted, might have been buried deeply beneath Structure 16 early in the 5th century, and elaborate tombs of other notables are found in the Copán urban core at the same time. Middle Classic Acbi pottery seems to develop out of earlier local forms, and an unresolved question, as already noted, is whether the predynastic population of the valley spoke Mayan or some non-Mayan language. If the latter, Copán would have been an unusually complex Classic Maya kingdom in ethnic terms.

Ruler 2, as the presumed son of *K'inich Yax K'uk Mo'* and a Copán woman, had firm links both to the local population and probably to prestigious Maya families elsewhere. He built the first ball court and also created the first elevated stages of the Acropolis by adding massive adobe and masonry constructions to the area of the founder's compound.

K'inich Yax K'uk Mo' and Ruler 2 firmly established royal rule and were followed by 14 successors, as shown in Table 2-2. Unfortunately for the archaeologist, the stelae and buildings of the first 11 kings were often destroyed or purposefully removed from public view by burial beneath successively more recent constructions. What we know about these rulers largely comes from architectural stratigraphy, tombs, and inscriptions on the monuments of later kings. The most important inscriptions are those on Altar Q, which depict each ruler in the order of dynastic succession. Agurcia (1998, pp. 352–353) provides a particularly recent and useful graphic depiction of the dynasty as it is presently understood, and the following dates are taken from his list.

At least by the early 6th century Copán's dynasty seems to have been widely recognized elsewhere in the Maya Lowlands. *Water-Lily Jaguar,* according to Nicolai Grube (1990), is mentioned in texts at the distant site of Caracol, in Belize. Many early kings were certainly great builders, and by the late 5th or early 6th centuries cut stone constructions increasingly replaced earlier buildings of adobe and river cobbles at the Main Group. Early phases of the great Copán ball court and the Temple of the Hieroglyphic Stairway were constructed in Acbi times, as was the splendidly preserved Rosalila building in the Acropolis, built by the 10th king.

TABLE 2-2
THE COPÁN DYNASTIC SEQUENCE

Succession Order	Names, Titles, and Variants	Important Dates or Estimated Reigns (all A.D.)
Ruler 1 (founder)	**K'inich Yax K'uk Mo'** Mah K'ina Yax K'uk Mo' Blue Quetzal Macaw Sun-eyed Green Quetzal Macaw	Accession and death dates unknown; accession in 426; death probably about 435.
Ruler 2	**Popol K'inich** Mat head	Accession date 435; death date unknown.
Ruler 3	Name unknown	Accession date unknown; death 485.
Ruler 4	**Cu Ix**	Accession date 485; death date 495.
Ruler 5	Unknown	Short reign at end of 5th century.
Ruler 6	Unknown	Short reign at end of 5th century.
Ruler 7	**Waterlily Jaguar** Balam-Nan	Reign at first half of 6th century (approx, 504–544).
Ruler 8	Unknown	Short reign in mid-6th century.
Ruler 9	Unknown	Accession date 551; death date unknown.
Ruler 10	**Moon Jaguar**	Accession date: 553; Death date: 578.
Ruler 11	**Butz' Chan** Smoke Snake Smoke Sky	Birth: 553, Accession: 578, Death: 628.
Ruler 12	**Smoke Imix God K** Smoke Jaguar K'ak'-Nab-K'awil	Accession: 628, Death: 695.
Ruler 13	**18 Rabbit** XVIII-Jog Waxaklahun Ubah K'awil Uaxaclahun Ubac C'auil	Accession: 695, Death: 738.
Ruler 14	**Smoke Monkey**	Accession: 738, Death: 749.
Ruler 15	**Smoke Shell** Smoke Squirrel Smoke Caracol	Accession: 749, Death: circa 763.
Ruler 16	**Yax Pasah** Yax Pac New Dawn Madrugada First Dawn Yax Sun-at-Horizon	Accession: 763, Death unknown, but prior to 820.

Despite clear continuity of rulership, the first nine kings had, on average, much shorter reigns than the last seven. René Viel (in press) believes the office shifted among royal lines. Another explanation for this pattern might be that succession passed to brothers rather than sons. Unlike Maya rulers at some other centers, Copán's kings were not very interested in recording kin relationships on their monuments, so we have no direct evidence concerning details of succession.

In A.D. 628 the great 12th king *Smoke Imix God K* ascended the throne. His extraordinarily long reign of 67 years inaugurated the period of Copán's greatest power and prosperity. He took part in rituals at Quiriguá, the nearest Classic Maya neighboring center in the Motagua Valley of Guatemala, and may have been instrumental in establishing the local dynasty there, to which he was probably related. In A.D. 652 *Smoke Imix God K* set up a series of seven stelae throughout the Copán pocket, apparently to mark out the core territory of his kingdom. His authority was also acknowledged by inscriptions found at the satellite center of Río Amarillo in the upper Copán Valley. Early constructions in Structures 4, 16, 22, and 26 may have been completed during his reign, which also ushered in changes in the local ceramic tradition. The most notable change is the widespread adoption of Copador polychrome pottery, an important chronological marker for archaeologists. This ware, along with other distinctive forms, defines the Coner ceramic complex. Although a few Coner pottery types are similar to those of the Maya Lowlands, and there are some imports from that region, Copán's strongest ceramic ties still lie with western El Salvador and central Honduras.

The 13th king, *18 Rabbit,* ruled between A.D. 695–738 and was probably the most powerful of Copán's rulers. The final layout of the Great Plaza in the Main Group is attributed to him, and this great open space is dominated by his stelae and altars (Figure 1-3). He also renovated the ball court, began the last phase of the Temple of the Hieroglyphic Stairway, and erected the famous Temple 22, replete with cosmological imagery, on Copán's Acropolis. Sudden catastrophe ended *18 Rabbit's* career in A.D. 738, when he was captured by his royal neighbor (and possible relative) *Cauac Sky* of Quiriguá. According to inscriptions *Cauac Sky* sacrificed *18 Rabbit* in an "ax-event" and also destroyed the statues of Copán's patron gods, which apparently had been carried along on the ill-fated expedition to Quiriguá (Schele and Mathews, 1998, p. 170).

Whether this debacle was part of a war or some lesser dynastic squabble is unknown. Any dependency relationship with Copán was severed, however, and Quiriguá thereafter experienced a long period of independent growth and prosperity. There are no signs that Copán itself suffered militarily or economically, but the loss of *18 Rabbit* must have caused great dynastic loss of face. The 14th ruler had a short reign, raised no stelae depicting himself, and seems to have had trouble mustering up labor for royal constructions.

Under the 15th ruler, *Smoke Shell,* there were signs of recovery, most notably the completion of the Temple of the Hieroglyphic Stairway. The inscriptions and associated sculpture on the stairway itself recount the dynastic history of Copán and celebrate its kings as warriors. On the summit was a temple dedicated to the founder, *K'inich Yax K'uk Mo'. 18 Rabbit's* inglorious fate is not mentioned, and the whole building seems to constitute a message aimed at reasserting the power of the dynasty and the splendor of its origins.

Yax Pasah, the 16th and last king, took power in A.D. 763 and distinguished himself as a builder during the first half of his reign. Somehow *Yax Pasah* seems to have patched up relations with Quiriguá because he carried out rituals there. Although we have no evidence of foreign conflicts, he took pains to depict himself as a warrior on his monuments, and in A.D. 775 he dedicated Altar Q, on which he is shown linked to all the previous rulers and metaphorically receiving a royal scepter from the long-dead founder. René Viel (in press) believes the specific theme is *Yax Pasah* being seated as a war and sacrifice leader.

A huge bench in the temple atop Structure 11 was also dedicated by *Yax Pasah* and might be another dynastic monument. It shows 19 figures in addition to *Yax Pasah,* and Schele and Miller (1986) suggest that these are former kings. Their numbers do not match those on Altar Q, however, and Viel thinks instead that they show the king surrounded by members of his court. If so, this bench offers remarkable insights into the political structure of 8th century Copán.

During the first half of his reign *Yax Pasah* managed to complete some very large construction projects, such as the final stages of Structures 11 and 16, as well as what was probably meant to be his own elaborate tomb. This recovery of royal power may be illusory, however, because at the same time the households of lesser elites became larger and more elaborate, and some of them sported carved stelae, thrones, and façade sculpture, normally the prerogatives of kings.

Many stresses in the polity eventually conspired to weaken both *Yax Pasah* and the central institution of rulership. He died under obscure circumstances in A.D. 820. According to some inscriptions other Copán nobles, including possible relatives of *Yax Pasah,* became politically assertive in the early 9th century. None, however, was able to stave off the abrupt end of dynastic rule, signaled by the last, uncompleted royal monument dated to A.D. 822, and at this point Copán's historical record ends and no more large construction projects were undertaken. Buildings in the royal residence at the south end of the Acropolis were apparently deliberately burned around A.D. 850–900, so some violence seems to have attended the end of the dynasty.

Until quite recently most archaeologists believed that the whole political superstructure of Copán disappeared at the same time as the royal dynasty collapsed. Following shortly upon these events a precipitous demographic decline was supposed to have essentially depopulated the valley by A.D. 859–900, although occasional offerings, including distinctive Ejar complex vessels, continued to be made in the now-abandoned Main Group by a few local survivors or visitors. Our settlement research and household archaeology, along with new ways of determining chronology, produced evidence of a very different story, as we shall see in later chapters.

CHAPTER 3

The History and Character
of Copán Research

INTRODUCTION

Copán is unique among Classic Maya centers because of its extremely long history of field research, which essentially incorporates the whole tradition of American archaeology. Also unusual is that this research has involved independent projects from many institutions, sometimes working simultaneously, each with its own goals, theoretical frameworks, and methods. (see Black, 1990, for a review). Such diversity has sometimes fostered scholarly debates leading to significant differences of interpretation, but in the long run even these debates have been productive. Varied research agendas, strategies and perspectives have greatly refined our understanding of ancient Copán society and culture, and continue to do so. Our own work owes a great debt to the data, thoughtful interpretations, and scholarly predictions generated by our archaeological predecessors and colleagues at Copán. What follows is a brief overview of Copán research that places our own contributions in context. Subsequent chapters discuss in detail the methods, data, and interpretations of much of the work introduced here.

ARCHAEOLOGICAL RESEARCH
AT COPÁN BEFORE 1980

Exactly what the name Copán means is unclear, but in 1530 a local chief called Copán Calel led an uprising against the Spanish; after his defeat his name became attached to the ruins (only recent decipherments revealed the original Classic Maya name *Xukpi*). Somewhat later the Copán Main Group was first described in a 1576 letter from Diego Garcia de Palacio to the Spanish King Philip II. After Palacio's visit the site was largely forgotten due to the inaccessibility of the region. The first illustrated description of Copán, complete with a map, cross-sections, structure plans, and sculpture drawings, is found in a 1834 report by Juan Galindo, who conducted excavations in the East Court. John Stevens and Frederick Catherwood visited the site in 1839 (Stephens, 1949) and cleared part of the Main Group in order to map buildings and record the sculptured monuments, depicted in Catherwood's now-famous lithographs (Figure 1-3). It was their work that brought the splendors not only of Copán, but of Maya civilization in general, to the attention of the wider world.

Pioneers of Early Archaeology at Copán

The first systematic excavations were directed by Alfred Maudslay, heavily supported by Harvard's Peabody Museum (Maudslay, 1889–1902). During field seasons from 1881 to 1895, Maudslay improved Stephens' map by locating and measuring Main Group structures more accurately. He also test excavated several of the more impressive buildings and made plaster casts of many of the monuments. Maudslay's colleagues George Gordon, John Owens and Marshall Saville continued excavations in the Main Group. They also exposed parts of Structure 36 in the Cementerios zone of the urban core (part of what is now called Group 10L-2) and investigated cave sites in the Sesesmil Valley, turning up the first evidence of Copán's early inhabitants (Gordon, 1896a, 1896b).

Sylvanus Morley (1920) was so impressed with Copán's sculpture that he made several trips to the site between 1910 and 1919. Morley concentrated his efforts on recording monument inscriptions and also conducted excavations at the Group 9 complex, now buried beneath the modern town of Copán Ruínas. He was convinced that Group 9, because of its early dated monuments, was the first capital of the Copán region, and that the royal center had later been moved to the Main Group. Morley also briefly described many of the more prominent outlying sites in the valley and provided the first systematic description of Copán's environmental setting.

The Carnegie Projects

The next major research effort was sponsored by the Carnegie Institution of Washington. As part of their larger program of Maya studies, Carnegie archaeologists worked at Copán from 1935 to 1946, with a two-year hiatus during World War II. They diverted the Río Copán away from the base of the East Court of the Acropolis, and many of the structures in the Main Group were excavated and restored, including the Hieroglyphic Stairway (Structure 26), the main Ball Court A (Stromsvik, 1942), and Structures 11 and 22 (Longyear, 1952; Trik, 1939). During the Carnegie excavations John Longyear (1952) developed the initial ceramic sequence for the Copán Valley, based primarily on artifacts recovered at the Main Group. Robert Burgh, a professional surveyor, made a map of the known mounds and other features found within the 18 sq km area surrounding the center. Burgh's map represents the first systematic record of structures outside the Main Group.

The Harvard Project

Gordon Willey of Harvard University initiated the most recent epoch of Copán research in 1977. Willey's project, which lasted for two years, was the first to

TABLE 3-1
HARVARD PROJECT SITE CLASSIFICATION

Type 4 sites: These sites consist of complex groupings of mounds, sometimes 40 or more, around one or more commonly multiple plazas. Construction includes much high quality dressed stone and vaulted ceilings; sculpture is associated with some of the buildings.

Type 3 sites: Mounds may be as high as 4.75 m and define one or more plazas. Dressed stone is abundantly used for construction.

Type 2 sites: These sites have one or more plazas and about 6 to 8 mounds, the largest of which are about 2.5 to 3 m high. Although usually built of rubble and undressed blocks, they may also include cut-stone construction.

Type 1 sites: These sites have two or more buildings (usually 3 to 5) grouped around one or more plazas. Buildings on the surface appear as low mounds no more than 1.25 m high, and are constructed of earthen fill and rough stone retaining walls.

focus intensive archaeological investigations on sites outside the Main Group. Harvard archaeologists surveyed and remapped the Las Sepulturas urban enclave, improving on Burgh's original survey. A major component of this survey was the accompanying collection of ecological data (Leventhal, 1979). Willey and his colleagues hypothesized that most of the structures visible on the Copán landscape were the remains of ancient households. They assumed that variations in the number of buildings, quality of construction, and the presence of sculpture and sophisticated building techniques (such as stone vaults) reflected the differential status and wealth of the original inhabitants. On this basis they constructed a heuristic site classification system still in use today, as shown in Table 3-1 (Willey & Leventhal, 1979, pp. 82–83).

This system was designed to impose some order on the surface manifestations of architecture being mapped. Excavations show exceptions to it—for example some Type 1 scale sites have dressed stone—but it has proved generally useful. With a few additions, such as aggregated and nonmound sites, subsequent projects have, as we shall see, adapted it to their own purposes.

During the Harvard Project several Las Sepulturas courtyard groups were partially excavated, initiating the subsequent tradition of household archaeology at Copán. Ongoing publications, most recently *The Ceramics and Artifacts From Excavations in the Copán Residential Zone* (Willey et al., 1994), summarize the Harvard work.

Architectural Mapping Projects

A long term, ongoing study of Copán's architecture was begun in 1970 by two Austrian doctoral students in architecture, Hasso Hohmann and Annegrete Vogrin. Employing unpublished fieldnotes, detailed photographs, and maps, Hohmann and Vogrin (1982) produced the most detailed architectural overview and construction analysis available for the Main Group. More recently, they extended their efforts to the Las Sepulturas urban enclave (Hohmann, 1995). Their survey techniques yield details of construction and levels of accuracy unmatched by previous cartography. The 1995 volume is particularly important because it includes the best architectural renderings of restored structures in the urban core. Many of these buildings figure in Abrams's (1994) construction models, which as we shall see later, have important implications for ancient Copán's social, political, and economic organization.

PAC I Research Project

In 1977 the Honduran government, through its agencies of the Ministry of Culture and Tourism and the Honduran Institute of Anthropology and History (I.H.A.H.), began a large-scale archaeological project at Copán. The Proyecto Arqueologico Copán (PAC) ran from 1977 to 1984 and was divided into two separate phases. The first phase (referred to as PAC I) was directed between 1977 and 1980 by Claude F. Baudez, of the French National Center for Scientific Research. During this phase the Main Group Structures 2, 4 and 18, and Ball Court B in the El Bosque urban enclave were all excavated and restored, and the stratigraphy of the Great Plaza explored (C. Baudez, 1983). René Viel (1983, 1993a, b) developed a detailed ceramic sequence refining the earlier one proposed by Longyear.

PAC I also saw the rapid expansion of landscape and settlement archaeology. Baudez initiated an important ecological and ethnographic survey of the region that provided much needed environmental and land-use data (Turner et al., 1983; I. Baudez 1983). PAC I archaeologists concurrently employed three different strategies to investigate the outlying rural Copán Valley settlements.

First, an ambitious survey and mapping project examined the 24 sq km Copán pocket (including the valley floor and the adjacent foothills) and eventually documented 3,437 structures representing 875 separate sites (Figure 3-1).

Second, in 1978 David Vlcek directed a preliminary surface survey of the 400 sq km area of the larger Río Copán drainage, an effort primarily aimed at recording archaeological sites known to local informants (Vlcek & Fash, 1986). Some 97 sites were mapped, but no test pitting or surface collection was done. Vlcek's exploratory rural survey was too brief to sample systematically the whole regional sustaining area, but it did provide much useful background information on the distribution and character of sites far from the Main Group.

Third, PAC I archaeologists test pitted 1% of the mounds located in the Copán Pocket, and 15 sites received more intensive excavations (Fash & Long, 1983). In addition to testing sites visible on the surface, Baudez designed a randomized subsurface probing project in the areas within and adjacent to the Copán pocket (Fash 1983a, b). This was an important innovation because, as we shall see later, the possible presence of buried buildings is a controversial issue in Maya settlement survey and central to demographic reconstructions. We will evaluate its effectiveness and implications in Chapter 6.

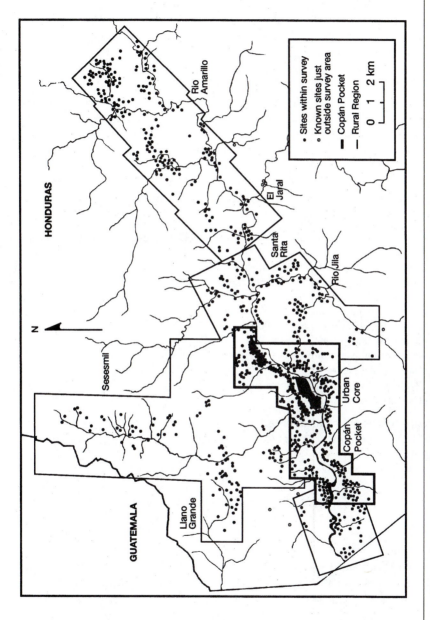

FIGURE 3-1 SURVEY REGIONS OF THE COPÁN VALLEY SHOWING SITES LOCATED BY SEVERAL SUCCESSIVE SURVEY PROJECTS.

In total, 182 test pits spread over an 86 sq km area were eventually excavated using these sub-surface sampling methods developed by PAC I. While generating a small sample of the subsurface remains in the region, these probes did provide extremely important information on early ceramics and other insights into early occupants of the valley. They also suggested that hidden or nonplatform sites did not exist in significant numbers in the Copán pocket, and that more random sub-surface testing for such sites would yield few positive results. This is an extremely important inference for our subsequent demographic reconstructions.

The PAC I project produced a wealth of new and detailed information on Copán, specifically its early history, sculpture, iconography, and settlement within the Copán pocket. Its findings have been reported in a three volume series edited by Baudez (1983), which includes an excellent map of Copán pocket settlement (Fash & Long, 1983). Baudez (1994) later published an analysis of Copán sculpture.

Most important for subsequent regional research were several preliminary conclusions about the evolution and decline of the Copán kingdom:

1. According to iconographic and ceramic data, the polity was founded shortly after A.D. 400, but reached its social, economic, and political climax during the Coner ceramic phase, or A.D. 700–800.
2. In Late Coner times the valley's population peaked, and the Copán pocket had by far the densest population of any zone, estimated by Fash (1983a) at 17,000–19,000 people.
3. The royal dynasty and associated nobles abruptly lost power at A.D. 800 or very shortly thereafter. By A.D. 850–900 the valley was virtually devoid of settlement and population (Fash, 1983a, p. 200).
4. An important cause of dynastic collapse and depopulation was human-induced environmental degradation.
5. Offerings of imported Ejar phase pottery were occasionally made in the Main Group after A.D. 900.

These conclusions seemed quite reliable when we began the Phase II Project in 1980, and we originally accepted them. Some, as it turns out, held up better than others.

THE PAC II PROJECT: GOALS AND RESEARCH DESIGN

The second phase of the PAC project (referred to as PAC II) was directed by William T. Sanders and David Webster of Pennsylvania State University between 1980 and 1984, and all of the authors became involved in Copán research during this stage. The results of PAC II, along with many ancillary projects, provide the central database we use in our reconstruction of the Copán's regional system.

From its inception, PAC II presented a unique opportunity to investigate Late Classic Maya society at Copán, in part due to the generous level of funding it enjoyed. Our Honduran sponsors wished to develop Copán further as a national archaeological park. More restoration in the Main Group was required, but permission was also granted for extensive surveys and excavations outside the Main Group.

As originally conceived, the PAC II project had several major goals, all of which were pursued simultaneously:

1. Large scale excavations at the Main Group;
2. Extensive household excavations at Las Sepulturas, known from earlier work to be an elite residential enclave; and
3. Surface settlement survey extended systematically beyond the Copán pocket to include much or all of the Río Copán and Río Sesesmil drainages.

Although we excavated one large set of buildings in the Main Group that turned out to be a dormitory complex for young elite men (Cheek & Spink 1986; see Group 3 in Figure 1-2), most of the PAC II work took place outside the Main Group, the first major project at Copán that had an almost exclusively non-center orientation.

The overall objective of the combined excavation/survey was to reconstruct the social, political, and economic institutions of Late Classic Copán society. At the same time, we wished to generate a model of the processes of colonization and resource utilization of the Copán Basin, or in other words to elucidate its demographic and agricultural history. Finally, we wanted to understand the collapse of the polity in more detail. Two strategies were employed to meet these objectives.

Household Archaeology at Las Sepulturas

First, we excavated several household groups in the Las Sepulturas urban enclave. As we have already seen, the Harvard Project generated both a typology of sites and a hypothesis that provisionally explained the variation inherent in it—i.e., variation reflected residences of social groups of different ranks. However sensible this hypothesis now seems, not too long ago groups of large, elaborate structures located near major centers were often thought of as minor ceremonial centers. Clearly the residential hypothesis needed more testing than had been possible during the Harvard project, and it had two major implications:

1. Excavations in most groups of whatever rank should yield unmistakable evidence of structures, facilities, artifact assemblages, refuse, and burials consistent with domestic activities; and
2. Groups in the putative elite ranks should provide evidence of high status vis-à-vis lesser groups as measured by increased labor input, more internal functional differentiation of facilities, higher quality construction, elaborate burials, display of elite iconographic and glyphic elements (especially on architectural sculpture), and increased richness of general artifact assemblages relative to groups in lower ranks.

Four sites, representing the full range of proposed status differences were selected for extensive excavation and restoration (Sanders, 1986–1990). These sites were 9N-8, a Type 4 site with 10 separate courtyards and over 60 structures (Figure 3-2); the 9M-22 complex, composed of one Type 3 and one Type 2 site (Figure 3-3a); and 9M-24, a small, single courtyard Type 1 site (Figure 3-3b). A

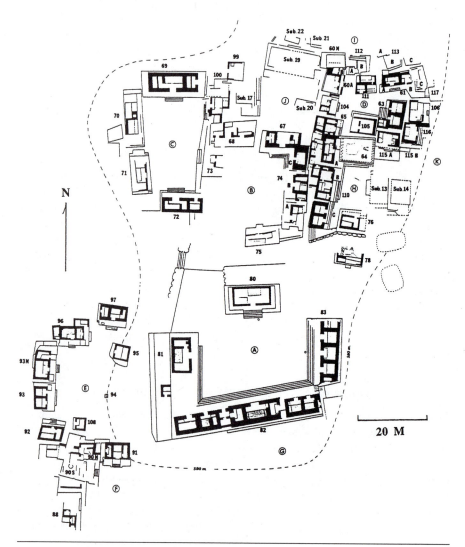

FIGURE 3-2   PLAN OF GROUP 9N-8, A RESIDENTIAL COMPOUND THAT HOUSED ELITE MAYA PEOPLE IN THE LAS SEPULTURAS URBAN ENCLAVE.

collateral Mexican effort led by Evelyn Rattray exposed the plaza of the Type 4 Group 8N-11.

In one sense there was nothing new about this approach. Excavation of outlying residential sites has a long tradition in Maya archaeology. A good example are household excavations at Tikal during the 1960s, summarized by Haviland (1985). Most such previous excavations, however, consisted of partial probes of individual structures (as did the Harvard work at Las Sepulturas). In our Las Sepulturas work we made one all-important innovation—extensive lateral stripping. Not only were all structures themselves completely excavated down to their

FIGURE 3-3

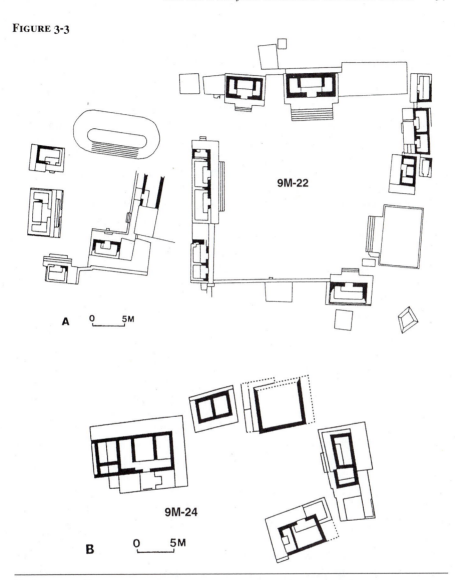

FIGURE 3-3   TWO RESIDENTIAL GROUPS OF DIFFERENT SCALE IN THE
LAS SEPULTURAS URBAN ENCLAVE. A SHOWS 9M–22, A TYPE 3 ELITE COMPOUND
WITH VAULTED BUILDINGS AND SCULPTURE; B SHOWS GROUP 9M–24, A TYPE 1,
A COMMONER SCALE, COMPOUND.

latest living floors, but so too were the patio surfaces around which buildings
were arranged, along with much other peripheral space. Our assumption was that
many activities took place outside the structures, as is commonly the case in
tropical climates. By digging whole groups, rather than just sampling buildings,
we were able to expose the full range of architectural features and remains of the
ancient behaviors associated with them. Structures were also trenched to reveal

internal phasing, as were the plazas, and special efforts were made to recover large, statistically robust burial samples for detailed analysis of diet, health status and household composition. Overviews and interpretations of the Las Sepulturas household excavations are mainly presented in Chapters 4 and 12.

Because a fundamental question in Lowland Maya research at the onset of PAC II was the degree of urbanization achieved by the larger centers, our excavation methodology was designed to produce data which could be employed to quantitatively measure such factors as status differentiation, population density, and economic specialization within the Late Classic Copán polity. Some of the Las Sepulturas residences included sculpture and inscriptions, so they also yielded very specific information about the social and political identities of their elite inhabitants, and one very precise date. Our excavations provided detailed information on how these residences were established and grew, and also how and when they were abandoned. As we shall see in later chapters, our Las Sepulturas work strongly supported the Harvard residential hypothesis and revealed much about Copán political, economic, and social organization in the urban core. It also provided a rather different picture of the collapse of the Copán polity than we expected.

Regional Settlement Survey

By the time PAC II started, we had an excellent grasp of outlying settlement in the Copán pocket—or at least its surface manifestations—thanks to the PAC I surveys. In order to understand the overall history of population size and distribution, as well as land-use patterns, more systematic surveys of the other parts of the valley were obviously needed. The Hondurans supported the survey of the outlying sections of the main valley in 1981, and two subsequent seasons (1983 and 1984) were funded by the National Science Foundation. During the latter period we surveyed the Río Sesesmil and Río Jila tributary valleys, and also undertook a major test-pitting effort. This was necessary because useful samples of artifacts usually cannot be picked up on the surface of Copán sites, which typically have a dense vegetation cover and are rarely plowed. Only test excavation could reveal the residential (or other) character of rural sites, and also provide chronologically sensitive artifacts to partition the rural sites in time. It was in conjunction with this phase of work that Freter began her ambitious obsidian hydration dating project, reviewed in Chapter 10.

Ethnographic and Landscape Research

Another goal of the PAC II project was to conduct ethnographic and ecological studies in the modern Copán Valley in order to gather information on modern land use, population distribution, and material culture. All these were necessary to generate models for the interpretation of the archaeological record. We were particularly interested in current land-use and land-tenure patterns, because these are triggering degenerative processes, including loss of soil fertility and erosion, that resemble those of Classic times. Such processes are much more rapid today than in the past, and provide clues concerning the final collapse of the Copán polity. Most important, William T. Sanders examined the households of subsistence farmers, surveyed their agricultural practices, and gathered informant information on crop yields through time.

Ancillary PAC II Research

Concurrently with the Las Sepulturas household excavations and the valley survey and test pitting, PAC II personnel pursued other, more specialized investigations we will enlarge upon later. Melissa Diamanti (1991), Andrea Gerstle (1988), Julia Hendon (1987), and Randolph Widmer all focused their work on various behavioral, social, and economic aspects of the Las Sepulturas sites. Rebecca Storey (1992, 1997) and Stephen Whittington (1989) initiated paleo-demographic and paleopathological analysis of our growing sample of Copán skeletons, one of the largest in Mesoamerica. David Lentz (1991) reconstructed the suite of plants used by the ancient Copán Maya from macrofossil remains in soil samples, and Eloisa Aguilar is now completing her study of the mineral contents of these samples.

Further afield, in 1981 John Mallory tested the site of El Duende, in the foothills near the Petapilla intermontane pocket several km to the northeast of the Main Group. Huge amounts of surface obsidian debris suggested that this little Type 1 site was not residential, but rather a workshop of some sort, and was central to Mallory's (1984) analysis of obsidian use and production. Stephen Whittington and Andrea Gerstle intensively probed two nearby sites in the Petapilla intermontane pocket. A little later, David Rue (1986, 1987) extracted a sediment core from the Aguada Petapilla that gave us our first glimpse—a very surprising one—into the vegetational history of the valley. Partly on the basis of this evidence, he and others (Abrams, Freter, Rue, & Wingard, 1996) assessed the extent and consequences of deforestation. Mary Spink (1983) investigated the quarrying of stone for manufacturing metates (food-processing stones), and Elliot Abrams (1984a, 1984b, 1994) studied the energetics and organization of construction and monument carving.

PAC II Regional Spin-off Projects

PAC II formally came to an end in 1984. Like so many other ambitious projects, however, it raised as many questions as it answered and stimulated new efforts to understand the regional Copán system. The first of these was the Copán Valley Rural Sites Project in 1985 and 1986, which extensively excavated eight rural Type 1 and single mound sites outside the Copán pocket (Gonlin 1993, 1994, 1996; Webster & Gonlin 1988; Webster, Gonlin, & Sheets 1997). Small residential sites of common people, particularly those far from royal centers, rarely receive much attention from Maya archaeologists even though they represent the households of 80 to 90% of the population of Maya polities. By excavating a sample of them we effectively complemented our earlier household sample from Las Sepulturas, which was heavily weighted toward the elite end of the residential continuum, and we also tested the specific inferences derived from our earlier test pitting.

At this point we faced an unusual sampling problem. At the end of PAC II we paradoxically had much better test pit information from rural sites outside the Copán pocket than inside it, where most of the people lived. Freter accordingly carried out a final test-pitting project in 1988 that focused on the Copán pocket settlement region. Her work was the logical extension of the previous settlement research by Harvard and PAC I and was the final step in acquiring artifacts from a statistically representative sample of sites in all settlement zones within the valley.

To expand our knowledge of elite residences beyond the urban core Stephen Whittington (1990) intensively probed the Type 4 and Type 3 sites Ostuman and Los Mangos just outside the Copán pocket to the southwest. In 1989 Webster investigated the character and timing of the erosional processes known from PAC I test pitting to have blanketed much of the northern Las Sepulturas zone. Later, in 1990 and 1997, Webster and his colleagues excavated large parts of the Type 4 8N-ll group at the end of the Las Sepulturas causeway, where Rattray had previously worked in 1982. More recent collateral projects include John Wingard's extensive soil mapping (Wingard, 1992,1996) and David Reed's (1994, 1997, 1998) determination of ancient dietary patterns based on stable isotope analysis of bone collagen.

Non-Penn State Related Projects Since 1980

Many colleagues from other universities have been active at Copán since 1984, and while much of their work is not directly germane to our regional reconstructions, it does collectively provide a rich background for many of our inferences. Wendy Ashmore (1991, 1992), then of Rutgers University, continued household studies by test pitting two elite rank groups in the northern foothills of the Copán pocket in 1989.

William and Barbara Fash began the Copán Mosaics Project in 1985, devoted to the conservation, documentation, rearticulation, analysis, and interpretation of tens of thousands of fragments of tenoned, mosaic façade sculptures which adorned the masonry royal structures at Copán (Fash, 1991). Restoration involving such important structures as the Temple of the Hieroglyphic Stairway (Structure 26) was the logical outgrowth of this effort, and continues to the present under the supervision of Rudy Larios, who earlier restored the excavated Las Sepulturas groups. Additional restoration and excavation in Main Group structures 9, 10, 11, 16, 21A, and 22 have also been conducted to date.

Beginning in 1990, the Mosaics Project broadened into the Copán Acropolis Project, sponsored by the Honduran government and also directed by William Fash, along with Ricardo Agurcia, Robert Sharer, David Sedat, and E. Wyllys Andrews V. The Acropolis Project has explored the architectural stratigraphy of the structures on the east side of the Copán Acropolis, and also excavated the royal residence in Group 10L-2 at the southern end of the Main Group. Archaeologists from Honduras, Tulane University, and the University of Pennsylvania have all participated in this research, which is still ongoing at important outlying sites such as Los Achiotes, Río Amarillo, and Piedras Negras.

Both these projects have greatly enlarged the known corpus of Copán's art and inscriptions. Epigraphers and iconographers, including Linda Schele, David Stuart, Berthold Riese, Nikolai Grube, Karl Taube, and Claude F. Baudez, have all contributed important insights about the meaning of the complex symbolic record left for us by the Copán Maya, and their work is essential to the reconstruction of the dynastic sequence outlined in Chapter 2. A magnificent new sculpture museum opened in 1996, allowing visitors for the first time to experience in unprecedented detail Copán's extraordinary heritage of architecture and sculpture.

SUMMARY

In summary, those of us who have been privileged to work at Copán, especially since 1975, have benefited immeasurably from the opportunity to carry out multifaceted, intensive work on an unusually large scale over many years. One reason we have been able to do so has been the exceptional funding available from the Honduran government and other agencies. That we know so much about Copán is also due to the fact that so many investigators have done so many kinds of research. Any particular line of archaeological evidence might be quite weak. Multiple lines of evidence bearing on the same issues greatly strengthen inferences, and we shall see many examples of this principle throughout the rest of this book. Archaeological research also tends to have a certain momentum which is all too frequently interrupted or stopped by lack of resources. At Copán we have been able to build on each generation of effort to gather more complete information. For example, surface surveys were supplemented by test pitting, and the results of test pitting were checked by intensive household excavations. Finally, our collective resources have allowed us to amass extremely large samples of architecture, artifacts, burials, art, and inscriptions. In the following chapters we discuss in greater detail specific aspects of research and the inferences about the Copán polity derived from them.

CHAPTER 4

Elite Household Archaeology

at Las Sepulturas

INTRODUCTION

One of the main efforts of PAC II was the extensive lateral excavation of large mound groups in the Las Sepulturas urban enclave. Earlier limited testing there by Harvard exposed impressive structures associated with apparent domestic assemblages, and contributed to the development of their typology of residential sites (Willey & Leventhal, 1979; Willey et al., 1994). The PAC II work sought to provide an independent test of the Harvard findings, and also to produce a much larger and more representative sample of elite-scale architecture and other domestic features. It is important to remember that in 1980 very little intensive work had been done anywhere on the residences of elite Maya people of non-royal rank, so determining the nature of such habitations was critical.

Ultimately, PAC II completely or largely excavated several impressive groups of elite rank according to the Harvard typology (Figures 3-2, 3-3, 3-4): the Type 4 group 9N-8, the Type 3 group 9M-22A, and the Type 2 group 9M-22B. Partly as a result of these excavations we now think that 9M-22A and B, along with a neaby unexcavated courtyard, are better seen as parts of a single large Type 3 compound. These groups are strung out along the Las Sepulturas causeway and so are connected directly to the Main Group. They were chosen because they incorporated considerable formal variation. Later on, Penn State projects excavated large sections of the Type 4 Group 8N-11, another very distinctive compound near the northeast end of the causeway (Webster et al., 1998). Hohmann (1995) presents the best plans, elevations, and reconstructions of much of the. exposed architecture.

DISTRIBUTION OF ELITE SITES

Before assessing what was discovered and how it can be interpreted, some very basic comments about our known sample of elite rank residential groups are necessary. One problem faced by archaeologists doing settlement archaeology is that of negative evidence. How does one know if one's sample of sites is reasonably substantial and representative? What might be missing? Fortunately this is not an issue with regard to large Type 3 and Type 4 Copán sites. The whereabouts of all surviving ones were known to archaeologists and local people long before formal surveys were made, for two obvious reasons. First, large mound groups are very obtrusive on the landscape. Their presence just cannot be missed. Second, because their architectural features are so massive, they are not as vulnerable to either natural or human destructive processes. We know that two impressive elite centers have been destroyed or buried by the growth of the modern towns of Santa Rita and Copán Ruínas, and also that some elite groups are partially buried by erosion washes along the northern fringes of the Copán pocket alluvial zone. These exceptions aside, we have an excellent sample of elite rank groups in the Copán Valley.

The second comment has to do with their distribution (Figure 4-1). Forty-nine Type 3 (n = 30) and Type 4 (n = 19) complexes have been identified. Of

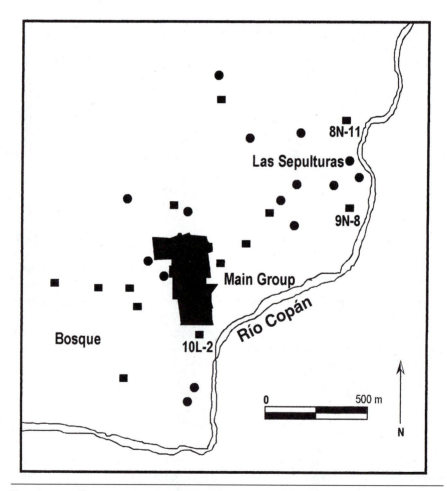

FIGURE 4-1   SCHEMATIC MAP SHOWING THE RELATIONSHIP OF ELITE TYPE 3 (CIRCLES) AND TYPE 4 (RECTANGLES) URBAN CORE COMPOUNDS TO THE MAIN GROUP, THE ROYAL COMPOUND 10L-2, AND THE RIVER.

these, 28 are located in the Copán urban core, all within about 800 m of the Main Group. Fourteen others lie outside the urban core, but at distances of less than 4–5 km from it. This is a striking and unexpected concentration. Residents of these elite compounds were within an easy hour's walk of the royal establishment, and most only a few minutes away. Indeed, the majority of Copán elites could have easily seen and heard what was going on at the Main Group (and residents of the royal household could similarly have monitored the behavior of lesser notables). In this distributional sense, elite sites as a settlement class "behave" very differently than sites of Type 2 and lower rank, which are both much more numerous and more widely distributed over the whole valley.

There are two main reasons for this concentration of elite establishments. The alluvial floor of the Copán pocket from the earliest times was the prime agricultural resource of the whole valley, and there were strong incentives to settle on or near it. Or, conversely, social groups fortunate enough to locate themselves early on this prime land and retain access to it stood an excellent chance of achieving high social rank. Once the royal household had been established at the Main Group in the 5th century, there were also powerful political and social incentives for lesser elites to have their own households nearby. Put simply, it was good (or prudent) to live near the king.

Both Las Sepulturas and El Bosque zones thus have the character of elite residential enclaves, but as William Sanders (1989, pp. 101–102) has pointed out, they are rather different from one another. The Las Sepulturas groups seem to be more discrete and they are on or near a very large causeway, apparently intended to tie them into the Main Group. While a causeway probably also extended west from the Main Group, only the northern El Bosque sites would have been connected to it. El Bosque groups are in a tight cluster in an area of about 33 ha, and in general give the impression of being closely linked to the Main Group itself or to the final royal residence (Group 10L-2) at the southern end of the Acropolis. Possibly the residents of these two zones stood in rather different relations to Copán's royal lineage.

There are a few elite scale residential sites at considerable distances from the Copán pocket. Three of these, tested by Freter, seem to have been isolated ceremonial constructions rather than residences, and so depart from the general pattern. Two elite households are located in the Río Amarillo East pocket about 20–25 km up valley. The most important of these is Río Amarillo, an imposing Type 4 site with its own emblem glyph and with sculptural themes derived from the Main Group. Another, now destroyed, was in the Santa Rita pocket. One impressive site of elite scale, not formally included in any of our surveys because it lies outside the Copán drainage, is locally called Agua Dulce. Situated on the north side of the divide that separates the Río Sesesmil drainage from the Río Monagua, this site might have regulated communication.

The overall distribution of elite residences is significant because archaeologists frequently assume that large sites in settlement hierarchies had administrative functions over particular parts of their regional landscapes. One could argue that the handful of distant elite Copán compounds were placed so as to administer outlying sections of the kingdom, but certainly this function cannot be ascribed to most of Copán's Type 3 and 4 establishments. Some important sub-regions, such as the Sesesmil Valley, have no residential sites of impressive elite scale at all. At Copán, then, there is a clear hierarchy of sites or residences, but not one that can be neatly described as an administrative one in spatial terms. Although the nobles who lived in them might well have had various managerial functions over the wider population and specific parts of the landscape, strategic location of their centers among outlying lesser sites does not appear to have been of prime concern.

One final point must be made here that is significant for our later demographic reconstructions. Some elite rank residential groups grew through accretion and expansion over many generations. Although we cannot usually detect in great detail what the earlier stages of the evolution of these compounds were like, many of them would have originally been equivalent to Type 1 or Type 2 sites.

Character and Functions of Elite Households

Rather than describe each Copán elite residence separately, we will instead focus on the general information we learned about them, and our interpretations of how they were used. For details see Webster (1989), Diamanti (1991), Gerstle (1988), Hendon (1987), Sheehy (1991), Hohmann (1995), and Webster et al., (1998).

Configurations of Sites and Buildings

Even before excavation it was clear that the Las Sepulturas elite compounds investigated during PAC II were quite different from one another in size and configuration. The largest and most complex of them all was Group 9N-8 (Figure 3-2). At least 11 linked patio groups originally comprised this elite residence, portions of which have been washed away by the river along its east and south sides. What remains covers an area of roughly 1.25 ha, most of which has been excavated. There are about 50 reasonably discrete structures, with about 111 rooms. The other two completely excavated groups, 9M-22A and 9M-22B (Figure 3-3) were originally mapped as separate sites, but are probably better conceived as a single unit of Type 3 scale with three conjoined courtyards, the western one still unexcavated. Altogether there are 20 structures with about 24 intact rooms covering an area of about 0.34 ha. The partly excavated Group 8N-11 (Figure 4-2) shows a third pattern—one courtyard with five very impressive buildings, and then a constellation of about 20 smaller structures on the east, west, and south sides, with no clear patio arrangements. In each group one patio cluster is clearly more impressive than the others. Patio A, for example, clearly dominates Group 9N-8.

Buildings in all of these groups consist of masonry substructures which support superstructures with one or more rooms. Individual buildings show varied construction. Each patio usually has a dominant building, or sometimes more than one, which is larger (some originally stood as high as 10 m) and has masonry

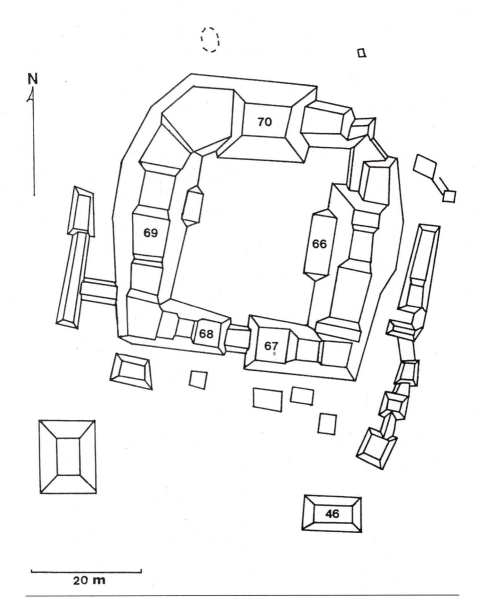

**FIGURE 4-2   THE TYPE 4 COMPOUND 8N-11 AS ORIGINALLY MAPPED BY THE HARVARD
PROJECT BEFORE EXCAVATION.**

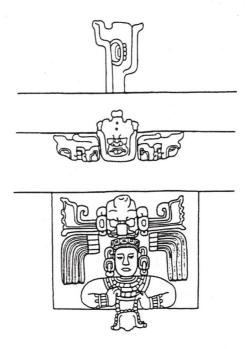

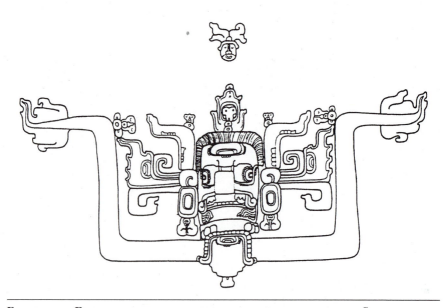

FIGURE 4-3   FAÇADE SCULPTURE RECOVERED DURING EXCAVATION OF STRUCTURE 66S, AN ELITE RESIDENTIAL BUILDING ON THE EAST SIDE OF THE MAIN PATIO IN THE GROUP 8N-11 COMPOUND. DRAWING AND RECONSTRUCTION BY BARBARA FASH.

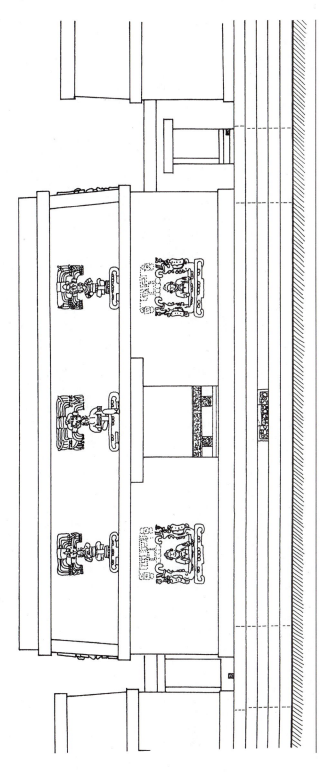

FIGURE 4-4 RECONSTRUCTION OF SCULPTURED NORTH FAÇADE OF STRUCTURE 9N-8-82 CENTER, KNOWN AS THE HOUSE OF THE BACABS. THIS VAULTED BUILDING IS LOCATED ON THE SOUTH SIDE OF PATIO A IN ELITE COMPOUND 9N-8. RECONSTRUCTION BY HASSO HOHMANN FROM ORGINAL DRAWINGS BY BARBARA FASH.

construction of exceptional quality. Such buildings are frequently vaulted, and a few exhibit elaborate façade sculpture (Figure 4-3). The best example is Structure 9N-8-82 center, called the House of the Bacabs, in Group 9N-8 (Figure 4-4). Rooms in all buildings are small, even in the most impressive superstructures. Some buildings, particularly around the smaller courtyards, are made of less refined materials such as natural river cobbles, and had largely perishable superstructures.

Scale of residential architecture is perhaps our best measure of the social rank of the occupants of Copán groups. Elliot Abrams has calculated that Structure 9N-8-82 center required the equivalent of almost 11,000 person-days of labor, and the largest building excavated in Group 8N-11 required almost as much. We will see shortly that considerable numbers of people lived in these noble compounds, but almost certainly the inhabitants were too few to provide all the labor necessary to build them, maintain them, and supply their own needs in terms of food and other resources. A strong inference is that all of these elite households were subsidized by the labor and products of lesser people living elsewhere in the region.

Artifacts, Features, and Burials

Our excavations in the Las Sepulturas sites, as predicted by the Harvard Project's residential hypothesis, yielded hundreds of thousands of potsherds and whole vessels, chipped stone tools of obsidian and chert, ground stone implements (including manos and metates for food processing) and other artifacts consistent with domestic use. Many of these were recovered from garbage middens around building peripheries or on plaza surfaces, where people had discarded refuse. In other cases distinctive concentrations of artifacts (features) or microdebitage showed where activities such as cooking and production of shell and stone ornaments took place. Hendon (1987) was able to discriminate statistically specific artifact assemblages whose distribution gives us a general grasp of the ways in which structures and their peripheral spaces were used. Most artifacts were from superficial deposits that represent only the final episodes of occupation, but others were from deep middens that had accumulated over considerable periods of time.

Although artifact assemblages from the Las Sepulturas elite compounds include some status objects not found in rural commoner sites, for the most part residential assemblages everywhere, and on all social levels, are quite similar (Gonlin 1993; Webster, Gonlin, & Sheets 1997). This is a pattern noted elsewhere in Mesoamerica as well (Hirth 1998). Of course people of high rank might have more objects of certain kinds than people of lesser rank, much as we do today, but there seem to have been few sumptuary rules that limited the character of domestic possessions. As an example, all Late Classic period households at Copán seem to have had access to polychrome painted serving vessels. Elite households, however, were involved in more intensive feasting and hosting, and so had numerically greater amounts of such vessels. The methodological lesson is that domestic artifacts alone are not good discriminators of status variation at

Copán unless very large collections are made and compared from different residential sites.

Skeletal remains of approximately 315 individuals have been recovered from the three Las Sepulturas elite groups. Most of these date from Coner phase times, although some came from a deeply buried Middle Preclassic cemetery (Fash, 1991), and there is one very rich burial from the 5th century, roughly contemporary with the founding of the dynasty.

Although studies of this large sample are not complete, it clearly includes infants, children, juveniles, and young and old adults of both sexes. Such a population is just what we would expect if, in typical Maya fashion, people were buried in their household compounds. The most elaborate burials came from well-constructed dressed-stone tombs covered with capstones, usually positioned under plaza surfaces fronting on impressive buildings. The simplest were interments placed in small pits in middens or construction fill, and between these extremes fall several other kinds of simple cists or rough stone tombs. Many burials lacked mortuary offerings, but others included both local and imported ceramic vessels, tools, ear flares and other ornaments, and what may be offerings of food. Pets were also buried. Patio E produced a dog purposefully buried with a small clay sphere. Even the individuals in the finest Coner phase tombs had comparatively few grave goods—usually a few ceramic vessels.

Building Functions

Although it is clear that all of the Las Sepulturas compounds were basically residential, this does not mean that all the buildings were houses in the strict sense. The Maya household tradition segregates activities among separate buildings, instead of concentrating them all under a single roof as Westerners usually do. Thus commoner Maya household compounds today, and in the past, often consist of dormitories (i.e., the house proper for eating, sleeping, and socializing), surrounded by detached kitchens or other work spaces, storehouses, and sometimes sweat baths and shrines. This pattern is archaeologically well-documented at Ceren (Sheets, 1992). Copán elite households of course needed the same range of facilities, and all have been identified in the Las Sepulturas sites. Dormitories are especially conspicuous because of the spacious interior benches that were used for sitting and sleeping, and kitchens by their associations with food preparation artifacts. Often such facilities were much more impressive than their counterparts in lower-ranked residences. For example, most large plaza compounds include large, well-built shrines and, in some cases, apparent burial structures. Structure 80 in Patio A of Group 9N-8 is such a shrine, possibly devoted to ancestors of the resident nobles.

Because of the high social and political status of their occupants, special facilities not appropriate for commoner compounds were also present. The House of the Bacabs on the south side of Plaza A, in Group 9N-8, was probably both an elite house and a building for political and ritual use. Right next to it on the west side of the courtyard was an apparent dormitory for elite young men, complete with ball game paraphernalia. Randolph Widmer identified a special workshop

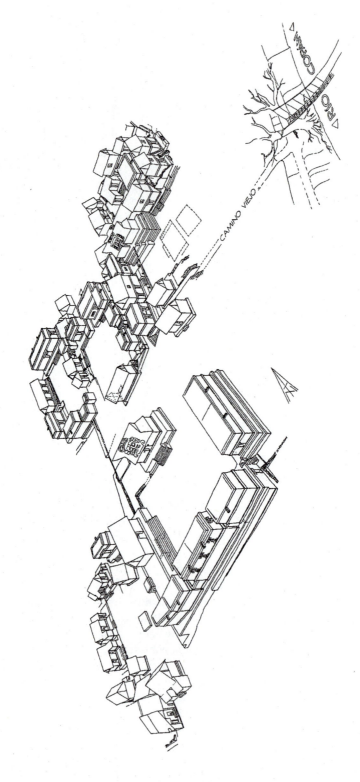

FIGURE 4-5   RECONSTRUCTION DRAWING OF THE ELITE RESIDENTIAL COMPOUND 9N-8 BY HASSO HOHMANN.

facility for making elite status lapidary and shell objects in Plaza H of Group 9N-8 that we will describe in a later chapter. Lords of the nearby Group 8N-11 had an extremely impressive political/ritual building separate from their elaborate house, and the façade of this structure appears to have been purposefully oriented to an important astronomical event—the setting of the sun at the time of solar zenith in about A.D. 785 (Bricker and Bricker, 1999; Webster et al., 1998).

Consistent with the concept of general residential functions is the fact that the Las Sepulturas elite compounds grew by accretion over time. Rooms were modified, old buildings enlarged, and new buildings, even whole new patio groups, were added to older ones. Ultimately, Group 9N-8 probably looked much like the reconstruction shown in Figure 4-5.

Chronology

Virtually all of the latest buildings in the excavated elite compounds sometimes were built after about A.D. 650–700 (although all have traces of earlier material, going back to Preclassic times in their fill), and it was only about this time that many noble residential sites began to exhibit fine construction. Taken individually, the compounds show considerable chronological variation. The locale of Group 9N-8 was occupied in Middle Preclassic times, and at least intermittently thereafter. In sharp contrast, Group 8N-11 predominantly dates after about A.D. 600–650, as does the 9M-22A/B complex. Obsidian, radiocarbon, and archaeomagnetic dates, along with other evidence, show that occupation and even construction continued long after the demise of the royal dynasty in the early 9th century. Elite status objects were still being made in Plaza H of Group 9N-8 until the mid-10th century, and so people we could reasonably call elites in some sense were still active until at least about A.D. 1000. After this time the compounds still show unmistakable signs of use, but we are not sure whether these late occupants retained any effective elite rank or functions. They did, however, use general Coner or Coner-like ceramics, along with a few Ejar phase wares, until the buildings were finally abandoned, which was at least as late as the 12th century.

The nature of abandonment is also suggestive. Floor and bench surfaces were usually well maintained until buildings collapsed. Artifacts in primary contexts on these living surfaces were very few, however, suggesting that rooms were cleaned out when people finally left them. For example, Hendon (1987) lists only about 90 whole or reconstructable vessels in all of the excavated 9N-8 rooms. By contrast, small commoner buildings at Ceren, which were abruptly abandoned, sometimes had dozens of associated vessels, along with a wide variety of other domestic artifacts (Sheets, 1992). Apparently the abandonment of the elite buildings we dug at Las Sepulturas was reasonably protracted and orderly, although there are a few signs of destruction. Façade sculpture on the House of the Bacabs was deliberately defaced by burning, (Fash, 1989). The adjacent young men's house also burned down, although not necessarily at the same time, and quite possibly as the result of an accidental fire. Widmer's workshop rooms (where many artifacts are *in situ* on floors and benches) collapsed suddenly in the mid-late 10th century, probably during an earthquake.

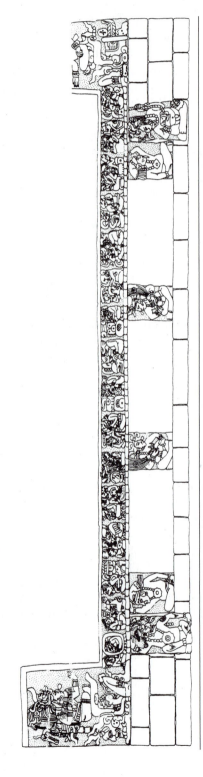

FIGURE 4-6 CARVED AND INSCRIBED BENCH FOUND IN THE CENTRAL ROOM OF STRUCTURE 9N-8-82 CENTER. ORIGINAL DRAWING BY BARBARA FASH.

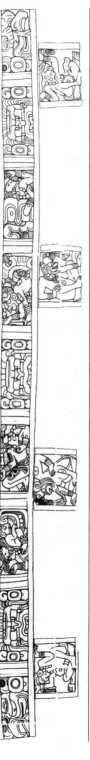

FIGURE 4-7   CARVED BENCH WITH A SKYBAND MOTIF FOUND IN STRUCTURE 66C, A VAULTED BUILDING ON THE EAST SIDE OF THE MAIN PATIO OF ELITE COMPOUND 8N-11. DRAWING BY BARBARA FASH.

Art and Inscriptions

To a degree unusual at other Maya polities, Copán's Late Classic elites were able to display their status with façade sculpture, altars, and elaborate carved thrones, all normally prerogatives of royalty. As we shall see later, this prerogative may signal royal weakness *vis à vis* nobles. The House of the Bacabs is the best example from Las Sepulturas. Its façade displays imagery associated with scribal persons or deities, and its interior bench (Figure 4-6) is inscribed with glyphs that give the date of its dedication (about A.D. 782), name the "owner" of the building, his parents, his scribal title, and link him in some direct fashion to the 16th ruler *Yax Pasah*. A similar, and almost contemporary bench was earlier found in a nearby elite group by the Harvard Project. Dominant buildings in Group 8N-11 have façade sculpture celebrating war, vegetation, and fertility, and one has a skyband bench that models the Maya cosmos and might also have warfare connotations. Whoever sat on this bench metaphorically was placed at the center of the universe (Figure 4-7), and might well have been a co-ruler of Copán and/or an important war captain (see Chapter 12). In Group 9M-22A the dominant building had elaborate sculpture that Karl Taube (personal communication to Webster, 1997) believes shows the tools used in sculpting.

Quite possibly scribal and sculptural imagery and titles point to the actual occupations or court functions of individuals living in these compounds, because we know from inscriptions at other Maya centers that nobles occupied such positions. David Stuart cautions, however, that these symbols might have more esoteric meanings. We do not yet understand exactly what the programs of art and inscriptions on elite household buildings at Las Sepulturas and elsewhere mean. Clearly, however, they show that the individuals who used the dominant patios and buildings were of extremely high social and political rank in the Copán kingdom. Some of them held high positions in the royal court, and it is possible that some were related, through descent or marriage, to the royal lineage.

Identity and Scale of Resident Populations

Who exactly presided over these elaborate households? Their inhabitants certainly included the political elite of Copán society below the level of the ruler. By political elite we mean generally those individuals or families freed from the necessity of manual work, able to employ the labor of others who provide them with elaborate household facilities, richer possessions, and more assured food supplies, and to whom lesser people pay deference. Some members of such a political elite undoubtedly had privileged access to important offices and titles, were attendants at the royal court, and either directly or indirectly influenced political decisions. No doubt many of these elite people also participated in a high culture of dress, speech, aesthetic taste, and general decorum that distinguised them from ordinary Copánecos, and were repositories of much of the esoteric knowledge of Classic Maya culture.

What we don't know is how these people were recruited. They might have acquired their positions through descent within larger kinship groups that included commoners. Alternatively, they might have been lesser members of the royal family, high officers or soldiers of the polity or favorite courtiers whose positions and wealth derived from royal appointment, or even people who had independently achieved wealth through trade. Presently we cannot discriminate among these kinds of recruitment, although we suspect that kinship was probably the most important element. These are issues that can only be resolved by future research.

Exactly how many people were permanent residents of the Las Sepulturas elite compounds is difficult to estimate, but it is clear that they housed social groups far larger than the nuclear or extended families that comprised most Type 1 households. Our best estimate, based on three people per residential room, is that there were about 250–300 people living in Group 9N-8 in the late 9th century, and probably about 100 people in the 9M22-A, B compound during the height of their occupations. The sizes of their populations obviously changed through time, as discussed in Chapter 11.

One thing is clear—not all of these people were nobles, despite the fact that they lived in impressive elite residences. In fact, judging from modes of burial and the low quality of some of the architecture, most people in Group 9N-8 were not particularly privileged. The concept of household, of course, does not imply that co-residents were related to one another. In all likelihood the Las Sepulturas elite compounds housed members of one or more noble family (or perhaps a noble lineage), whose members would themselves have been of greater or lesser social rank. Their households probably also included a wide range of unrelated servants, retainers, or guests (see Diamanti, 1991 for ethnographic examples of this pattern). Andrea Gerstle (1988), for example, believes she has found evidence of nonlocal people from central Hounduras who resided in Patio D of Group 9N-8. Although we cannot at this point determine the degree of kin versus nonkin relationships in our burial population, this may become feasible in the future through the application of DNA analysis.

Some Maya nobles appear to have been polygynous, and some of the 9N-8 patio groups show unusually high ratios of buried women and children to adult men. Such a pattern is found in Patio F, right next to the dominant Patio A. Quite possibly the lesser wives or consorts of the principal lord lived there, while Patio A itself housed the lord himself, along with his highest-ranking wife, children, and other close relatives.

SUMMARY AND INTERPRETATIONS

Household archaeology at Las Sepulturas by PAC II abundantly supports the Harvard residential hypothesis, and supplements the results of the early Harvard household excavations. By Coner times this part of Copán's urban core was dominated by the establishments of elite social groups, whose privileged rank and wealth were particularly evident after A.D. 650–700, when many of them lived in or otherwise used facilities that we can accurately describe as palatial. Indeed, groups such as 9N-8 compare very favorably with the presumed royal residential compound 10L-2 at the Main Group. Assuming that future research in the El Bosque enclave turns up similar patterns, the whole urban core has the appearance of a residential zone occupied by elite people and their retainers or adherents of lesser rank. As discussed later, there might have been as many as 9,000–12,000 such people clustered around the Main Group by the end of the 9th century. Because this whole area measured only 1–1.5 sq km, overall population densities were of urban proportions, although the sociological and economic character of the enclave was very different from that of major urban centers elsewhere in Mesoamerica, such as the Aztec capital of Tenochtitlan or the great Classic city of Teotihuacan (Sanders and Webster, 1988). In this respect Copán is unique. No other Classic Maya center has a comparable urban-like concentration.

In Chapter 3 we remarked that it is useful to think of Classic Maya polities as composed of households of various ranks. As a result of Las Sepulturas household research we now have a much firmer grasp of the identities, lifestyles, and functions of social groups that, while not of royal status, were certainly exceptionally prestigious, wealthy, and powerful in Copán's sociopolitical hierarchy. Although we infer that such groups were heavily supported by people living elsewhere in the polity, we unfortunately have no direct insights into the nature of these wider relationships. One possibility is that powerful elite families taxed unrelated commoners, a situation known ethnohistorically elsewhere in Mesoamerica. William Sanders (1989, 1992) has argued persuasively that instead Copán elites were heads of large kinship groups, or maximal lineages, that included hundreds, or in some cases thousands, of people outside their immediate households. According to this model, elite households were in a sense miniature versions of the royal household in that they were engaged in administration of their own dependents and corporate resources, most importantly land.

That some elites clearly survived the royal collapse suggests that they had their own effective support independent of the dynasty. As we shall see later, they might in fact have played a potent political role in the collapse itself.

What is needed next at Copán are similar extensive excavations at elite residences outside the urban core. Ashmore's (1992) tests of outlying Type 3 and 4 residences in the Copán pocket revealed patterns strongly reminiscent of the Las Sepulturas sites. Similar work at the center of Ostuman, however, showed the unusual pattern of large buildings of Type 4 scale, but low-quality construction and with virtually no sculpture. Obviously there are still uninvestigated dimensions of variation in Copán elite residential arrangements.

Finally, our examination of elite households helps us understand the process of urbanization at Copán. The urban core (the Main Group included) had royal or elite households as its dominant organizational features. Certainly nonelite people were present as well, but they lived on a social landscape dominated by the presence of numerous elite individuals, by the tangible and permanent manifestations of elite authority and wealth, and were often themselves directly attached to elite households.

People of all kinds for thousands of years been have attracted to cities or their peripheries. But we cannot see the concentration of people in Copán's urban core as due to the same processes that attracted people to more conventionally urban places in Mesoamerica such as Tenochtitlan or Teotitihuacan, the great centers of the Basin of Mexico. If something like Sanders's system of maximal lineages existed at Copán, then elites had to balance three major sets of relationships—their connections with the royal dynasty, with their fellow elites, and with their lesser kinspeople. To the extent that they actively chose to live where they did, the first two considerations seem to have been very strong. Such spatial concentration no doubt created tensions, in the sense that most elite households were not spatially imbedded among the more rural households so important to them. Nevertheless, as we will see later, they probably did live within a few hours walk, at most, from the bulk of the sustaining population of the kingdom.

CHAPTER 5

The PAC II Regional Settlement Survey: Setting, Methodology, and Results

INTRODUCTION

Much research has been devoted to the study of Classic Maya settlement patterns since Gordon Willey's (Willey et al., 1965) pioneering survey of the Belize River valley. Settlement projects of the 1960s and 1970s carried out at Tikal, Yaxha, Dzibilchaltun, Lubaantun, Becan, Seibal, and Altar de Sacrificos, as well as around numerous smaller sites, provided many new insights concerning major Maya centers and the nature of Maya polities. Once the site cores and their immediate surrounding peripheral zones had been adequately mapped and tested by excavation, it became obvious that they did not conform to the earlier model of "vacant ceremonial centers." Centers instead served a variety of political, social, economic and religious functions, but most especially that of royal residences, an inference further confirmed by the increasingly clear understanding of Classic Maya texts.

Surveys also revealed that outlying settlement around Maya centers tended to drop off in density and become more dispersed as distance from site cores increased. Although populations were often quite dense within a km or two of the major concentrations of large architecture, Classic Maya centers were less urban in their settlement arrangements than the great cities of highland Mexico, such as Tenochtitlan, Teotihuacan, and Monte Alban (Sanders & Webster, 1988).

A major difficulty confronting these early surveys was simply recording an adequate sample of surface remains on landscapes covered in dense tropical forests, such as those of the Petén of northern Guatemala, or by the impenetrable scrub of northern Yucatán. Knowledge of some celebrated Maya polities, such as Palenque, is confined almost entirely to their central, monumental precincts. Occasionally, as at Dzibilchaltun, clearing for agriculture and shallow soils allowed rapid survey coverage and easy identification of sites over large, continuous areas. More commonly, archaeologists were forced to adopt the strategy of laboriously cutting long transects radiating from centers, or sometimes between them. Surveys accordingly progressed slowly, and it was often difficult to know where to stop because there were usually few clues to the boundaries of any given settlement system. Slow work meant high costs, which in turn limited scale and effectiveness, and extrapolating from the surveyed zones to those still unsampled was always problematical. Such limitations are in stark contrast to the situation throughout much of the Mexican highlands, where regional surveys cover hundreds and even thousands of square kilometers on landscapes minimally obscured by vegetation.

When we began our PAC II surveys at Copán in 1981 archaeologists still did not know very well what the overall settlement domain of any Maya polity looked like, nor how it was internally differentiated. Even less clear were the processes by which a local polity was defined and settled, and the kinds of socio-political relationships that occurred between ruling elites within and among polities. One advantage that Mayanists possessed was the generally excellent preservation of sites of all kinds on landscapes minimally disturbed by modern populations, urban development, or agricultural activity. Morever, most sites consisted of structures visible on the surface, rather than the scatters of artifacts common on highland Mexican landscapes. Where landscapes were not heavily altered by erosion or deposition of soil, surface inspection usually provided a reasonable approximation of site layout and scale.

THE PAC II SURVEY

From a methodological perspective the Copán region presents an almost perfect setting for settlement and landscape archaeology compared to other parts of the Maya Lowlands. The contoured sections shown on the regional base map (Figure 1-5) cover a total area of about 485 sq km. The rugged upland topography demarcates a natural survey universe centered on the main drainages—one with clear boundaries and small enough so that it can be sampled effectively. Using modern roads one could walk to the headwaters of the Río Copán or the Río Sesesmil from the Main Group in about two days.

Ancient features are quite accessible and visible because deforestation has produced a much more open landscape than found in the Petén. Good topographic maps exist, as does aerial photo coverage. Because the valley was essentially abandoned for so long, ancient Maya sites are not heavily obscured by more recent settlement remains. Site preservation is remarkably fine, and in some zones, such as the Copán urban core, the sheer density of structures has inhibited plowing, thus minimizing destruction. Adjacent uplands are used, as we shall see in a moment, in ways that minimally disturb archaeological features. The valley supports a well-developed system of roads and paths, so all parts of it are reasonably accessible. Some zones, especially in the Copán pocket, have been affected by colluvial and alluvial erosion that buried some sites and washed away others, but such processes are localized.

Ancient Copañecos built most of their structures on durable stone platforms, and even the lowest and most inconspicuous of these are often visible, as we shall see in Chapter 7. Because of the density of the modern population and the long history of archaeological research in the valley, most sites of large scale have long been known, although two of them have been destroyed by the growth of the modern towns of Copán Ruínas and Santa Rita. Last but not least, local people are used to archaeologists and are almost always extremely accommodating when strange-looking foreigners festooned with maps suddenly appear in their fields or even their houselots.

In 1981 we had an additional, all-important advantage—the excellent work of our predecessors of the Harvard and PAC I projects. From them we inherited a good ceramic sequence and the main outlines of Copán's dynastic history. Even more important, the urban core had been thoroughly mapped and tested, the settlement distribution in the Copán pocket was known, and a valuable heuristic model of households established. Our own survey strategies were a logical next step in all these efforts. Finally, we benefited enormously from the parallel PAC II excavations in the Las Sepulturas urban enclave; in effect, constant feedback between the survey efforts and the urban core residential excavations provided a much richer picture of the past than either could have on its own.

Goals of the Survey

The specific goals of the PAC II survey were:

1. To acquire a systematic and representative sample of settlement or other cultural features in those parts of the Copán drainage located outside the Copán pocket;
2. To clear and map all outlying sites found, and collect surface samples of artifacts if possible;
3. To collect detailed data concerning patterns of modern land-use and ecological characteristics in the surveyed areas;
4. To carry out a program of test excavation at a large percentage of the sites located in order to establish control over the chronology of occupation and the range of site functions, with special emphasis on any signs of economic specialization; and
5. To employ data from both the survey and test excavations to reconstruct the settlement history of the polity and ultimately to explain more fully the rise of the Copán kingdom, its character at its height in the 8th and 9th centuries, and especially the process of its decline.

A specific and fundamental goal of our operations in the regional sustaining area of the Copán Valley was to test a central assumption of settlement research: the "principle of abundance." Edward H. Thompson (1886) first expressed the common sense idea that most small mound sites surrounding large Maya centers must represent the residences of commoner households because they occur in such high frequencies. Only in recent years has the assumed residential function of such sites been systematically tested through excavation and artifact analyses. For any non-industrial, agrarian society such as the ancient Maya we make the further assumption that a very large percentage (usually well over 50%) of the population must have been engaged in agriculture on the landscape. Dispersed rural settlement of the kind found in the Copán Valley is thus heavily determined by agricultural resources and practices. In addition to putative residential sites, we also expected to encounter remains of ancient Maya agroengineering practices, such as agricultural terraces.

Settlement Survey and Land Use

Both settlement and landscape research are ideally carried out in environments unaltered by humans since the ancient inhabitants abandoned them. Most archaeologists never enjoy such optimal conditions but many parts of the Maya Lowlands had, for all practical purposes, been so abandoned. Even today some projects operate in locales virtually untouched since Classic Maya times, as around the great center of Piedras Negras in western Guatemala. The Copán Valley is not such a region.

In pursuing our goals we had to accommodate ourselves to the unique circumstances of the landscape of the modern Copán Valley, which, as described in Chapter 1, is not only unlike that of any other ancient polity in the Maya Lowlands, but has also been heavily altered by humans in ancient and recent times. Copán's topographic setting itself is not unique—Maya settlement surveys have been carried out elsewhere in river valleys, most notably in Belize. These regions, however, have much better upland soils, different kinds of vegetation, and are in reasonable proximity to marine environments, so they do not serve as good predictors of Copán's settlement patterns. Complex hydrographic and topographic conditions at Copán produce a variety of significantly different ecological zones within a comparatively small region, with a corresponding complexity of settlement patterns and agricultural practices.

We also knew from the Harvard and PAC I surveys that modern land-use systems in the valley influence the preservation and visibility of archaeological sites. In order to understand the context and methodology of our regional research and the simulations of agricultural history presented later, we must review in more detail both recent patterns of land use and how these have evolved. Many of these patterns provide important analogs for our conceptions of the decline of the ancient polity.

Intensive commercial agriculture, primarily involving dry-season irrigation, the use of fertilizers, and mechanical plows, is conducted on the deep alluvial soils of the active flood plain and older alluvial terraces. The principal cash crop, tobacco (for which Copán has been famed since the 18th century), is grown during the dry season. During the wet season the same parts of the landscape are used to grow maize and other subsistence crops. They are the prime agricultural soils today as they were in the past, and heavy cultivation of them has caused most of the serious destruction of archaeological sites on the floodplain, especially of the smaller mounds. Fortunately, as already noted, such destruction has been limited by the large size, density, and stone construction of many mounds, particularly those of the urban core in the Copán pocket. Even when sites have been plowed they are often still identifiable as distinct scatters of construction material and artifacts.

Small-scale, short-fallow subsistence farming (swidden agriculture) takes place primarily in the foothills and some of the intermontane valleys and is usually carried out using household labor. Vegetation is removed with machetes and piled until ready for burning at the end of the dry season. Hand hoes are then used to turn the ash into the soil, and planting is done with metal-tipped digging

sticks. Maize and beans are the principal outfield crops, and vegetables and orchard crops are grown in houselot gardens. Dispersed households of rural farmers are found in many parts of the valley today, although people often live in
large towns or other settlements and travel to their distant fields.

Destruction of upland sites by such traditional cultivation is minimal and surface visibility is excellent. Erosion, however, is increasingly a problem, especially
on the preferred soils that develop on limestone bedrock. Many such zones have
been reduced to pockets of soil on otherwise bare limestone slopes. Because of
the high density of the modern population, fields are seldom left fallow very long
and are often cultivated every year, so essentially what is cleared and burned are
grasses and low scrub. According to Sanders's agricultural surveys, yields often
drop by 60–75% over as little as a decade under such intense cultivation.

Despite thin and often infertile soils and the ever-present danger of erosion,
rural farmers seldom make efforts to maintain or enhance productivity through
the construction of terracing or other soil conservation measures, although they
are aware of these methods. One possible reason for such neglect is that many
rural subsistence farmers had, until recently, no secure rights to land and thus few
incentives to improve it. Contour hoeing is practiced in restricted locales, and low
stone terraces are built across natural swales to capture eroding soils and mois-
ture (Plate 5-1). Often eroded upland fields are immediately adjacent to the river
and present a stark contrast with the deep, productive alluvial soils (Plate 5-2).

PLATE 5-1   PEOPLE TODAY BUILD SMALL CHECK DAMS LIKE THESE ON STEEP
HILLSIDES IN THE COPÁN VALLEY TO INHIBIT EROSION AND CREATE DEEPER DEPOSITS
OF USABLE SOILS.

PLATE 5-2   NOTE THE EXTREME CONTRAST BETWEEN THE DEEP, FLAT, ALLUVIAL SOILS ALONG THE RIVER AND THE STEEP, THIN-SOILED SLOPES. ALLUVIAL LAND, THOUGH LIMITED, IS THE PRIME AGRICULTURAL RESOURCE AND CAN BE IRRIGATED AND PLOWED. HILLSIDE LAND IS MUCH LESS PRODUCTIVE, MORE SUSCEPTIBLE TO EROSION, AND MUST BE CULTIVATED WITH HAND TOOLS.

Since Stephens's and Catherwood's time there has been a distinctive evolutionary process of land use that structures the local political economy. Nineteenth century colonists of the valley staked out extensive holdings, including both prime bottom lands and adjacent uplands, on an essentially vacant landscape. Stephens in 1839 recorded one such parcel of 6,000 acres, or just over 24 sq km, that probably included most of the Copán pocket. Large landowners needed labor to capitalize their commercial efforts and attracted it by giving workers, who often were recent migrants into the region, the right to clear upland cornfields, or *milpas*. Newly cultivated upland fields were quite productive as long as population density was low, with farmers shifting their fields frequently to maintain productivity.

Such a system of economic relationships for a long time benefited both landowners and laborers, but the equation eventually changed. Landowners introduced cattle into the upland zones cleared by subsistence farmers, effectively transforming vast upland tracts into cattle pasture. This process had two beneficial effects. Although it prevented reforestation, it also inhibited upland erosion caused by subsistence agriculture because grasses and herbaceous vegetation quickly formed dense ground cover, nourished in part by the fertilizer provided by cattle. In the long run, the expansion of pasture also benefited archaeologists by rendering much of the landscape more open and accessible, while not destroying ancient sites. On the other hand, of course, it increasingly restricted shifting cultivation, leading to the extremely short fallow periods of permanent cultivation that are widespread today.

Commercial farming of coffee, and to a lesser degree pineapple or sugar cane, occurs on slopes and in some intermontane valleys. Coffee is shade adapted and cultivation requires the removal of undergrowth vegetation, leaving only the larger trees for shade. Sites are easily visible in coffee plantations, although the steepness of slopes where coffee is often planted frequently discouraged ancient occupation. Sugar cane and pineapple fields are virtually unsurveyable because of poor visibility and difficulty of movement, but fortunately cover comparatively few parts of the valley.

Pine forests in the higher elevations and on the steepest hillsides tend to develop on the thinnest, poorest soils. These zones are not very attractive to subsistence or commercial farmers, although they do provide some grazing, and are often damaged by runaway fires. Much recent deforestation has been caused by such fires, as well as by logging and the demands for fuel, particularly for drying tobacco. Today large zones of upland forests are protected by the Honduran government so fuel and building materials are in increasingly short supply.

When we began our work in 1981 about 60% of the Copán Valley had been significantly altered by agriculture, cattle raising, or logging. About 10% of the valley remained in undisturbed tropical forest and about 30% was in relatively open oak and pine forests. These conditions contributed significantly to the success of the Copán PAC II survey.

Copán Settlement Survey Design and Methodology

The initial decision in designing settlement research is defining the region to be surveyed. This can be a difficult task since the survey zone must be large enough to yield the data needed to address questions of regional settlement dynamics, but small enough to be adequately sampled given limited time and other resources. We had to decide which parts of the approximately 400 sq km drainage of the Río Copán in Honduras to include. Here the results of the earlier surveys were extremely useful. We knew that the modern population was heavily concentrated on the alluvial lands of the streams or the immediately adjacent piedmont/foothill zones, and that this seemed to be the ancient pattern as well. Even in the densely settled Copán pocket the PAC I surveys found very few traces of ancient settlement in the pine forest uplands. Our strategy, therefore, was to define survey strips along the Río Copán and its major tributaries. While this decision did not exclude coverage of some of the higher, more remote sections of the valley, it was based on informed assumptions about where ancient settlement was concentrated and omitted most zones of steep pine forest well away from permanent streams.

Fortunately we already had a good set of black and white aerial photographs at a scale of 1:16,000 taken by flights along the major streams. Three sets of overlapping photographs were selected that incorporated *vega,* foothill, and mountain zones along the Río Copán from Río Amarillo to the Guatemalan border (photos 6, 7, 9, 11, 18 and 25); the Sesesmil drainage (photos 28, 30, 32, 34, and 38); and the Río Jila valley (photo 99). The space contained within these zones was 129.8 sq km (Figure 3-1) and constituted the *survey universe*—the region to be sampled. Not only was this a very large area, but it covered all valley ecological zones and fell outside the already surveyed Copán pocket. Because we had overlapping sets of photos, they could be examined with stereoscopes to provide three dimensional perspectives.

The archaeological ideal, rarely achieved, is 100% surface coverage of any survey universe, but this was far beyond our capabilities. Much of our defined survey universe could not be covered on the ground because the landscape was inaccessible due to vegetation cover, terrain (e.g., extreme slopes or swamps), or cultural features (e.g., roads or modern settlements). Even if the landscape had been totally accessible, our funding was insufficient to provide the labor to examine all of it. Time was short as well because surveys can only be done effectively during the dry season from January through early May.

We decided to use a systematic, stratified, non-random sampling method to reduce the area covered. "Systematic" means that all major sections of our universe were sampled to ensure adequate coverage. "Stratified" means that some environmental zones received greater attention than others based on our informed assumption that the distribution of the modern population and land use overlapped significantly with those of the ancient Copañecos. "Non-Random" means that survey areas were selected based upon current land use and accessibility, not by a randomly designed statistical sample, which given the size and diversity of the universe, was not feasible.

MODIFICATIONS OF THE SITE TYPOLOGY   In Chapter 3 we reviewed the Harvard project site typology, and because we used a variant of it as the basis for the rural surveys, some additional discussions of its implications are necessary.

The typology was created as a heuristic device to categorize sites quickly. While the basic assumption was that almost all sites on the landscape were residences, this functional criterion is not essential to the use of the typology. Much more important are several formal attributes. Some of these, such as numbers of buildings or patio groups, are only weak indicators of site rank. While the biggest Type 4 sites do have the largest numbers of buildings and patios, there is much overlap between the categories in these characteristics. Height of the largest mound at a site (which usually also correlates directly with mass of the structure) and quality of construction (fine cut stone, evidence of vaults, façade sculpture) are the essential correlates, and these must co-occur to define elite sites.

Any rough and ready classification system of this kind obviously obscures much internal variation. Such variation has been documented at Copán (indeed, it was evident to the Harvard archaeologists before they made the classification). Our excavations at Las Sepulturas revealed distinctive elite compounds, and variation in small rural sites is discussed in Chapter 7. The typology also suggests discrete rather than continuous clusters of sites. In fact, there is considerable continuity in site attributes both in energetic (Abrams, 1994) and qualitative terms. As an example of the latter, some Type 2 buildings have finely cut stone and vaulted roofs. Finally, surface indications sometimes are poor guides to site scale and configuration. Some buried sites of elite scale (reviewed later) appear on the surface to be much more modest. We nevertheless found the typology to be appropriate for our purposes, and retain it here as an organizing feature of our data.

The Harvard typology was largely based on observations of sites located within the Copán urban core. Because differences at the simpler end of the site scale were not as apparent in Las Sepulturas as they were in the outlying rural regions, we modified the typology somewhat to fit the purposes of our rural surveys. Two site types were added: 1) *non-mound* sites (which were not recorded by the Harvard or PAC I projects) and 2) *aggregate* mound sites. Most non-mound sites were discrete scatters of artifacts (usually pottery) that had no apparent associated construction debris. Such sites were typically found in plowed fields where visibility was good (if a site had both artifacts and a debris scatter, we recorded it as a single mound site). We also occasionally applied the nonmound label to special sites such as caves that showed signs of human use. The aggregate category refers to two or more mounds of Type 1 scale that are in close proximity, but do not appear to form a coherent courtyard group. During the analyses of settlement that follow, we lump aggregate mound sites with Type 1 sites because during the excavation phases we determined them to be essentially similar except for the difference in site layout.

Field Procedures

The most essential field tool was the set of aerial photos that oriented survey teams and on which sites were recorded. Each of the individual 1:16,000 photographs covers approximately 14 sq km, but at this scale small features cannot easily be seen. We therefore enlarged each photo to a scale of 1:4,000 and cut it into four quadrants, labeled A, B, C, or D, to make them easier to handle in the field (Figure 5-1). Each quadrant photo covered an area of 3.45 sq km, and was placed on a board with a tracing paper overlay. At this scale individual fields, houses, trees, fence lines, paths, and roads were clearly distinguishable. Even the specific kinds of crops in a field and their stage of growth could be recognized.

SURVEY UNITS   Quadrant maps were subdivided by visual inspection into *survey units,* the basic spatial units of the survey. All survey units shared four characteristics. First, each one was clearly visible on the photo and had clearly defined boundaries, such as fence lines, field borders, rivers or roads. Second, each unit was fairly uniform in its ecological characteristics; it might be a corn field, a patch of pine forest, or a zone of fenced pasture. Third, each was accessible and allowed reasonable surface visibility. Finally, each unit was sufficiently small so that it could easily be walked over by survey teams composed of one or two archaeologists and several workers.

While most survey units were wholly or partly determined by cultural factors, more "natural" units were included as well. For example, small zones of uncut deciduous forest and extensive zones of upland pine forest often appeared as islands of natural vegetation defined by surrounding settlements and fields, and were included as survey units. We quickly learned that Maya sites in the Copán Valley tend

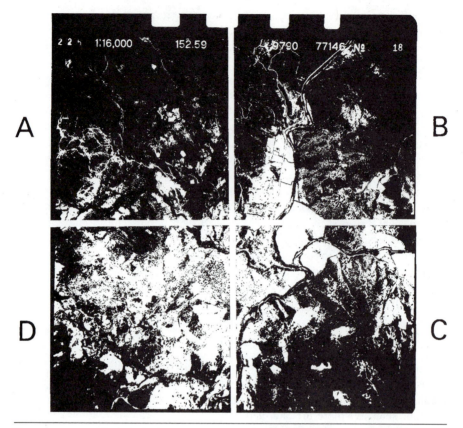

FIGURE 5-1   1 : 16,000 SCALE AERIAL PHOTOS WERE BASIC TOOLS OF THE COPÁN
SURVEYS. THESE WERE DIVIDED INTO FOUR QUADRANTS AS SHOWN (A–D), AND EACH
QUADRANT WAS THEN ENLARGED TO A 1 : 4,000 SCALE MORE USEFUL FOR LOCATING
SITES AND OTHER LANDSCAPE FEATURES IN THE FIELD.

to be located in quite predictable places. Our field procedures, however, obliged us
to traverse virtually every kind of terrain imaginable as we moved across or between survey units. This is an important point because we were not only looking for
habitation sites, but for any ancient human alterations of the landscape.

Each survey unit was traced right on the aerial photo overlay and given a se-
quential number within the quadrant. Survey units were walked over by field
crews and locations of all sites within the unit were recorded on the quadrant
tracing overlay. If a site was detected its location was marked on the map with a
spatial error usually not greater than about 10 m. This kind of photo record made
relocating sites quite straightforward and thus facilitated later test-pitting reviewed in Chapter 6. We also made other notations about slope, land use, and visibility right on these traced maps; a cleaned up example is shown in Figure 5-2.
When each survey unit had been covered and all the sites within it mapped, a survey unit form was filled out that recorded all the pertinent environmental data on

that survey unit, such as topography, vegetative cover, soil depth, soil erosion, current crop usage, nearest available water source, and modern structures or disturbances. We repeated this procedure until all of the surveyable units within each photo quadrant were covered.

Unsurveyed areas were also traced and the reasons why they were not surveyed were recorded (e.g., greater than a 40 degree slope, heavy tropical forest cover, pine forest, under modern constructions, swamps, etc.).

Because survey units are heavily (but not entirely) defined on the basis of modern land use, it might be objected that our sampling strategy is distored by the historically and culturally contingent activities of recent populations that might not be spatially coextensive with ancient patterns of settlement and land use. There is some truth to this criticism—the ancient Maya no doubt did use different parts of the landscape in distinctive ways. Remember, however, that the recent historic process of opening up much of the natural landscape—initially cleared for subsistence crops by maize farmers with hand tools—almost certainly reproduced the basic process of colonization of ancient times, and involved many of the same kinds of decisions that ancient people made. That such lands have now been devoted to cattle pasture or coffee plantations is not relevant to the quality of the settlement sample.

RECORDING OF SITES   Site forms were filled out for every site located, the mound sites were mapped using tape and compass readings, and surface samples were taken whenever available. Sites were designated by using the aerial photograph number, quadrant letter, survey unit number, and site number. Thus, 28C-13-1 refers to aerial photograph 28, quadrant C, survey unit 13, site 1 within that survey unit.

To complete the environmental data a *survey quadrant sheet* was filled out when the entire quadrant was finished. On this form we recorded more generalized environmental data such as the primary land use in the area, locations of nearby springs, streams and creeks, soil information, and general field observations about the distribution of archaeological sites. In addition, any special resources located in the quadrant were noted, such as outcrops of tuff, chert or jasper, or the presence of clays suitable for pottery production.

Although not all of the landscape in each aerial photograph was surveyable, all photos had significant surveyable land within them. We applied the same criteria of judgment to the selection of survey units in each quadrant, guided by the simple principle that if we could get to it and walk over it, it was surveyed.

While in the field, we developed a reliability index for the survey units so that the degree of ground surface visibility could be systematically recorded. The reliability index consisted of a series of letter codes describing the degree of surface visibility. These codes could be used consistently by all members of the survey crews. This allowed us to control for areas where mound sites might be seen if they were present, but where non-mound sites would not have been noted due to the ground cover, such as pastures or year-old milpas. It was also used to indicate the likelihood of finding mounds of various sizes, thereby controlling for the fact that the surface visibility of a 4-m-high mound and a 50-cm-high mound

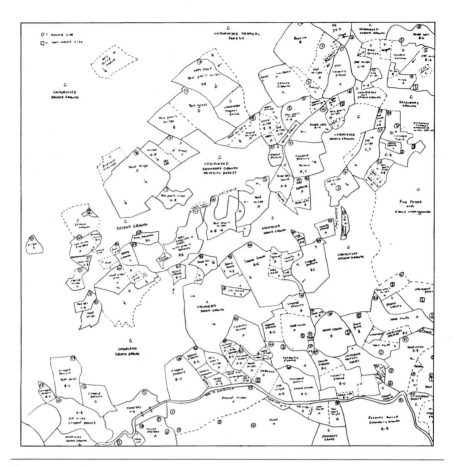

**FIGURE 5-2   SECTION OF FIELD TRACING MADE DURING THE SURVEY FROM THE
1:4,000 PHOTO QUADRANTS. LOCATION OF SURVEY UNITS, SITES AND OTHER
INFORMATION WAS RECORDED DIRECTLY ON THESE SHEETS.**

in chest high vegetation are not the same. The reliability index system was used
to record data on the areas that were not surveyed as well, again for the sake of
consistency. These data allow extrapolations for areas where non-mound sites
would not have been visible or where poor surface visibility restricted the obser-
vation and recording of smaller mounds. They will also help future resurveys that
might encounter more favorable conditions.

Despite the advantages of our field procedures, there were two disadvan-
tages as well. Recorded sites can be easily relocated, but they cannot be automatically keyed into the coordinate systems of the 1:50,000 base maps, as would be
possible had GPS technology been available. One could, of course, now revisit
each site with a GPS unit, but this would be a big job. A second disadvantage is
the distortion that occurs on the edges of photos, which somewhat displaces peripheral features. Overlaying the actual distribution of sites on a base map thus

incorporates some errors, but not enough to seriously affect the general patterns of site distribution.

We earlier noted the distinction between surveys that are site-centric, and those focused on landscape features. Most surveys, in fact, combine elements of each approach, but are weighted toward one extreme or the other. In some cases, archaeologists record sites that are reported to them by informants, are visible through remote sensing imagery, or are found on pre-selected parts of landscapes where sites are presumed likely to exist. All these strategies produce very site-centric data. Our own Copán surveys were much less tied to where we knew, or expected, sites to occur. We explored many survey units where we ourselves (correctly, as it turned out) thought the likelihood of finding any sites at all was very low. Many other more potentially fruitful survey units, for whatever set of reasons, had no sites associated with them. If landscape archaeology partly consists of looking where sites are *not* found, then we did a lot of looking.

RESULTS OF THE RURAL SURVEY

We applied the methodology reviewed above to three sections of the Copán Valley. The focus in 1981 was the main valley, including all of the non-surveyed alluvial pockets, the section of the drainage immediately adjacent to the Guatemalan border, and the lower section of the Mirasol Valley. In 1982 we surveyed the valley of the Río Copán's principal northern tributary, the Río Sesesmil, and the Llano Grande sub-region on its western margins. Finally, in 1984 we surveyed the lower portions of the Río Jila, the major southern tributary that joins the Río Copán in the Santa Rita pocket. The results of these surveys are included in Table 5-1, which also lists sites found by previous surveys.

At the conclusion of the three stages of survey work we had covered 37.66 sq km using our stratified, non-random methods, amounting to 29% of the whole 129.8 sq km survey universe. A total of 1,106 structures was located and mapped, and 550 separate sites recorded. Areas not surveyed consisted primarily of extremely steep slopes, swamps, and forests high up in the foothill and mountain

TABLE 5-1
COPÁN VALLEY SITE SUMMARY

Region	No. of Sites	No. of Strs.	% of Strs. in Whole Valley
Main Valley	330	762	16.7%
Río Sesesmil	152	225	5%
Río Jila	68	119	2.6%
Copán Pocket	735	2,369	52.2%
Urban Core	149	1,068	23.5%
Totals	1,425	4,543	100%

zones where very few archaeological sites exist. Clearly a larger sample would be desirable. Some tributary valleys with permanent streams have only been surveyed along their lower courses, and coverage is better along the northern side of the main valley than along the south. Nevertheless, we are confident that our surveys covered most of the parts of the valley attractive for dense human settlement and agricultural exploitation, and that we can reasonably extrapolate from our findings to those regions not surveyed.

It is useful to contrast our general results with those of the informal and opportunistic PAC I rural survey conducted in 1978. That survey recorded 97 sites, while ours recorded 550. Our intention here is not to make an invidious comparison, but simply to point out the much more comprehensive results of systematic settlement research, which is especially effective in recording small rural sites.

Survey Findings: The Copán Valley Settlement Zones

We are now able to compare settlement in all parts of the Copán Valley. Known sites fall into three general settlement zones, the urban core, the peripheral Copán pocket (i.e., sites inside the pocket but outside the Main Group and urban core) and the rural sustaining area. A summary for all three zones is presented in Tables 5-1 and 5-2.

THE URBAN CORE ZONE   We described the basic character of this zone in Chapter 1 and will discuss its features in more detail in Chapter 6.

For now, it is important to note its settlement density as shown in Table 5-1. Some 1,068 urban core buildings were mapped by the Harvard/PAC I projects over an area of about .75 sq km—23.5% of all the known structures in the Copán Valley. Overall settlement density is therefore about 1,425 structures per sq km.

TABLE 5-2
NUMBERS AND LOCATIONS OF RECORDED COPÁN SITES
(DESTROYED ELITE SITES NOT INCLUDED)

Region	NM	SM	Type 1*	Type 2	Type 3	Type 4	Type 5	Totals
Copán Pocket/ Urban Core	3**	271	448	111	25	16	1	875 (61%)
Main Valley	68	107	139	13	2	1	0	330 (23%)
Sesesmil	56	46	44	4	2	0	0	152 (11%)
Río Jila	24	19	19	6	0	0	0	68 (5%)
Totals by Region	151	443	650	134	29	17	1	1,425
% of Total Sites	(10)	(31)	(46)	(9)	(2)	(1)	(.07)	(100)

*Includes aggregate sites.
**Non-mound sites were not recorded during the PAC I survey; these sites, recorded as "other," are locations of stelae.

Originally the urban core covered about 1–1.5 sq km, and while we do not know if similarly dense concentrations of architecture occupied those areas that have been washed away or buried by erosion, it was nonetheless a zone of striking settlement nucleation, especially of elite scale residences.

THE PERIPHERAL COPÁN POCKET SETTLEMENT ZONE   This zone covers 23.25 sq km and its 735 sites comprise 52.2% of all the mounds located and mapped in the valley, including most of the Type 3 and Type 4 sites found outside the urban core. Peripheral pocket sites are concentrated along the alluvial terrace, vega and foothill ecological zones, (Fash & Long, 1983) with a very few sites situated in the higher, steeper mountain elevations. The foothills northeast of the Main Group have site densities about half those of the urban core, and far fewer elite rank sites. As we shall see later, some excavated sites on this northern periphery served as work areas for craft production (Mallory, 1984; Spink, 1983).

THE RURAL SUSTAINING AREA   The rural sustaining area is defined here as the 130 sq km covered by the rural survey and test pitting projects or the photo universe previously discussed. Nearly a quarter (24.3 %) of the mounds recorded within the Copán Valley surveys are located in this relatively large region, and 6% of the Type 3 or Type 4 sites are found here (Table 5-2). Moreover, sites in the rural area are not evenly distributed over the landscape but rather form discrete clusters of settlement in several regions.

Along the periphery of the Copán pocket, in the southern Río Sesesmil, Santa Rita and the Guatemalan border areas, the rural sites are fairly evenly scattered over the vega and foothill zones. Settlement in these outlying areas constitutes a transition from that of the Copán pocket, with site densities gradually decreasing with distance. Sites within this transition zone have many of the characteristics of the Copán pocket sites, including the use of generally better construction (more dressed stone, and higher mound platforms), and a slightly higher frequency of imported and fine ware ceramics than more peripheral sites.

"Emic" boundaries are probably represented by several of the seven stelae set up in A.D. 652 by the 12th ruler, *Smoke Imix God K:* Stela 13 and Stela Centinela at the Santa Rita border, and Stelae 10 and 19 near the Guatemalan border.

Farther away from the Copán pocket, rural sites form several relatively discrete settlement clusters centered on the El Jaral and Río Amarillo pockets and associated foothills, as well as in favorable parts of the Río Sesesmil, Llano Grande, and Río Jila drainages. These areas contain the most productive agricultural land outside of the Copán pocket, and centrally located within each of them is at least one elaborate Type 2 or Type 3 site that appears to have served as a residential/ceremonial center.

Between these settlement clusters are scattered smaller sites, usually located in the higher foothills, mountains, or intermontane valleys. These sites vary from field huts and simple Type 1 residences to some surprisingly elaborate Type 2 sites. We will examine the finer details of the rural site distribution later after reviewing results of the test excavations and chronological analyses.

SUMMARY

Favorable environmental conditions enabled us to sample effectively by 1984 most of the suitable areas for ancient human habitation outside the Copán pocket. Adding our data to those of the previous survey projects resulted in one of the most comprehensive pictures of settlement distribution then available for any Classic Maya polity. Many peripheral regions of the drainage remain unsurveyed and should be examined in the future, and such omissions introduce a source of potential error into our following reconstructions of demographic and agricultural history. Some specific gaps in our knowledge are clear—for example the higher, more remote upland zones might well yield sites situated for special kinds of extractive purposes or other specialized functions.

Nevertheless, we believe that the present sample is broadly representative of settlement character and distribution as a whole. Certainly the locations of most sites of any scale are known. Moreover, because of the obvious concentration of sites, and by inference population, in the Copán pocket and its immediate transitional zone, any errors that occur because of limitations of peripheral survey will have comparatively small effects on our later estimates.

Our surveys confirmed what had long been suspected—the heavy concentration of elite-rank sites in the urban core and the Copán pocket. In contrast, sites of Type 2 and lower rank "behave" much differently in spatial terms in that they are found in all parts of the valley. This difference independently supports the utility of two important segments of the Harvard typology.

Despite all that we learned from the several successive surveys, in 1984 settlement patterns anywhere in the valley, with the exception of the urban core, were mainly known only from surface indications. The next steps were obvious. First, we needed a comprehensive program of test excavations to test the assumption that most mapped sites had primarily residential functions. Second, we needed detailed control over the chronological dimensions of our sample. Finally, we needed extensive excavations of small rural sites as a check on our impressions derived from surface inspection. It is to these operations that we now turn our attention.

CHAPTER 6

Test Excavations: PAC II
Methods and Results

INTRODUCTION

Knowing where sites are located and what they look like on the surface are merely the first steps in understanding ancient settlements. Such data provide only rough impressions of population size, history, and land use. More detailed interpretations require artifact samples, but at Copán it is usually impossible to collect systematically samples of well-preserved artifacts without excavation. By 1982 it was obvious that however successful we were in recording surface features we still faced several fundamental questions. Were rural sites predominantly residences, as we hypothesized both from the "principle of abundance" and the Las Sepulturas excavations? Did some sites have special domestic functions, or did extradomestic activities take place at some residences? Were there variations in construction or site configuration undetected by surface mapping? Finally, we knew that all mapped sites could not possibly be contemporary. How could we partition them in time? Like most archaeologists, we relied on test pitting to help resolve these issues.

TEST PIT RESEARCH
DESIGN AND METHODOLOGY

Test-pitting operations are essentially sharp, minor, surgical excavations that provide essential information with minimal disturbance. They are usually focused on cultural features, but may also be placed elsewhere on landscapes to investigate natural stratigraphy or geomorphological processes. Although almost always desirable, programs of test excavations are much more costly and time-consuming than surface survey and many projects cannot afford them. We fortunately possessed the resources, but had to plan our excavations very carefully to get the best results. In doing so we capitalized on an earlier testing program.

PAC I Test Excavations

PAC I archaeologists tested less than 1% of the structures in the Copán pocket, and 15 sites received more intensive excavation (Fash, 1983a, 1983b). An innovative feature of the PAC I work was a randomized set of sub-surface probes devised by Baudez and applied to locales in the west end of the Copán pocket and much of the adjacent uplands. Grids of 52 × 52 m blocks were superimposed on these areas, and four test trenches, each 2 × 2 m, were excavated in randomly selected sections of each block. This effort was innovative because it did not assume that the only places of archaeological significance were those visible on the surface, or that archaeologists could necessarily prejudge where they should excavate. About half of the first 51 test trenches contained no artifacts (Fash, 1983b), and some of the randomly placed units fell on steep slopes where erosion probably would have eliminated signs of habitation or other use even had they existed.

After recognizing this problem, the strategy was modified for the steeper piedmont, foothill, and intermontane valley regions. Twenty-five ha blocks were employed as grid units, and the 2 × 2 m test probes were nonrandomly placed in locales deemed most suitable for prehistoric occupation.

A total of 182 test trenches over an area of about 86 sq km were ultimately completed during PAC I. These generated a small sample of sub-surface remains and provided extremely important information on the beginnings of the ceramic sequence and the early occupants of the valley. They also demonstrated that hidden, non-platform structures did not seem to appear in significant numbers in the Copán pocket except on the valley floor.

The Rural Test Excavation Program

Our own subsequent test pitting operations were conducted in two phases under the direction of AnnCorinne Freter. The goal of the first phase in 1983 and 1984 was to sample a representative portion of the 482 rural sites located during the PAC II surveys of the Main and Sesesmil River Valleys discussed in Chapter 5 (the Río Jila region was not included because it had not yet been surveyed). We adopted a site-centered approach built on the experience of the PAC I project. We reasoned that while many ancient activities were not reflected on the surface, excavation of a large sample of known sites would most efficiently produce the kinds of information necessary to reconstruct population and agricultural history of the outlying settlement zones.

We stratified mapped sites on the basis of geographic location (to sample as many different zones within the valley as possible) and site type (to investigate all levels of site complexity visible on the surface). We decided to select and test a random sample of 20% of the numerous non-mound, single mound, and aggregate mound sites within each aerial photograph quadrant, as well as 50% of the less numerous sites of Type 1 and higher ranks. While the ideal was to test all randomly selected sites, realities of fieldwork did not allow this on rare occasions. Sometimes a chosen site could not be tested for some reason (e.g., it was destroyed, flooded, located in a modern cemetery, or in a field of mature crops). Under these circumstances we selected the nearest site of the same type in the quadrant as its alternate.

PROCEDURES   At each randomly selected site we placed a 2×2 m trench either in front of or behind most of all visible structures (Plate 6-1). These trenches were positioned to intercept, but not disturb, the retaining walls of the buildings and any adjacent living surfaces. We knew from the Las Sepulturas excavations that midden debris tended to accumulate in these places, and also that burials were frequently placed in pits along wall lines. When time allowed, a test pit was also excavated in the center of the patio.

Test trenches next to buildings automatically exposed information about construction techniques, either in the form of standing masonry walls or collapse debris from them. Quality of construction is one dimension of the Harvard typology, and we expected that most rural buildings in the Type 1 or lower range sites would be roughly built and would yield no sculpture. Non-mound sites were tested by placing a single pit in the center of the visible artifact concentration.

Ideally, we should also have dug through each mound to acquire artifacts from the construction fill and evidence of internal architectural stratigraphy—a common practice in other research projects in the Maya Lowlands. We did not do this because such trenching destructively accelerates erosion and we did not have the resources to restore rural buildings. Later, as a result of our large-scale excavations of rural sites (see Chapter 7), we discovered that testing through small buildings would not have been very productive. Most test pits, no matter where they were placed, were excavated down to sterile soil and so provided the widest possible chronological range of artifacts.

PLATE 6-1   PHOTO OF RURAL TEST EXCAVATION UNIT REVEALING INTACT STONE ALIGNMENTS ALONG THE EDGE OF A LOW MOUND.

TABLE 6-1
COPÁN VALLEY SITES AND TEST PITS BY SETTLEMENT REGION

Region	Number of Sites	Number of Structures	Number of Sites Tested	Percent of Sites Tested
Urban Core	140	1,068	8	0.5
Copán Pocket	735	2,369	102	13.9
Main Valley Rural	330	762	94	28.4
Sesesmil Valley	152	225	48	31.5
Río Jila	68	119	0	0
Totals	1,425	4,543	252	17.7

The Copán Pocket Test Pitting Program

By late 1984 an embarrassing imbalance became apparent. We possessed an excellent test pit sample of outlying rural sites, but no comparable information for the Copán pocket settlement outside the urban core, where the earlier PAC I testing had been very minimal. We knew from PAC I surveys, however, that an extremely large percentage of the polity's ancient population resided in this settlement zone. To correct this problem we randomly selected 102 sites in the Copán pocket for test pitting, along with eight sites in the urban core itself, and again stratified our sample on the basis of site type and geographic location. This phase of the project was finished in 1988.

Summary of the Test Pitting Operations

Table 6-1 shows the overall results of our work. By the end of 1988 we had completed 688 test pits at 252 sites. Fully 29.5% of all sites mapped outside the Copán pocket had been tested, while coverage of the outlying sites in the Copán pocket amounted to 13.9%.

From the larger perspective of Maya settlement archaeology the most important result or our work is the very large proportion of tested sites beyond the urban core. It is precisely these outlying zones of settlement that are typically underrepresented in excavations in many other regions. Not only is our excavated sample quite large—nearly 18% of all Copán mapped sites—but we believe it also to be very representative of the whole site inventory.

IDENTIFICATION OF SITE FUNCTIONS

A principal goal of our test-pitting effort was to assess how sites were used, and more specifically our assumption that most sites were residences. The whole notion of site function is a tricky one, however, and deserves some consideration.

We assumed that people in all ancient Copán households must have carried out a broadly shared set of activities associated with domestic life, including the

TABLE 6-2
GENERAL SITE FUNCTIONS IN THE RURAL SUSTAINING AREA AS REVEALED BY TEST-PITTING

Site Type	# Tested	Residences	Field Huts	Ritual	Other
Nonmound	28	0	8	0	20
Single Mound	33	22	11	0	0
Agg/Type 1	89	88	0	1	0
Type 2	13	12	0	1	0
Type 3	3	0	0	3	0
Type 4	1	1	0	0	0
Totals	167*	123	19	5	20

*Includes 25 rural Copán pocket sites which overlapped the rural sustaining area survey.

preparation, consumption and storage of food; construction and maintenance of houses and other facilities; processing raw materials into tools or other necessary objects; and carrying out domestic social events and rituals. We also assumed that people living in most sites outside the Copán urban core were farmers who primarily devoted their time and domestic labor to agricultural tasks, and who supported elites with their products and labor.

The archaeological expectation is that all residences should produce artifact assemblages that are therefore broadly similar. Of course we would expect some assemblage variation even among low-rank households because some were more well-established, larger, or more prosperous than others, nor were they all contemporary. Residences of people of high rank might also exhibit rather distinctive domestic artifact assemblages.

By the time we began our test pit operations we already had a pretty fair idea about what the "richer" end of the domestic assemblage range looked like from work in the urban core. Freter quickly began to anticipate a quite predictable domestic assemblage signature during the first phase of test pitting. A little later, in 1985 and 1986, we extensively excavated eight small rural sites (see Chapter 7) that provided very extensive collections of artifacts from residences and a field hut. By 1988, then, we were pretty sure that we could properly infer residential functions from test pit data.

The test pits collectively produced three very general, distinctive assemblage profiles that we interpret to represent three different primary site functions: (1) residential occupations, (2) field huts, and (3) outlying ritual places. These identifications are based on a combination of three factors: site location, architecture, and associated artifacts (Table 6-2).

Residential Sites

The vast majority of the single mound, aggregate, Type 1 and Type 2 sites test pitted in the Sesesmil, Main Valley, and Copán pocket areas had artifact inventories and architecture indicating that they were primarily residences. Test pits placed in these sites produced a wide range of artifacts all strongly indicative of domestic functions. These included the full range of utilitarian ceramic forms (jars, bowls, griddles, basins, and cylinders of various sizes) and also a small percentage (usually consistently about 10%) of ceramic fine wares. In addition, obsidian blades, obsidian and chert flakes, manos, metates, serpentine celts, spindle whorls, occasional animal bones (usually deer), and charred vegetable material were found in the middens associated with structures. Burials were also encountered, but not in large numbers, although of course the chance of recovering a burial context with any particular test pit was quite low. If we have correctly identified this range of materials as signaling domestic functions, 74% of all the sites shown in Table 6-2 were residences. The proportion rises to 95% if nonmound sites are ignored, as they should be because most appear not to be residences.

Field Huts

In many parts of Mesoamerica, including the Maya Lowlands, farmers today build and maintain small structures in or near their fields for situational shelter and storage during the agricultural season (Plate 6-2). Sometimes these are *ramada*-like buildings consisting of little more than corner posts and a thatch roof, with no prepared floors or foundations. In other cases considerable care is lavished on them, and they resemble small, isolated, traditional houses. Farmers in the Copán Valley today construct simple structures *(champas)* for shade from

PLATE 6-2   PHOTO OF A FIELD HUT, A KIND OF SMALL, PERISHABLE STRUCTURE USED BY COPÁN FARMERS TODAY FOR SHELTER AND STORAGE DURING THE AGRICULTURAL SEASON.

the noonday sun and to live in while they clear their fields and protect their crops during the last few weeks before harvest. In one sense field huts are special purpose structures, but in another they are simply spatially distant extensions of the normal domestic facilities of farming households.

Test pits showed that although many of the non-mound and single mound sites in the Sesesmil and Main Valley were occupied, the full range of expected domestic activities was not represented in the artifact samples. These sites lacked manos, metates, and celts, and had very low frequencies of chert flakes or obsidian blades. They did have ceramics, but almost all the sherds recovered (over 85%) were from utilitarian jars. Location was also suggestive, because these sites were isolated on steep slopes in the foothill or mountain zones. Construction (when any evidence for it was present) was extremely crude, typically small, low platforms with single-course retaining walls of rough stone. At two non-mound sites we found postholes, indicating that perishable structures had been built right on the ground.

We interpret 19 sites exhibiting these features as field huts, and later tested this proposition by a large scale excavation (see Chapter 7). They are particularly correlated with steep topography and are especially numerous in the Sesesmil survey subregion.

Ritual Sites

Five sites of Type 2 and 3 rank sites in the Copán and Sesesmil survey zones had large mounds with elaborate architecture and were centrally located on mountain mesas, or on the floors of intermontane pockets. One such site in the El Jaral/Río Amarillo West region consists of a single mound measuring 15 x 15 m at the base and over six m in height. It has two staircases running up to a small summit structure and is constructed of dressed tuff blocks. Artifacts from test pits were few and almost exclusively ceramic sherds, including censer fragments and part of a Copador cylinder. We interpret this isolated building as a ritual structure.

In the other four cases, similarly impressive buildings are more closely associated with residences. One site, Llano Grande, consists of two mounds over 3 m high facing each other across a 50 m long plaza. A series of large boulder terraces or stairs provides access from the plain below. Our seven test pits produced only 175 artifacts, most of which were sherds of basins and incense burners. This unique site appears to have been an "empty" ritual place, but it is clearly associated with a nearby contemporary settlement. At three sites large, elaborate structures are surrounded by residences. We have listed them in Table 6-2 as ritual places because of these unique features, but they obviously had both ritual and residential functions.

SITE CONFIGURATION

Small test trenches located adjacent to buildings visible on the surface cannot be expected to reveal very much about buried platforms or non-mound structures because exposures are just too small to predictably capture such features. Some hidden platforms were exposed, however, and we estimated that minimally about 15% of the structures present at small rural sites were not "counted" on the basis of surface inspection alone. Either some very low platforms were totally covered by soil accumulation, or more commonly, what was mapped as a single mound turned out to be two separate buildings.

We did confirm our expectations about construction techniques. Test trenches in sites of Type 1 or lower rank showed that substructures generally had retaining walls of rough stone, sometimes only one or two courses high, that construction quality was much inferior to that of many low-rank buildings in the urban core, and that sculpture was absent. In some cases there were prepared surfaces such as cobble floors or low terraces attached to platforms. These patterns are consistent with the assumption that buildings were the products of domestic labor of commoner households.

Test trenching was essential in figuring out the functions of nonmound sites. Our nonmound survey designation obviously means merely that we could see nothing but artifacts on the surface. Excavations at eight nonmound sites produced evidence for low, hidden platforms or, very rarely, postholes for nonplatform structures (perhaps for in-field storage). It was on this basis, as well as the character of the associated artifacts, that Freter interpreted all eight as field huts. The remaining 20 nonmound sites appear to have either been places where there was secondary deposition of artifacts, or where some sort of specialized activities took place away from residences. These sites are simply listed as "Other" in Table 6-2. While more extensive lateral stripping of nonmound sites might reveal a different picture in some cases, we believe that they generally have little relevance for the reconstruction of ancient population history in the valley (see Chapter 11). As we will see, however, they might be critical in reconstructing details of the Copán economy.

GENERAL SITE CHRONOLOGY

Test pitting does, fortunately, produce immediately obvious indications of gross site chronology in the form of recognizable and temporally sensitive potsherds. Archaeologists participating in the PAC I surveys and test pitting in the Copán pocket formed the conclusion that an overwhelming proportion of the sites visible on the surface were occupied during the Coner ceramic phase. Many sites, of course, might also have had less obvious, earlier occupations as well. None were assumed to have been occupied after A.D. 850–900, by which time the valley was believed to be largely depopulated. Our later household excavations in Las Sepulturas showed the last building phases of all structures to be of Coner date, but also revealed older buildings and artifacts that were blanketed and obscured by the later buildings.

Freter's own field observations and her later laboratory analysis of artifacts showed that only about 5% of all her excavated sites completely predated the Coner phase—i.e., showed no signs of Coner occupation. Some 15% of the remaining test-pitted sites showed pre-Coner material (mainly Acbi phase) mixed with, or stratified beneath, the Coner remains. No sites were found that had Ejar domestic assemblages (such assemblages have never been defined), and only a handful of Ejar fine ware sherds of any kind were identified among the thousands from our test pits.

One possible explanation for these distributions is that pre-Coner, and especially Acbi phase people resided in different locales than those favored for settlement in Coner times. We reject it for three reasons.

First, if pre-Coner populations were large in the outlying zones we tested, where are the surface manifestations of their settlements? Second, even in the densely settled Copán pocket the random PAC I tests revealed little hidden habitation. Third, Coner phase sites are so numerous that they occupy most of the choice settlement locations. For this explanation to work, one would have to assume that Acbi people built structures very much unlike those of Coner times and chose not to locate them in the obvious locales favored by Coner householders. A much simpler explanation is that Acbi (and earlier) population was comparatively small outside the floor of the Copán pocket, and that sites of these phases were often dismantled by Coner settlers for building materials and/or buried beneath later Coner household constructions.

These chronological insights were both reassuring and frustrating. On the one hand they abundantly confirm the conclusions from much earlier work. On the other hand, if virtually every site was dated to the Coner phase (a period then believed to be 150–200 years long), how could one tease apart any sort of detailed settlement history of the Copán Valley, and especially the dynamics of the collapse? Ceramic seriation was a possible solution, but the surfaces of many sherds were heavily altered by acidic soils, making such an effort impractical. Fortunately the test pits and other excavations provided obsidian samples to solve this problem which in turn gave us very surprising new insights into the collapse of the Copán polity, although we did not realize it at first. We will return to the larger implications of the obsidian hydration dates in Chapter 10.

The general conclusion about settlement history that derives from our work outside the urban core is that pre-Coner population was very limited in this zone. We identified Late Preclassic sherds (and very occasionally Preclassic buildings) in several parts of the valley, including the Sesesmil subregion and the Eastern Río Amarillo pocket. Apparently Preclassic people were widely but thinly spread over the drainage as a whole, although future work might identify impressive settlements of this period buried beneath later deposits on the Copán pocket floor. Interestingly, Early and Middle Classic populations seem more heavily concentrated in the Copán pocket than their Late Preclassic predecessors, although the large and rather enigmatic center of Los Achiotes near the El Jaral pocket is mainly of pre-Coner date.

EVIDENCE OF ECONOMIC SPECIALIZATION

A fundamental issue in Maya archaeology is how specialized economic activities (i.e. those not widely shared as basic activities of most households) were organized and spatially partitioned. Architecture and artifact assemblages at Copán suggested the presence of full- or part-time economic specialists such as potters, weavers, woodworkers, shellworkers, lithic tool and ornament makers, stonemasons, sculptors, and carpenters whose products were not made merely for their own households. In the urban core excavations we found evidence of artisans who made objects from imported marine shell associated with elite households. Did craftspeople of whatever rank pursue their specialized activities as part of their domestic economies?

Until recently Maya archaeologists have had very few data relating to rural household economies. A principal goal of the test excavation program was to answer some important questions. Were some sites not residences at all, but rather special production facilities or places where raw materials were extracted and/or prepared? If so, could we identify such places archaeologically? We hoped to reconstruct what kinds of activities were carried out at the household level and how they were organized through analysis of the rural artifact assemblages recovered from excavations in rural sites.

Two problems are preservation and sample size. On the gross level of test pitting, one is likely to be able to recognize in the field only those specialized activities that involved either unusual numbers of durable artifacts, such as chipped stone, ground stone, or pottery, or durable facilities such as kilns for the production of pottery or plaster. Intensive scrutiny of artifacts or soil samples in the laboratory might reveal less obvious evidence for specialized activities. Conclusions would still be ambiguous, however, because it would be difficult to distinguish production of, for example, pottery or stone tools for household use from more intensive production on the basis of test pit exposures alone. Conversely, one might simply miss any such evidence entirely because excavations were too limited in extent. Our expectations of identifying specialized activities were not accordingly high. As it turned out the test pit data provided information about three kinds of economic specialization: Coner-phase utilitarian ceramic production, obsidian lithic processing, and lime plaster production.

The Rural Ceramic Production System

As at other Maya sites, ceramics are by far the most abundant artifacts at Copán. They are also extremely variable in form and function and so are useful in reconstructing the lives of the ancient Maya. Unfortunately, archaeologists seldom recover direct archaeological evidence showing how and where pottery was manufactured. During our Copán research, we accordingly placed special emphasis on the analysis of rural ceramics, resulting in a better understanding of both how they were produced and used. As with all aspects of material culture the best place to begin is with the raw material.

CLAY SOURCES   Two primary pottery clay sources were identified by Gail Mahood during the PAC I geological survey of the valley (Turner et al., 1983). The first was a deposit of pure, fine gray clay weathered from white volcanic tuff

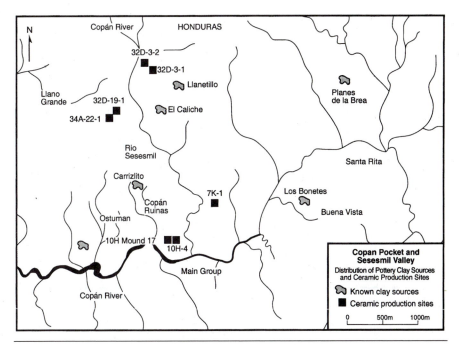

FIGURE 6-1   MAP OF THE COPÁN VALLEY SHOWING LOCATIONS OF CLAY SOURCES AND CERAMIC PRODUCTION SITES. MODIFIED FROM FRETER 1996: 212, FIGURE 2.

located near Planes de la Brea (Figure 6-1). Mahood observed that the fine clay matrix eroded downslope and was redeposited in flat, low-lying areas, a process that resulted in numerous small isolated patches of clays with variable purity and fineness. A second deposit of light gray clay was found near Llanetillo, where it is still used for pottery production. Mahood noted that this clay was the result of the same tuff weathering process, and that the Llano Grande and Buena Vista locales probably also contained clay deposits because of their similar geological characteristics.

Several additional clay sources were identified during survey as part of our own routine recording of environmental information. These included a light brown clay in El Caliche, a fine white clay in Carrizalito, and a red-brown clay source southeast of Ostuman. While we did not observe any clay sources in the Río Jila, El Limon or Río Amarillo pockets of the valley, geological surveys suggest that they also contain small patches of weathered, tuff-based clays.

Rural Utilitarian Ceramic Production Sites

Seven tested sites produced direct evidence of small scale pottery production (Figure 6-1). Three were specialized non-mound or single mound sites with no evidence of residential facilities, and four were Type 1 or 2 sites with primary residential functions accompanied by evidence of ceramic production. These sites appear to form paired patterns, with each specialized non-mound or single mound site located within 100 m of a Type 1 or 2 site that also showed evidence for ceramic production. Figure 6-2 illustrates one of these paired sets of sites. The distribution of these sites strongly correlates with the location of known pottery clay sources, and all were utilized between A.D 800–1000.

No evidence of formally constructed kilns was encountered. Rather it appears that the non-mound sites were loci for the open firing of ceramics, as indicated by waster sherds and burned floor surfaces. Alternatively, ceramic activity areas associated with the residential Type I and II sites contained pigments, basalt slabs stained with pigments, fragments of small serpentine celts (probably used to burnish vessels—see Freter, 1996), and some waster or misfired sherds.

The stratified random sampling design of the test pitting program allows us to extrapolate the possible number of low-level ceramic production sites in operation

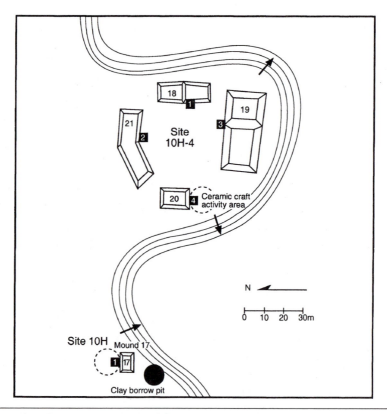

FIGURE 6-2   SKETCH MAP OF SITE 10H-4, WHERE TEST PITTING REVEALED EVIDENCE OF CERAMIC PRODUCTION. ARROWS POINT DOWNSLOPE. MODIFIED FROM FRETER 1996: 224, FIGURE 7.

at Late Classic Copán. We think that about six such production loci existed in the Sesesmil Valley, and about 15 others in the Copán pocket. These figures are conservative, however, for two reasons. First, ceramic production activity areas at residential sites were limited in extent and appeared to be spatially isolated. We thus had to be very lucky to encounter them in test pits, and so our sample is undoubtedly a minimal one. A second source of error is a methodological one. The PAC I Copán pocket survey did not record non-mound sites because artifact scatters were so numerous. This type of site is associated with specialized ceramic production in outlying parts of the valley, so our extrapolation of the number of ceramic production sites in the Copán pocket represents a very minimal estimate.

We can now make several inferences about Late Classic ceramic production at Copán. First, pottery was simultaneously produced at many different sites in the Copán pocket and Sesesmil Valley where the best pottery clays are found, and probably in other parts of the valley as well. Second, each ceramic production site was utilized by part-time specialists on a very small scale and probably produced a limited number of vessels for local, domestic consumption. Third, production was probably carried out by household members, or possibly lineage groups, rather then organized in some larger, more centralized manner. That clays suitable for pottery production are scattered in many small deposits would encourage this kind of production because no single community or group could effectively monopolize them. Finally, the paired production sites suggests that vessels were fired near but not in residences, probably for basic safety reasons. Even our extensive excavations at Las Sepulturas and some rural sites (see Chapter 7) might therefore fail to uncover firing areas, which were far from buildings.

The Obsidian Production System

There is no local source of obsidian in the Copán Valley. Retouched obsidian artifacts such as scrapers, knives, piercing tools, or projectile points are rare at Copán. Prismatic blades and associated cores, and debitage, and utilized flakes make up the vast bulk of the obsidian assemblage, which in turn comprises about 75% of all chipped stone tools. Plate 6-3 shows a sample of typical obsidian artifacts.

Lithic assemblages from rural sites support earlier studies (e.g., Mallory, 1984) indicating that obsidian was imported in the form of prepared cores or prismatic blades during the Late Classic period. The primary known sources of obsidian in Mesoamerica have unique properties of color, clarity and crystallization that affect their usefulness for manufacturing various forms of artifacts. Glossy, clear black, obsidian from Ixtepeque, and cloudy purple-black obsidian from El Chayal were both imported into the Copán Valley from the highlands of Guatemala. Banded black obsidian came from San Martin Jilotepeque, also in Guatemala, and green-gold Pachuca obsidian from faraway Central Mexico.

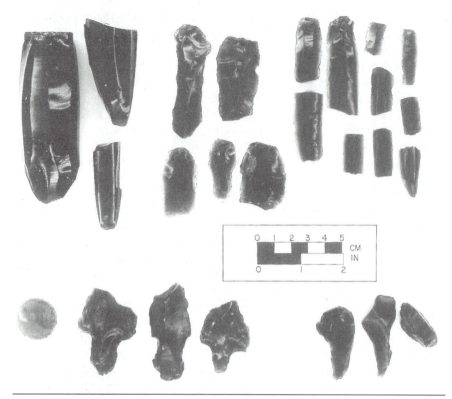

PLATE 6-3   COPÁN OBSIDIAN ARTIFACTS, INCLUDING CORES (UPPER LEFT), PRISMATIC
BLADE FRAGMENTS (UPPER RIGHT) AND RETOUCHED TOOLS (BOTTOM).

Copán Obsidian Sourcing

In 1984 Freter selected 60 blades from Coner phase test pit assemblages recovered from all parts of the valley. These artifacts represented the full range of visually distinctive obsidian encountered (e.g., black, dark gray, banded, opaque). Freter used atomic absorption spectroscopy to determine the chemical profile of each blade. The element profiles were then compared to those of the major sources in southern Mesoamerica: Ixtepeque, El Chayal, La Esperanza, and San Martin Jilotepeque. All 60 blades sourced to Ixtepeque, which appears to be the primary source for Late Classic Copán.

Because other obsidian sources might have been used in earlier times, Freter did a second sourcing experiment in 1986, this time focusing on a sample of 24 obsidian artifacts from primary occupation levels in deep stratigraphic excavations in Courtyard A of Group 9N-8, excavated by William Fash (Fash,1991). Samples from Early Classic and Preclassic periods were sourced to a variety of flows, including Ixtepeque, El Chayal, and San Martin Jilotepeque.

Independent sourcing experiments carried out at the nuclear reactor facility at the University of Missouri by Michael Gallscock and Hector Neff, and by

Harbottle et al. (1994), lead to the same basic conclusions as Freter's: the obsidian sources used in the Copán valley changed over time. Preclassic and Middle Classic obsidian came from a variety of sources, but during the Late Classic period the Ixtepeque source was by far the most important one.

A few artifacts made from green Pachuca obsidian were encountered in our excavations. Only five Pachuca artifacts were dated via hydration due to their rarity and all were made during Late Classic or later times. An enlarged sample of dated Pachuca obsidian would probably show that it was used over a longer time span.

Obsidian Tool Manufacture in the Copán Valley

Analyses of Coner phase obsidian artifacts from several Copán projects, including those from our rural excavations, revealed that less than 1% show any signs of natural cortex. It thus appears that obsidian tools were imported either as blades, or in the form of roughly prepared cores which were rendered down into blades as needed within the household. The latter is most probable, both because exhausted cores are found in rural sites and cores would be the most durable form to transport from the Ixtepeque source.

Two obsidian workshop sites have been located in Copán, only one of which was excavated. In 1981 John Mallory (1984) partly excavated the small Type 1 site 5M-1, locally known as "El Duende," high up in the foothills of the Copán pocket on the edge of the pine forest. Thousands of obsidian tools were visible on the surface near buildings of Type 1 scale. His exposures showed that incredible numbers of obsidian tools were produced and consumed at El Duende. Mallory concluded both on the basis of the obsidian assemblage itself and the low numbers of domestic artifacts and burials that El Duende was not a full-time residence, but rather a specialized economic production site that either specialized in the production of obsidian tools directly, or some perishable product that required large numbers of obsidian blades to make. Interestingly, El Duende continued to be used well into the late 10th century, long after the valley was originally thought to be depopulated.

A second obsidian processing site (non-mound) was located during the Main Valley survey, situated on a small knoll distant from any residential sites. Hundreds of lithic fragments were scattered over an area of about 12 sq m. The high density of obsidian cores, flakes and blade fragments indicated that the processing of cores into blades had occurred there.

Despite its distant origins, obsidian was used in all parts of the valley, during all time periods, and by people of all social ranks. However it was procured and distributed, it was a "cheap" material that probably was not produced or controlled by some centralized body of specialists.

The Lime Plaster Production System

The third kind of specialized economic activity revealed by the test pit program was the production of lime plaster for the construction and surfacing of buildings.

While testing a single mound site near the Copán river about 1 km north of Las Sepulturas, Freter exposed about a quarter of a circular earthen kiln, the floor of which was covered with burned lime and ash (Figure 6-3). This kiln was used for the burning, or calcining of limestone, a necessary step in producing lime. Plaster, as opposed to mud, was used to coat the surfaces of high quality buildings at Copán. Without the addition of lime to crushed limestone and water, the plaster is too weak to protect masonry walls from seasonal rains, an especially important consideration at Copán where only mud was used as mortar for masonry.

This single kiln could have produced a considerable amount of lime. Its interior volume was 17 cu. m, and would have contained between 6–10 cu m of limestone—which when calcined would have produced an equivalent amount of

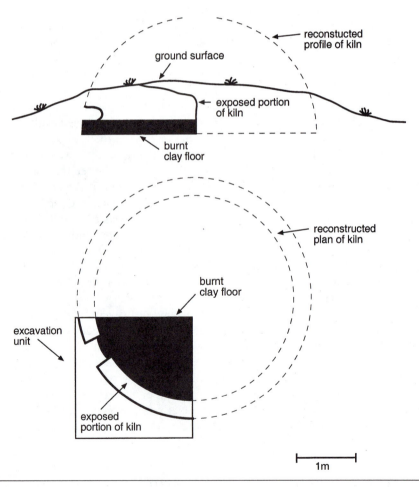

FIGURE 6-3   PROFILE (TOP) AND PLAN (BOTTOM) OF RECONSTRUCTED LIME KILN
UNCOVERED DURING TEST EXCAVATION. FROM ABRAMS AND FRETER 1996: 426,
FIGURE 4.

plaster cement. Because lime plaster is a mixture of one part lime to two parts aggregate (generally at Copán this is crushed stone or *sascab,* a naturally decomposed limestone), the kiln could have generated material to produce about 24 cu m of lime plaster at each burning, an amount which would cover an average size Copán masonry building (see Abrams & Freter, 1996 for a more detailed discussion).

The kiln was part of a single mound site that otherwise showed no signs of residential use. As in the case of the ceramic loci, the kiln site was located within 50 m of a small residential Type I site that we also test pitted. Obsidian hydration dating shows the two sites to be about the same age (A.D. 750–900). Because plaster (as well as masonry architecture) could only be produced in the dry season, plaster producers necessarily worked on a seasonal basis. Part-time specialists who resided in the Type 1 site probably operated the kiln as needed during the dry season (plaster must be used within a short time after its mixing), and it appears that these plaster workers were of commoner status.

SUMMARY

Our goal of acquiring a large and representative artifact sample from the hundreds of archaeological sites outside the Copán urban core was accomplished by our two phases of test pitting. Few if any Classic Maya polities are as well documented in this regard as Copán. We also convincingly showed that the overwhelming majority of mapped sites had residential functions by isolating a rather narrow range of distinctive domestic artifact assemblages. Of course we anticipated this result, and few Maya archaeologists would find it surprising, but now the assumption has been tested at Copán. More important for our later population reconstructions, we can now manipulate our settlement sample by using empirically derived numbers to extrapolate to the untested site universe.

Despite the spatial limitations of test pitting, we did discover that construction details of sites were consistent with expenditures of domestic household energy, thus strongly reinforcing the central logic of the Harvard site topology. More important, we began to appreciate the extent to which structures even at small sites were underestimated by surface counts. Finally, we confirmed the heavy Coner phase occupation of the valley as a whole.

Insights into economic specialization were possible based on the test pit data. We were able to identify sites that seem to have had special ritual functions, and determine that most nonmound sites were probably field huts or some other kinds of specialized places. Our model of the Copán utilitarian ceramic production system is consistent with reconstructions of other utilitarian production systems in the valley during the Late Classic period, all of which appear to have been conducted as part-time activities and as components of the domestic economy of common people. In Chapters 12 and 13 we discuss additional information on kinds of specialization more closely related to elite and royal segments of society. Data on economic specialization for the Copán polity are still very limited, and further investigation into the production and distribution of important commodities is needed. Still, our data help us re-evaluate excavation methodologies and re-assess our assumptions about the use of space by Maya households.

Satisfying as these results were, many nagging doubts remained—doubts related to the most intransigent problem faced by archaeologists: what haven't we found? Had we simply missed evidence for pre-Coner levels stratified beneath Coner ones? Did we really have an adequate handle on the numbers of hidden structures and the range of variability present at small sites? Were burials around residences really as infrequent as they seemed? There was only one way to find out—we had to excavate extensively a sample of small, outlying sites, just as we had done at Las Sepulturas.

CHAPTER 7

Rural Household Excavations
in the Copán Valley

INTRODUCTION

In 1985 and 1986 we extensively excavated eight small rural sites in the Copán Valley as a follow-up PAC II project (Webster and Gonlin, 1988; Gonlin, 1993, 1994, 1996; Webster, Gonlin, and Sheets, 1997). The term "rural" is usually used in opposition to the term "urban" in referring to ancient complex agrarian societies. The latter connotes high population density, heterogeneity of community or household functions, cultural sophistication and dynamism, and complexity on many levels. By contrast, "rural" usually implies comparatively low population density, homogeneity in functions, and less sophistication, in the sense that rural people were spatially distant from centers where political decisions were made, trade and commerce were concentrated, intellectual and aesthetic patterns were most strongly expressed.

Excavation of rural sites was necessary for both general and strategic reasons. Robert Wauchope, one of the pioneers of Maya household research, commented long ago that

> Surprisingly little attention has been given to the study of the mode of living of the vast majority of the Maya people. Expeditions to the Maya area, with few exceptions, have devoted their interests and their labors almost exclusively to the more spectacular civil and religious centers of the sites investigated. Although this concentration on the main ruins of Maya centers is entirely justified by its important results regarding migrations, chronology, religious customs, architecture, and art, it has furnished us with the knowledge of the customs of only the very highest social stratum, the priests and the chieftains, who always form a very small percentage of any population (Wauchope, 1934, p. 113).

Not much had changed by 1985, so our general goal was to redress this neglect.

Although rural household excavations were desirable in their own right, they were also dictated by the historic logic of the Copán research program itself. By 1984 we had an excellent sample of excavated elite households in the urban core, and the obvious next step was to complement it with a similar rural settlement component. Freter had finished mapping and test pitting hundreds of these little sites by that time, turning up convincing support for the "principle of abundance" discussed in Chapter 5. Only extensive lateral stripping could ultimately test her inferences from test pitting, however, and also address other issues unresolved by

PLATE 7-1   MODERN HOUSES AND HOUSELOT FIELDS ON HILLSIDE OF COPÁN POCKET. ANCIENT HAMLETS IN THIS REGION PROBABLY LOOKED MUCH LIKE THIS.

her previous work. These included the overall character of small sites, how much variation existed among them, the range of activities that took place at them, refinement of site chronology, how household social groups were organized, and the thorny problem of buried or nonplatform structures. Another goal was to recover larger and therefore more representative samples of both artifacts and burials.

Earlier surveys showed that in the Copán Valley houses tend to be fairly dispersed, but are sometimes distributed in neighborhoodlike concentrations. A similar pattern was ethnographically recorded by Wisdom (1940) for the local Chorti Maya and still can be seen today (Plate 7-1).

RESEARCH DESIGN

To investigate urban-rural contrasts, and also gain information for demographic reconstructions, we decided to dig the humblest, most unprepossessing household remains we could find. We concentrated our efforts on eight sites in the Type 1 (n = 6) and single-mound (n = 2) ranks. Using Freter's survey data, we chose sites that showed considerable variation in terms of numbers, sizes, and arrangements of buildings. All the Type 1 sites consisted of single patio groups of two to five buildings located in varied geographic parts in the valley. For seven sites we already had artifact collections from Freter's test-pitting or from

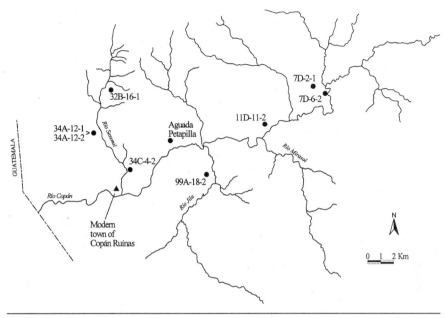

FIGURE 7-1 MAP OF COPÁN VALLEY SHOWING THE LOCATIONS OF EIGHT SMALL RURAL SITES EXTENSIVELY EXCAVATED IN 1985–86. ALSO SHOWN IS THE AGUADA PETAPILLA, FROM WHICH THE SEDIMENT CORES DISCUSSED IN CHAPTER 8 WERE RECOVERED.

surface collections. These collections were consistent with domestic use, although we suspected that one of the single-mound sites might be the remains of a field hut used for temporary shelter during the agricultural season.

An advantage of such small sites is that they can be nearly completely excavated, or at least very heavily tested, in a reasonably short time. Moreover, cultural deposits are typically shallow and the stratigraphy is minimally disrupted. After working a month or so at one of these small rural sites one is unlikely to be seriously fooled by what one has *not* found.

The sites chosen were located both in the main and tributary valleys of the Río Copán (Figure 7-1), at different elevations (from 700 to 950 m asl), and each in a different topographic situation. All were reasonably accessible by road—always an important practical consideration. The closest site was 2.2 km from the Main Group, and the most distant was 22 km, with an average distance of 11 km (these are surface travel distances—direct air distances would be shorter). Most of the rural sites were widely separated from their closest neighbors, so there would have been plenty of room for agricultural production in the immediate vicinity.

Excavation Methodology

As in the Las Sepulturas elite household investigations, we used horizontal stripping to expose all (final phase occupation) buildings at each site, along with associated patio and other peripheral spaces. Ultimately we exposed all or parts

TABLE 7-1
SUMMARY OF RURAL SITE DATA 1

Site Number	Locational Data	Distance from Urban Core	# Structures Before/After Excavation	Peripheral/ Total Space Excavated	Raw Obsidian Hydration Range*
11D-11-2	El Jaral pocket; tropical forest; 750 m asl.	11km	3/6	303/430sq m.	A.D. 686–1020
7D-6-2	Río Amarillo; tropical and pine forest; 700m asl.	22km	2/3	413/496sq m.	A.D. 854–1058
7D-3-1	Río Amarillo; tropical and pine forest; 700m asl.	21km	2/3	254/320sq m.	A.D. 687–899
34A-12-1	Sesesmil Valley; pine forest; 800m asl.	5.8km	1/1	170/180sq m.	A.D. 624–694
34A-12-2	Sesesmil Valley; pine forest; 5.8km; 820m asl.	5.8km	1/2	253/272sq m.	A.D. 614–723
32B-16-1	Sesesmil Valley; pine forest; 950m asl.	10km	1/5	337/380sq m.	A.D. 535–791
34C-4-2	Sesesmil Valley; tropical forest; 730m asl.	2.2km	4/5	550/744sq m.	A.D. 582–1013
99A-18-2	Río Gila; tropical forest; 720m asl.	8km	2/2	143/212sq m.	A.D. 861–1025

* For example, error ranges not included.

of 27 structures at the eight sites. Next we trenched into each building to determine its architectural history, and then excavated along the outer foundation walls where the Maya frequently placed burials. Artifact collections were basically controlled by 2×2 m grids, with spatial adjustments made for features or other special finds. These grids also formed the basis for simple contour maps of the site surface. While screening excavated soil is always desirable, it would have greatly diminished the size of our exposures. Our compromise was to take many soil samples for later laboratory analysis, screening only soil from burials and some other features in the field.

In ancient behavioral terms, we investigated what archaeologists call house lots (Santley and Hirth, 1993; Johnston and Gonlin, 1998). House lots, commonly used by contemporary Mesoamerican rural people today, are complexes of domestic buildings and open spaces, sometimes surrounded by a wall or other boundary. It was especially important to test areas outside of structures because we know from ethnographic accounts that many outdoor activities occur in house

TABLE 7-2
SUMMARY OF RURAL SITE DATA 2

Site Number	Size of Structures (L x W x H)	Energetic Cost (person-days)	Inferred General Function
11D-11-2	Str. 1: = 3.8 x 3.56 x 1.2m Str. 1-sub = 4.4 x 5.85 x .75m Str. 2 = 6 x 3.78 x .30m Str. 3 = 3.87 x 3.26 x .30m Str. 4 = 4.52 x 4.52 x .50m Str. 5 = 9.6 x ? x .20m	Str. 1 = 42pd Str. 1-sub = 51pd Str. 2 = 36pd Str. 3 = 19pd Str. 4 = 38pd Str. 5 = 37pd	Str. 1 = residence/ritual Str. 1-sub = residence Str. 2 = residence Str. 3 = kitchen/storage Str. 4 = kitchen/storage Str. 5 = residence
7D-6-2	Str. 1 = 4 x 4.38 x .75m Str. 2 = 5.8 x 9.75 x .55m Str. 3 = 5.8 x 4.4 x .20m	Str. 1 = 32pd Str. 2 = 96pd Str. 3 = 32pd	Str. 1 = residence Str. 2 = residence Str. 3 = kitchen
7D-3-1	Str. 1 = 4.6 x 4.9 x .25m Str. 2 = 4.5 x 6.2 x .15m Str. 3 = 4.3 x ? x .20m	Str. 1 = 35pd Str. 2 = 43pd Str. 3 = 29pd	Str. 1 = residence/kitchen/ storage Str. 2 = residence Str. 3 = residence
32A-12-1	Str. 1 = 3.6 x 2.8 x .20m	Str. 1 = 12pd	Str. 1 = field hut
34A-12-2	Str. 1 = 6.4 x 2.4 x .20m Str. 2 = 2.7 x ? x .20m	Str. 1 = 18pd Str. 2 = 16pd	Str. 1 = residence/storage Str. 2 = residence/kitchen
32B-16-1	Str. 1 = 4 x 4 x .30m Str. 2 = 5 x 4 x .30m Str. 3 = 3.8 x 3.4 x .25m Str. 4 = 2.5 x ? x .25m Str. 5 = 4 x ? x .25m	Str. 1 = 22pd Str. 2 = 26pd Str. 3 = 18pd Str. 4 = 20pd Str. 5 = 22pd	Str. 1 = residence Str. 2 = residence Str. 3 = kitchen/storage Str. 4 = residence Str. 5 = residence
34C-4-2	Str. 1 = 10 x ? x 1.0m Str. 2 = 8 x 7.6 x .35m Str. 3 = 9.6 x 5.8 x .75m Str. 3-sub = no estimate Str. 4 = 10 x 6.6 x .75m	Str. 1 = 148pd Str. 2 = 129pd Str. 3 = 133pd Str. 4 = 148pd	Str. 1 = residence/kitchen Str. 2 = residence Str. 3 = residence Str. 4 = residence
99A-18-2	Str. 1 = 6 x 6.6 x .50m Str. 2 = 5 x 5.8 x .75m	Str. 1 = 56pd Str. 2 = 87pd	Str. 1 = residence Str. 2 = kitchen/residence/ storage

lots, and that they are often used for gardens. Payson Sheets (1992) documented such use archaeologically at Ceren. About 81% of the total area excavated at the Copán sites—3024 sq m—accordingly consisted of patio or peripheral spaces. One reason why it was possible to clear such extensive spaces is that the overburden accumulated on the ancient living surfaces or features was rarely more than 50 cm deep.

A related issue was trash disposal. We assumed that few artifacts would be in their primary contexts but rather would have been moved about and redeposited, especially in middens. While specific concentrations of artifacts might not directly indicate the locations of activities, we did anticipate finding concentrations of discarded trash immediately around the buildings and patios. Some ethnographic studies suggest, however, that modern Maya keep their houses and patios swept clean, a dismal prognosis from the archaeological perspective. By digging lines of trenches out from the site cores, we tested how artifact densities varied with distance.

We do not have the space here to describe each rural site. Because fully excavated small rural sites are so uncommon, however, we briefly describe and illustrate four of them to show the range of variation. Then we give our general interpretations of this household sample. Basic information about all sites is shown in Tables 7-1 and 7-2.

A SAMPLE OF RURAL SITES

Like their more elite counterparts, common Maya people in the ancient Copán Valley built almost all of their domiciles, kitchens, storehouses, or other domestic facilities on substructure platforms. People still build in the same manner in the valley today (Plate 7-2) and a house without a platform is regarded as substandard and undesirable. At Las Sepulturas, substructures often made up most of the mass of the buildings and could be up to several meters high. In our rural sites the platforms were much smaller. Prior to excavation, some were visible only as lines of stone virtually flush with the ground, and the highest stood only

PLATE 7-2   PHOTO OF TRADITIONAL COPÁN HOUSE AND ITS HOUSELOT GARDEN. ROOFING IS PALM THATCH AND LOWER WALLS ARE POLES PLASTERED WITH MUD. WALLS REST ON LOW STONE FOUNDATIONS. THE CYLINDRICAL OBJECTS HANGING FROM THE SIDE WALL OF THE HOUSE ARE BEEHIVES.

about 1.2 m. All substructures had retaining walls, usually of rough natural stone, that contained earthen fill, sometimes mixed with rubble.

Superstructure features were almost entirely absent, except for occasional stone wall bases or the infrequent remains of interior benches. Originally most superstructure buildings probably consisted of heavy, upright corner timbers joined by walls of lighter poles and saplings liberally slathered with mud plaster. Such construction, still widely used today, is called *bajareque,* or wattle and daub. Roofs would have been of some light thatching material such as palm fronds, grass, or even cornstalks, which were the most common material observed by Stephens and Catherwood at Copán in 1839. Needless to say, nothing remains of these superstructures except occasional pieces of burned mud from the walls which retain impressions of poles, saplings, and grass.

In the Las Sepulturas elite compounds, the patios and some other ambient surfaces were paved with cobbles set in mud mortar and sometimes covered with thick layers of limestone plaster. Rural sites sometimes had crude pavings of stones around some structures, but usually the patios and other outdoor surfaces were simply hard-packed mud. Despite all these similarities, small sites each have their own unique characteristics, as the following examples show.

Site 7D-6-2 (Operation 31)

Site 7D-6-2 (Figure 7-2; Plate 7-3) is located in the Río Amarillo East pocket, not far from the stream of the same name, on level ground at the foot of a small, pine-covered hill. One would have to walk about 22 km to get to the Main Group from this locale. The PAC II survey recorded the site as a two-mound aggregate in 1981, but excavation turned up three strikingly different buildings.

Structure 1, on the north, was nearly square—measuring about 4 × 4.38 m— with retaining walls about 70–80 cm high. A small stairway led up to the platform from the south, and remains of stone superstructure walls and a stone bench were on the summit. Unusual for a rural building, much of its substructure was composed of well-cut rectilinear stones, possibly looted from an abandoned site of higher rank such as the nearby Type 4 center of Río Amarillo.

Across a wide courtyard was the sprawling Structure 2, which covered an area of about 9.75 × 5.8 m. This building was very complex and obviously had grown by lateral expansion. Ephemeral wall lines were uncovered on the building's surface, hinting at its original interior complexity.

The previously undetected Structure 3 was a low, crudely-built, T-shaped building on the east side of the patio. Inside it were the remains of a hearth, the only one we found anywhere inside a building. This feature, along with the building's associated artifacts, its position relative to Structure 1, and its unusual shape, led us to provisionally identify it as a kitchen.

Although site 7D-6-2 had a very large patio, it was composed of tamped earth. Excavations into it produced large quantities of sherds and other artifacts, and high densities of such material continued to the west. We found no clear signs of construction on this side of the patio but there were piles of cobbles, which might represent stones being stockpiled for a building project that was abandoned, or a

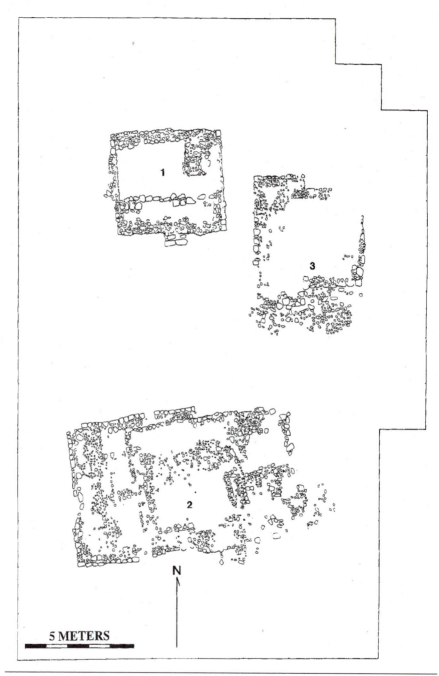

5 METERS

N

FIGURE 7-2   PLAN OF THREE EXCAVATED FOUNDATION PLATFORMS AT RURAL SITE
7D-6-2. NOTE THE LARGE AREA OF EXCAVATED AMBIENT SPACE AS SHOWN BY THE
BLACK LINE AROUND THE BUILDINGS.

PLATE 7-3   PHOTO OF SITE 7D-6-2 DURING EXCAVATION, LOOKING TOWARD THE SOUTH.

destroyed platform from an earlier time period, looted for the stone used at the site. Two sets of chipped-stone artifacts stood out at 7D-6-2. Among the hundreds of obsidian blade fragments were 20 with a distinctive greenish gold color—almost certainly imported from the Pachuca flow in the Basin of Mexico, about 1000 km to the northwest. Such obsidian is widely but sparsely distributed at Copán, and very unusual in concentrated amounts at a small rural site. Also notable were 20 bifacially-flaked projectile or spear points, artifacts not conspicuous in household inventories elsewhere. Although they may have been used for hunting, they also could have served as weapons in conflicts against other humans.

Taken together with the apparent looting of cut stone from sites of higher status, these artifacts suggested to us that 7D-6-2 was occupied quite late in the Coner phase. As we shall see later, independent evidence supports this view.

Sites 34A-12-1 (Operation 33) and 34A-12-2 (Operation 34)

In 1986 we turned our attention to two adjacent sites in the Río Sesesmil tributary valley which we excavated concurrently in the interests of efficiency. Both these sites were in foothill locations on the south side of a seasonal tributary stream flowing into the Río Sesesmil, a locale of limestone bedrock. Freter originally recorded them as single mound sites, and the visible architecture was very minimal—a few wall lines of rough stone almost flush with the ground. Her test pits showed that 34A-12-2 seemed to have the normal complement of artifacts, but much less was found at 34A-12-1, only a short distance away to the north. This interesting contrast was partly responsible for our decision to excavate here.

34A-12-2   Structure 1 was located near the top of a steep hill, and upon excavation turned out to be the most modest dwelling we ever excavated at Copán (Figure 7-3). Its basal platform, one stone course high, was originally only 3.8 m long and 2.3 m wide. Later a small extension with a *cascajo* surface was added to its eastern end and almost doubled its length. Domestic artifacts, however, were abundant, both in a midden immediately uphill from the building and on the lower slopes to the north, where they had been washed by erosion.

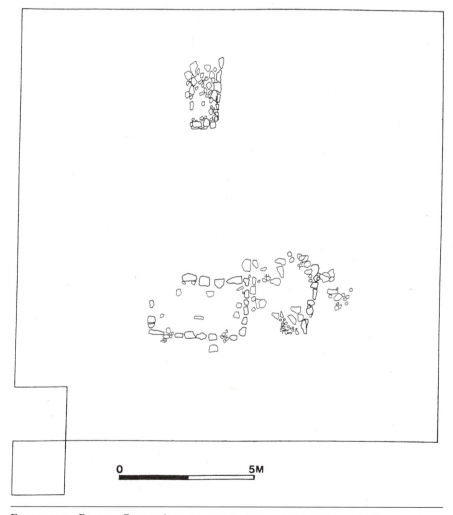

0   5M

FIGURE 7-3   PLAN OF SITE 34A-12-2, WHICH HAS THE SMALLEST PERMANENTLY USED RESIDENTIAL BUILDINGS THAT WE EXCAVATED ANYWHERE AT COPÁN.

On survey Freter thought she saw remains of another building about 5 m downslope from Structure 1, but could not be sure. We excavated this area and uncovered the partial remains of Structure 2, a little building originally about the same size as Structure 1. We think Structure 2 was occupied slightly earlier and was partly dismantled to get construction material for the later Structure 1.

Up to this point we had uncovered no burials at any of our rural sites, despite systematic attempts to locate them. What we found at Operation 34 therefore surprised us. We identified five burials in the field, all in shallow pits. Two were just outside the north wall of Structure 2, one was beneath the floor of Structure 1, and two more were buried near the south wall of Structure 1. Because the bones were in very poor condition, most were removed along with their matrices and later cleaned and analyzed in the laboratory by Rebecca Storey. She identified remains of nine individuals, including five adults, two juveniles, and two infants.

Burials were simple flexed, and extended inhumations where position could be determined. Mortuary offerings were very sparse. Most significant were whole vessels recovered with two of the burials. Both of these vessels were types that began in the Acbi phase, then disappeared in early Coner. These vessels, along with other ceramic finds, strongly suggested that Site 34A-12-2 was occupied in the 7th to the early 8th centuries, a prediction that, as we shall see shortly, was independently confirmed.

34A-12-1   This little single platform site occupied a knoll about 65 m to the northeast of 34A-12-2, and its preserved sections were roughly rectangular (3.6 × 2.8 m) with walls only about 20 cm high. We encountered no features or burials, and artifact densities were extremely light. There were no chert or ground stone implements at all, and only 11 fragments of obsidian. The sparse ceramic collection consisted mainly of large Coner jar sherds and lacked the expected range of domestic types. As we suspected from test pitting, 34A-12-1 seems not to have been a residence. It might have been a storage structure for 34A-12-2 but seems inconveniently distant for that purpose. The alternative explanation we favor is that it represents a field hut, used for short periods during the agricultural season. If this inference is correct, it must date to an interval when 34A-12-2 was not occupied.

Site 99A-18-2 (Operation 38)

In 1984 Webster recorded a small, two mound group in the foothills of the Río Jila, a southern tributary of the Río Copán, and collected surface material from it (Figure 7-4). The site occupies a little limestone ridge about 700 m from the stream on a hillside that, until recently, supported broad-leaf tropical forest. We cleared and mapped both well-preserved structures but could only intensively investigate Structure 2. This building measured 5 × 5.8 m, and was slightly smaller than its neighbor. Its maximum height was about 1 m, and it had been damaged by looters. Along its south side we found steps running the width of the front wall. These gave access to a front terrace, beyond which there were traces of

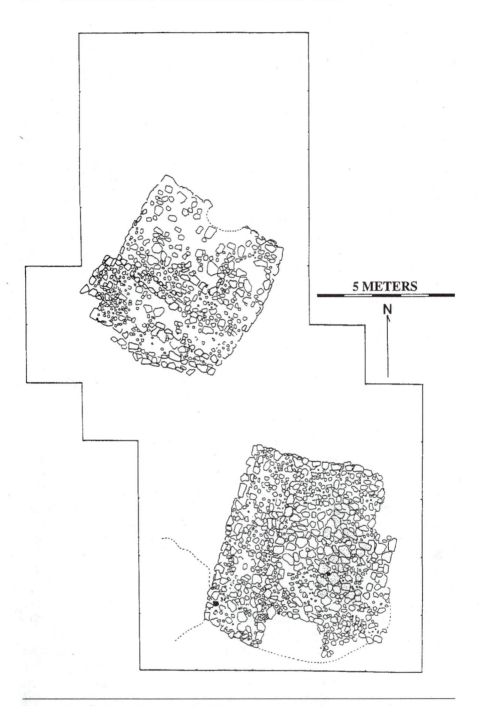

FIGURE 7-4   PLAN OF SITE 99A-18-2. THE NORTHERNMOST BUILDING OF THIS SMALL TWO-MOUND SITE YIELDED SOME OF THE RARE BURIALS FOUND DURING THE EXTENSIVE EXCAVATION OF RURAL HOUSEHOLD REMAINS.

superstructure walls and an interior bench—only the second one we excavated in a rural site. A little western projection of the substructure may have been a food preparation area, given the abundant artifacts and remains of a hearth found there. Our probes of Structure 2 revealed evidence of an earlier construction phase, but of greater interest are five associated graves with seven identified individuals. These burials, most of which lacked mortuary offerings, were placed in shallow pits, sometimes with rough-stone, cist-like linings or markers, along and partly beneath the northwest substructure wall. Preliminary analysis by Rebecca Storey shows two or possibly three elderly adult females, two additional unsexed adults, a juvenile aged 3 to 4 years, and an infant of less than 1 year old.

RESULTS AND INTERPRETATIONS

Site Functions

The most important conclusion from our rural excavations is that the inferences drawn from test pitting were correct: seven of the eight sites yielded clear domestic assemblages, and the eighth was identified as nonresidential (field hut) as inferred from earlier test pitting. Potsherds were the most numerous artifacts (over 125,000 altogether), representing a consistent range of food storage, food processing, and serving vessels, along with a few for ritual use. Chipped-stone tools for cutting, scraping, and sawing were, with a handful of exceptions, made of imported obsidian and predominantly took the form of broken prismatic blade fragments. Retouched or bifacial tools and chert artifacts were rare. All seven residential sites produced manos, metates, and greenstone celts, and there were many miscellaneous finds as well. As expected, the hypothetical field hut site 34A-12-1 stood out from the rest, with a very restricted, special purpose artifact assemblage.

Inventories of domestic artifacts show striking overlap with those found in the elite Las Sepulturas sites, which are, however, richer in the range of specific artifact forms. While rural people may have had less access to sophisticated material possessions than some of their more urban counterparts, they do appear to have had equal access to the implements and commodities used in everyday activities, including polychrome pottery and imported materials such as obsidian blades. Highly ranked people might have possessed more of these things, but there seem to have been few sumptuary rules that rigidly denied certain kinds of possessions to common people.

All of the sites we investigated appear to have been gradually abandoned. Interior floors were mostly clean, and no doubt most useful household possessions were carried away when people moved. On several occasions we observed modern episodes of abandonment and noted that even the old wood wall materials and main house posts were carried away, the former probably for firewood and the latter for construction material at a new location.

Sheets's excavations of suddenly abandoned household facilities at Ceren remind us of how much has been lost to the archaeological record (Sheets, 1992;

Webster, Gonlin, and Sheets, 1997). Just what any particular building was used for is thus difficult to determine on the basis of artifact distributions. Intact features that clearly show specific activity areas outside the buildings are also rare, although statistical analysis by Gonlin (1993) revealed general patterns. The Maya themselves probably had rather flexible notions of how to use the indoor and outdoor spaces of their house lots. For example, they probably shifted their outdoor hearths from one place to another, and did certain tasks indoors or outdoors as the seasons dictated.

At no site did we recover any obvious signs of specialized economic or other activities, although we know from Mallory's work at El Duende and from Freter's test pitting that such sites exist (see Chapter 6).

Fortunately the ancient Maya inhabitants of the sites we excavated were not, as we had feared, overly concerned with cleanliness. Although surfaces of structures were quite clean, plenty of artifacts were trodden into patio floors, discarded in middens adjacent to buildings, or in a few cases, seemingly left where activities took place. Wherever we dug lines of trenches extending out from site cores, we detected extremely steep dropoffs in artifact densities with increased distance.

Flotation of soil samples also provided useful information about rural life—particularly diet—that we will review in Chapter 9.

Site Character and Associated Social Organization

Despite their similar low ranks in the Harvard typology, the sites collectively show considerable variation in architectural form. Some of this variation is attributable to length of occupation (see below) but no doubt also reflects varied household composition of the inhabitants. Site 34A-12-2 could hardly have housed a social group larger than a nuclear family—say four to six people. At the other extreme, sites 11D-11-2 and 34C-4-2 must have accommodated households several times this size—perhaps extended or joint families (see Chapters 11 and 12 for detailed discussions of social and political organization).

Gonlin (1993), using a variation of Abrams' methods, estimated the labor investment in 20 of the rural structures (including their perishable superstructures). Construction costs showed a range of 16 to 148 person-days, with a mean of 54 person-days. Such investments are well within the capabilities of small domestic groups, but pale by comparison with the labor investments made in the largest elite palace buildings described in Chapter 4, which Abrams calculates required investments on the order of 10,000 person-days.

Two residential features associated with Copán elite dwellings in the urban core, and at some smaller sites in the Copán pocket, were only infrequently represented in our rural sites. Interior benches, which we associate with domiciles, were found in only two buildings. Their limited number indicates either that rural Maya householders used interior space differently than people closer to the Main Group, or that features such as benches were made of perishable materials, a possibility suggested by Sheets's domiciles at Ceren.

More puzzling is the general lack of burials. Although we purposefully searched for them, we found burials at only two of the eight intensively excavated rural sites. Burial of the dead away from households is not characteristic of the ancient Maya, and in fact some scholars (McAnany, 1995) have suggested that burial around households had essential symbolic, social, and economic functions. Two possibilities are that there were distinctive burial practices of Copán rural people on the southeastern Maya frontier, reflecting some sort of ethnic differences; or alternatively, that people who lived in rural households had strong relationships with the core population and buried their dead in more central locales.

One significant methodological insight involves the number of structures present at small sites. Surface inspection suggested a total of 16 structures at all sites collectively, but excavation increased the total to 27. Buried platforms obviously are numerous at Copán, even in upland sites, and our rural excavations helped us to correct for this problem in our demographic simulations. In two cases (Ops. 34 and 35), excavation showed that what looked like single mound sites on the surface actually had multiple mounds, and so these sites should be upgraded to aggregate/Type 1 status. On the other hand, we found no evidence of nonplatform structures at any of the sites.

General Chronology and Length of Occupations

An extremely important issue is the chronology of small Copán sites, because it is central to our later demographic reconstructions.

CERAMIC PHASING   All of the rural sites produced overwhelmingly Coner ceramics, sometimes with a little admixture of Acbi or earlier material. Not a single sherd of the Ejar complex was recovered in our huge sample (although such sherds were found during test pitting at other rural sites). We will return to the implications of this fact shortly. We concluded that most occupations dated after A.D. 600–650, except for Site 34A-12-2, which was transitional between Acbi/Coner. The methodological problem was to narrow down specific occupations still further, especially because the Coner phase seemed to be of longer duration than previously suspected.

ARCHITECTURAL STRATIGRAPHY   One clue about the length of site occupation is architectural stratigraphy. In only one case (Op. 36) did we find a clear pre-Coner phase building, and instances of one Coner phase construction superimposed over another were also rare at rural sites. More common was lateral expansion of structures, along with additions and renovations to adjacent patio surfaces, just as we would expect in house lot facilities. Trenches in mounds frequently produced sterile or almost sterile fills, suggesting that when they were built there was little or no previous occupation debris in their immediate locales. A methodological lesson is that trenches through structures during the test-pitting operations reviewed in Chapter 6 would not have repaid the effort.

No doubt the larger sites also grew by the addition of whole structures over time, but the lack of connecting features such as paved patio floors makes such phasing difficult to untangle. In two Operations (34 and 35) we detected hidden buildings that seem to have been partly dismantled for material to construct new ones.

Obvious variation in the number and character of structures, as well as density of artifacts, shows that some were occupied much longer than others. Site 34A-12-2, for example, must have been an extremely ephemeral place compared, say, to 34C-4-2 or 11D-11-2. Of course there is always the problem of confusing continuous occupation with multiple occupations. Quite conceivably a little place such as 34C-4-2 was occupied for a while, abandoned, then reoccupied. We cannot presently detect any such fluctuations of occupation in our sample.

GEOCHEMICAL DATES   Although we frequently encountered carbon and other organic remains, none came from particularly reliable contexts and so were not very useful for radiocarbon dating. Nor could we have afforded the many radiocarbon determinations necessary to assess occupation intervals. We thus turned to obsidian hydration dating. This method and its applications at Copán are critically evaluated by Freter in Chapter 10, but we will review briefly its results for the rural sites here.

Figure 7-5 shows the spread of 210 dated obsidian blade fragments derived from all the sites. Four conclusions stand out. First, most sites were occupied (continuously or intermittently) for extended periods of time—typically a century or two. Second, despite the fact that all had predominantly Coner ceramics, they were not all contemporary. Third, the hydration dates beautifully capture the Coner/Acbi transition at Op. 34, as well as the trace of pure Acbi occupation in Op. 36. Fourth, some sites, especially those in Río Amarillo and Río Jila (Ops. 31 and 38), were founded after the dynastic collapse and occupied until almost A.D. 1100, thus supporting the extended use of Coner or Coner-like ceramic assemblages.

In 1996 and 1997 we independently tested the hydration dates against AMS (Accelerator Mass Spectrometer) radiocarbon determinations run on bone collagen from burials (Webster, Freter, and Storey, 1997). Although only two of our

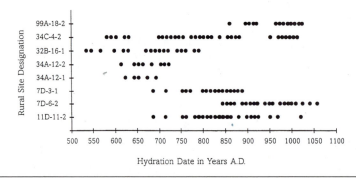

FIGURE 7-5   DISTRIBUTION OF 210 OBSIDIAN HYDRATION DATES ON SAMPLES OBTAINED FROM EXCAVATION OF THE RURAL SITES WE EXTENSIVELY EXCAVATED IN 1985–1986. EACH DOT REPRESENTS ONE OR SEVERAL DATES.

TABLE 7-3

CALIBRATED AMS RADIOCARBON DETERMINATIONS FROM
BURIALS AT SITES 34A-12-2 AND 99A-18-2 (ALL FROM THE
UNIVERSITY OF ARIZONA AMS LABORATORY):

Radiocarbon Age	One Sigma Span	Two Sigma Span
34A-12-2		
1375±50 B.P.	A.D. 642–689	A.D. 680–772
1600±60 B.P.	A.D. 415–540	A.D. 357–615
99A-18-2		
1030±50 B.P.	A.D. 985–1029	A.D. 897–1154
1115±60 B.P.	A.D. 883–997	A.D. 778–1025
655±50 B.P.	A.D. 1288–1393	A.D. 1278–1411
1260±65 B.P.	A.D. 649–792	A.D. 649–978
1345±60 B.P.	A.D. 646–768	A.D. 603–856

rural sites (Ops. 34 and 38) produced burials, these were, fortunately, among the earliest and latest ones occupied according to the hydration dates. Calibrated determinations from seven burials are shown in Table 7-3.[1]

Assuming that the burials represent people who lived at the sites, the hydration chronology is strongly supported. The two dates from Op. 34 nicely overlap with the hydration dates and are consistent with the ceramic chronology. One date suggests undetected earlier occupation of the site. The five dates from Op. 38 incorporate the entire hydration-determined occupation span. They similarly suggest that we missed some earlier occupation, but also that one burial was placed in this site as late as the 13th to the 15th century. Had we burials from the other sites, we are confident they too would be in general agreement with the obsidian dates. Clearly the Coner phase began about the time predicted by Viel (1993a, 1993b), but Coner-like ceramic assemblages, without any Ejar subcomplex forms, were used by people in the valley much later than expected.

SUMMARY

In summary, our rural household excavations have enlightened us about Maya commoner household remains in a general sense and provide rich information on the nature of such sites at Copán, and on their inherent variability. Freter's earlier conclusions about the basic functions of the sites were strongly supported.

---

[1] Hydration dates were determined using a 1985 baseline, and radiocarbon dates using a 1950 baseline. We show the raw dates here, but to properly compare these data sets either the whole radiocarbon array should be pushed forward 35 years, or the hydration arrays for each site pushed back 35 years (Webster, Freter, and Storey 1997). See Chapter 10 for a more complete discussion.

We also understand much better two issues essential to the proper estimation of population using settlement data—the hidden structure problem and the issue of contemporaneity of occupation within the Coner ceramic phase. Finally, the obsidian hydration method gave very plausible results, both as tested against expectations from the ceramic sequence (the Acbi/Coner transition) and against radiocarbon determinations, a reliable, independent dating method widely used in archaeology. As we shall see, all these positive results have important implications for many of our most fundamental conclusions abut the Copán regional polity.

While we can reasonably conclude some important things about the occupants of these little sites, it is difficult to know exactly what to call them in terms of the larger political economy of the Copán polity. Certainly they were people of the lowest social ranks and hence as individuals of little political influence. We could accordingly call them "commoners." Collectively, of course, they represented the bulk of the population and provided most of the goods and labor that supported Copán's political elites, so they could also appropriately be called "basic producers." Subsistence farmers of low social status in many societies are labeled "peasants" by some anthropologists (Wolf, 1966), and "smallholders" by others (Netting, 1989). The latter is an attractive term in one sense, because clearly the occupants of our little houses had only modest possessions and facilities and cultivated only small fields. On the other hand, we cannot know, in the absence of written records, to what extent they "held" rights of access to agricultural (or other) resources. Did they in any sense "own" land of their own? Was access to land delegated by more highly ranked people? We simply do not know.

Whatever we choose to call them, the common people represented by our little sites no doubt lived lives very similar to those of the predynastic farmers of the valley, and they long outlasted Classic period kings and elites, as we shall see in Chapter 12.

CHAPTER 8
The Ancient Environment of Copán

INTRODUCTION

A central tenet of landscape archaeology is that environments are dynamic, both because of changing natural processes and because of human activity. We cannot assume, therefore, that all of the environmental characteristics described for the Copán Valley in Chapter 1 were the same in the past. In fact, we know this was not the case. Evidence of environmental change is easy to see if one looks for it. Deeply buried Classic Maya house floors are visible in the roadcuts of the modern highway, and even during our own projects the landscape noticeably changed, most dramatically through continued deforestation.

In this chapter we review the evidence for environmental change and some of the ways we can detect it. Farmers are particularly important agents of environmental change in preindustrial agrarian societies anywhere, and of course such changes in turn affect their strategies of deriving a living from their land. As we shall see, humans are strongly implicated in ancient environmental changes at Copán.

RECONSTRUCTING ANCIENT ENVIRONMENTS AT COPÁN

To appreciate how dynamic environments can be, one only has to consider the recent history of the Copán Valley. When Stephens and Catherwood explored the Copán pocket in 1839, they encountered only a few local inhabitants, and much of the valley floor was covered with dense, deciduous tropical vegetation, while pine and oak covered the uplands. By World War I only remnants of these forests were left (Popenoe, 1919). Since then the human population has vastly increased, and virtually all of the valley floor and most of the nearby lower slopes have been cleared of natural vegetation for agriculture or cattle pasture. These processes are so rapid that those of us who have worked in the valley for many years are struck by how much it has changed. In particular, deforestation and erosion are very obvious and widespread.

Many more long-term, historically unrecorded changes have also clearly occurred since Classic Maya times. Most conspicuously, the main channel of the

river has moved. At some point it flowed farther to the south and east. Later, perhaps partly because of human-induced changes, it shifted its course and washed
away parts of both Las Sepulturas and the Main Group. To take another example,
anyone walking along the modern highway at the edge of the northern foothills of
the Copán pocket can see Classic Maya house floors and platforms exposed in
roadcuts, deeply buried by ancient erosion.

Rene Viel and his colleagues have recently begun studies of the geomorphol-
ogy and hydrology of the Copán pocket. They provisionally conclude that in Late
Preclassic times the river flowed at a higher level, flooded frequently, and that
the Copán pocket floor was rather poorly drained. These conditions are somewhat like those of the floor of the modern Río Amarillo East pocket.

Evidence Used in Reconstructing
Ancient Environments

Archaeologists have many ways of detecting and measuring what ancient environments were like. Remote imagery from satellites or aircraft can detect ancient
features such as old, silted-in river channels. Sediment cores recovered from bodies of water contain samples of plant material useful for reconstructing vegetation
history. Changes in oxygen isotopes from such cores can be used to reconstruct
fluctuations in temperature or rainfall. Stratigraphic sequences exposed in archaeological or other excavations tell complex stories about hydrological and
geomorphological processes. And, of course, archaeological data in the form of
plant and animal remains, tools, agroengineering features, and even settlement
patterns, provide us with indications of what ancient landscapes were like.

Many such methods were developed by scientists in other fields and require
not only specialized technology, but special skills, if they are to be properly applied and their results understood. Partnerships between archaeologists, geographers, and natural scientists are therefore essential, and many specialists have
been involved at Copán right from the beginning of the most recent phase of research (Turner et al., 1983). Comparatively few of the available methods of environmental reconstruction have been systematically and widely applied at Copán,
but what we have done gives us some insights about what the valley was like in
the past.

Evidence from Sediment Cores

Old bodies of water, especially those that are anaerobic and not turbulent, often
build up deep deposits of well-stratified sediments over time. Rates of sedimentation and the character of the nonorganic sediments have environmental implications, as does plant material in the form of preserved pollen, macrofossils, or
phytoliths. Palynology, the study of fossil pollen, can be used to reconstruct
vegetation history and indirectly other processes such as changes in climate or
human alterations of the landscape. Organic material from the sediment cores
can be radiocarbon dated, providing convenient chronological control.

Comparatively few sediment cores are available from southeastern Meso-america and northern Central America. Three were recovered by Penn State re-searchers during PAC II or later related projects and have important implications both for the Copán Valley as well as a much larger region (Rue, 1986, 1987; Webster et al., 1997). Two of the cores come from a small, circular bog called the Aguada Petapilla, located among limestone hills in a small intermontane valley about 4.5 km northeast of the Copán Main Group (Figure 7-1). Both were ex-tracted by David Rue, one in 1984 and the second in 1989. Rue also took a third core from Lago Yojoa, a large lake in central Honduras in 1984. Rue studied all three cores in conjunction with Alfred Traverse of the Department of Geo-sciences, who maintains a palynological facility at the Penn State campus.

PETAPILLA CORE I   This sediment sample, full of well-preserved pollen, was taken by Rue from the northern edge of the bog. Because the coring device hit impenetrable clays at a shallow depth, the core is only 1.35 m long, and we knew it would therefore tell us only about the last part of the Copán regional sequence. Two standard radiocarbon dates from the 70 and 130 cm levels show respective uncalibrated radiocarbon ages of 595±160 and 940±160 B.P.[1] On the basis of the uncalibrated dates Rue estimated that the deepest zone of the sediments was formed about A.D. 1000; the calibrated dates suggest the basal sediments are slightly later—11th or 12th century. Interpreted either way, the sediments post-dated the proposed demographic abandonment of the valley, which in 1984 was thought to have occurred between A.D. 850 and 900.

Given the original abandonment scenario, significant regrowth of natural vegetation, and particularly broad-leaf, deciduous and semideciduous tropical forest, should have been conspicuous throughout the pollen profile (Figure 8-1a). Instead, the pollen in the lower sections of the core shows high percentages of *Gramineae* (grass) and the presence of *Zea* (maize). Expected tropical, broad-leaf tree species, such as *Meliaceae* (mahogany family), are nearly absent. Even pine pollen percentages are low, suggesting that the montane forest may have been heavily depleted. These patterns strongly indicate the continued presence of farmers in the valley. Not until after A.D. 1250 (or slightly later according to the calibrated dates) did reforestation occur, at which time the bog also expanded into an extensive forested wetland. Above the 30 cm level modern disturbance is signaled by the reclearance of deciduous trees and the re-emergence of a strong *Compositae* (aster family) pollen signature.

Rue's interpretations are supplemented by a very short core taken at Copán during the PAC I project. This core did not penetrate to sufficient depth to sam-ple sedimentation processes during the Maya occupation of the valley, but its post-Maya zone agrees well with that of Petapilla core 1.

---

[1] One sigma calibrated dates for these samples are A.D. 1303 (1397) 1414, and A.D. 1022 (1046, 1097, 1115, 1144, 1153) 1177.

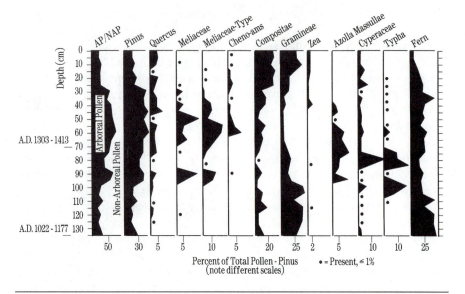

FIGURE 8-1A POLLEN PROFILE FROM PETAPILLA SEDIMENT CORE 1. THE TWO ASSOCIATED C14 DATES ARE EXPRESSED AS CALIBRATED ONE SIGMA RANGES.

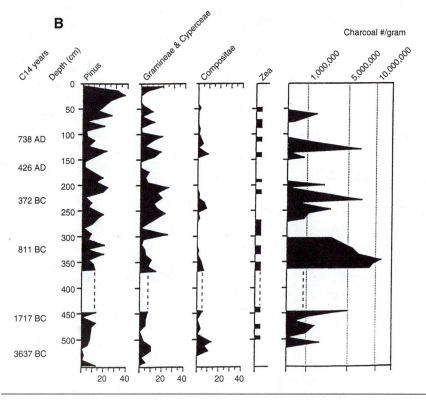

FIGURE 8-1B POLLEN AND CARBON PROFILE FROM PETAPILLA SEDIMENT CORE 2.

EXTENT OF DEFORESTATION   On the basis of the first Petapilla core and simulations of amounts of wood needed simply for household fuel, construction material, and plaster-making, Abrams and Rue (1988, pp. 391–392) argue persuasively that by A.D. 800 ". . . no pine would have been standing for the entire 12 km length of the Copán pocket for a distance of nearly 1.0 km away from any zone of settlement on either side of the Copán River." Their estimates are conservative, and of course, do not take into consideration the deforestation for subsistence agriculture that had been going on for centuries by A.D. 800.

PETAPILLA CORE 2   The second core was extracted from closer to the center of the bog and at 5.3 m is much longer than the first one. Eight AMS radiocarbon samples were run on samples from the core in 1996. The lowest (from 511 to 513 cm) yielded a calibrated one sigma date of 3662 to 3527 B.C. and the highest (111–113 cm) a date of A.D. 669–860. Basal sediments may be as old as 4500 B.C. This core, unlike the first, incorporates not only all of Copán's dynastic and postdynastic history, but in all probability most of the entire interval of prehistoric human occupation.

   Unfortunately the second core had very low absolute (pollen) amounts of all kinds for reasons we do not understand (Figure 8-1b). In addition, a very high percentage of the pollen recovered consists of fungal and fern spores, rather than the angiosperm (flowering plant) or gymnosperm (conifer) pollen useful for environmental reconstruction. Nevertheless, two other kinds of evidence were very revealing. Heavy concentrations of charcoal are apparent in this core from the beginning (i.e., well before 3600 B.C.), and what appears to be the pollen of domestic maize shows up at or before 2000 B.C. If humans set the fires that produced the charcoal, as seems likely, and if the maize pollen is correctly identified, horticulturists occupied the valley much earlier than we believed only a few years ago, and anthropogenic environmental changes are much older than we thought. Such evidence at Copán is paralleled by similar findings recently reported from Belize and elsewhere in the tropical lowlands of Mesoamerica and Central America (Pohl et al., 1996).

LAKE YOJOA CORE   In 1984 Rue also extracted a 1.5-m-long core from Lago Yojoa, a shallow lake about 100 km due east of Copán. He found early pollen signatures of forest clearance at about 4500 B.P. in this core. Then there was a period of further agricultural intensification until 3000 B.P., after which few identifiable trends in the pollen sequence can be seen, suggesting long term stability. Although the Yojoa sediment sequence has little direct relevance for local environmental changes at Copán itself, it does support the conclusion that there have been no major regional climatic shifts since about 3,000 years ago. This is an important point, because as we shall see later, some paleoclimatologists (Hodell, Curtis, and Brenner, 1995; Curtis, Hodell, and Brenner, 1996) have argued that such changes, specifically severe droughts, can be detected in sediment cores from Yucatán, and that they are implicated in the Classic Maya collapse.

Evidence of Erosion

Despite heavy rainfall and steep slopes, erosion would not be a serious problem in the Copán Valley in the absence of farming populations because dense vegetation would inhibit soil loss. Test pitting and soil studies during the Harvard project (Olson, 1975), the PAC I project, and by Freter during PAC II, however, revealed evidence of significant erosion in association with Coner phase sites along the northern edge of the Copán pocket alluvium. In 1989 Webster carried out a small project expressly designed to test systematically the depth of erosion in this zone, and if possible, to date it.

At Las Sepulturas there are many mapped mounds on the northern fringe of the urban enclave, but not as many as we might expect. Furthermore, mapped mounds in this sector tend to be low. Webster chose to test one conspicuous mound (Structure 9M-101) in a modern cornfield in this zone. Though it appeared to be only about 1.5 m high, it covered an extensive area and had well-cut masonry, suggesting a much more impressive, partly buried building. A 4-m-long trench was laid out along the north side of the mound perpendicular to its anticipated wall line and excavated to a depth of several meters.

A clear sequence of events is shown by the profile of the west wall of this trench (Figure 8-2). The earliest construction feature is a cobble floor, upon which two separate structures were built—9M-101 itself and the small cobble Platform A. These buildings were aligned with each other but separated by a narrow corridor. A thin, dark midden deposit containing many artifacts had built up in the corridor, as commonly occurred at urban core elite residences. Later a very distinctive layer of almost sterile silty clay covered this midden trash. From artifacts in its upper levels and from a large stone slab (not shown in the profile) purposely laid on top of this deposit in ancient times, we know that the Maya were still active in the locale. At some later time the upper sections of Structure 9M-101 collapsed, and eventually silt and humus accumulated to the level of the modern cornfield, about 2.8 m above the original cobble floor.

The silt in Layer B and the much deeper accumulation in the cornfield were obviously deposited by natural processes. The river could not have transported this material, because other, nearby elite Las Sepulturas sites are lower in elevation and have no similar sediments. Only sheet erosion from the adjacent foothills to the north could have been responsible. The most likely scenario is that many of the deposits along the northern fringe of the Las Sepulturas are coalesced colluvial fans composed of soil washed from the hillsides. The causeway in effect acted as a dam that protected the groups to the south from this slopewash, but much of the local hydrology of the Copán pocket must have been disturbed by this and later erosion.

But when did this happen? We have three main chronological clues. First, Structure 9M-101 was constructed of fine, cut-stone masonry and sported mosaic façade sculpture. Such buildings at Las Sepulturas are common after A.D. 700, and particularly after A.D. 750, but probably were seldom built after the royal collapse in A.D. 822, so the erosion probably began sometime in the 8th century. Fortunately, we recovered obsidian blade fragments from the trash deposit

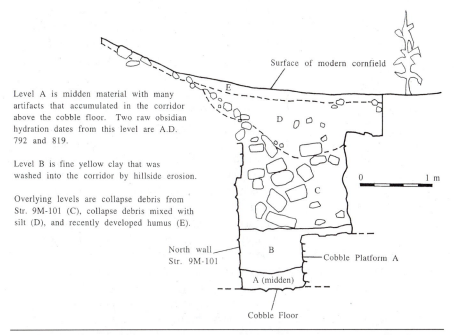

Level A is midden material with many
artifacts that accumulated in the corridor
above the cobble floor. Two raw obsidian
hydration dates from this level are A.D.
792 and 819.

Level B is fine yellow clay that was
washed into the corridor by hillside erosion.

Overlying levels are collapse debris from
Str. 9M-101 (C), collapse debris mixed with
silt (D), and recently developed humus (E).

**FIGURE 8-2   PROFILE OF THE WEST WALL OF THE EROSION TRENCH EXCAVATED NEXT
TO STRUCTURE 9M–101, ON THE NORTHERN FRINGES OF THE COPÁN URBAN CORE.**

below the eroded soil, and Freter dated two of these to A.D. 792±140 and
819±140 (two sigma error intervals). Both dates are in excellent agreement with
the inferred date of the building. Finally, as we shall see in Chapter 11, a simulation of agricultural and population history predicts a major erosion event about
this time.

In all likelihood the erosion process began to affect 9M-101 soon after it was
constructed in the mid-late 8th century and continued long after it was abandoned and collapsed. This conclusion, of course, applies only to erosion in the
immediate locale of this group, where the effects may have been felt long after
more general processes of erosion began elsewhere in the valley.

This little experimental excavation not only told us something important
about environmental change but also had implications for our later simulations of
Copán population. We now know that many Las Sepulturas sites (and probably
others in the urban core) are undetected or incorrectly classified because they
have been wholly or partly buried. Appropriate alterations are accordingly made
to our simulation of population in Chapter 11.

Evidence from Prehistoric Flora and Fauna

Ancient flora and fauna remains recovered from Copán excavations provide another window into the general similarity or dissimilarity of the ancient environment compared to that of today.

FLORA   David Lentz examined tiny fragments of charcoal from soil samples at Site 11D-11-2 (discussed in Chapter 7) and determined that they came from hardwood and pine species such as found in the area today. He also (Lentz, 1991) identified a wide range of wild and domestic plants that we review in Chapter 9.

FAUNA   Similarly, remains of many animal species have been recovered from archaeological contexts (Feldman, 1994; Gerry, 1993; Pohl, 1994). Some of these represent species exotic to the valley, such as marine mollusks or fish, but local fauna are well represented. These include herbivores such as white-tailed deer, coati, tapirs, peccary, and paca; predators such as jaguars, pumas, and ocelots; and a wide variety of small snails and riverine mollusks. Although some of these animals are now rare, they were much more common only a few decades ago and well remembered by our older Honduran workers.

Many species of plants and animals are very sensitive to both large scale and local environmental changes. Our identified samples mainly come from post-A.D. 600 contexts and indicate that the broad parameters of temperature, precipitation, seasonality, and vegetation were not very different when the Copán polity was at its height than they have been as recently as the 1950s. Of course, such samples tell us little about the actual abundance or distribution of these species. For example, deer may have been virtually absent from the main valley pockets in Late Classic times and obtained only at considerable distances from the sites where their remains were eventually deposited. Future fine-grained analyses of particular species and the implications of their distributions would contribute greatly to our understanding of detailed microenvironmental changes in the Copán Valley.

SUMMARY

Much more paleoenvironmental work is needed at Copán before we fully understand ancient processes and patterns of change, but for now the following conclusions seem warranted:

1. There is no convincing evidence that over the last 3 to 4 millennia the region has been affected by pronounced regional or worldwide climatic shifts of the kind postulated elsewhere in the Maya Lowlands. Specifically, there are no signs of unusual drought at or around the time of the dynastic collapse.
2. Human activity began to alter Copán's environment much earlier than we thought— well before 2000 B.C.
3. Forest clearance for agriculture, as well as for other purposes, stimulated massive sheet erosion in the Copán pocket at least by A.D. 750–800, if not earlier.
4. Blanketing of alluvial soils by comparatively infertile upland soils probably reduced the productivity of much of the valley floor, adversely affected some settlement zones in the urban core, and even altered the river system and its course.
5. Increasingly dense settlement and land use created a more impoverished environment for wild terrestrial species of animals and plants, rendering them less useful to humans.

6. Seasonal tributary streams carried more runoff and became more deeply entrenched as deforestation and erosion intensified.

What we reasonably infer from many lines of evidence about changes in the Copán regional environment is a rather grim picture of long-term, human-induced degradation of a fragile tropical environment. Later we will discuss the implications of these changes in connection with Copán's demographic and agricultural history and the decline of the polity.

CHAPTER 9

Bioanthropology at Copán:

Paleopathology, Paleodemography,

and Diet

INTRODUCTION

For more than a century Mayanists have routinely encountered human burials in their excavations, even when not deliberately searching for them. Burials turn up so frequently because the ancient Maya rarely used cemeteries that were spatially segregated from their households or other community features, the places where archaeologists habitually dig. Sometimes early burial collections were quite large, internally varied, and were well documented in published reports, such as the sample recovered from the excavations of Group A-V in the 1930s at Uaxactun, Guatemala (Smith, 1950). Until quite recently, however, analyses tended to emphasize cultural attributes such as the type of burial structure, the arrangement of the body, mortuary offerings, and purposeful alterations to the skeleton (cranial deformation and dental mutilation).

Attempts were sometimes made to record and analyze basic biological attributes such as stature, age, and sex, but often such work was unsystematic and carried out by researchers who were not trained as human anatomists or bioarchaeologists. For example, John Longyear (1952) believed he could detect a reduction in stature over time in male skeletons from Copán. Such provisional efforts were often hampered by poor preservation of much skeletal material due to the high humidity and temperature of tropical environments. However well or inaccurately burials were studied, it is fair to say that many Mayanists have been intensely interested in them, because they assumed that the collapse of Classic Maya civilization had a strong biological component—catastrophic demographic loss.

Over the last 30 years there has been a revolution in the study of the biological dimensions of Maya burials (for a summary, see Whittington and Reed, eds., 1997). Archaeologists have made systematic recovery of large, representative samples of Maya burials an essential component of research design. Just as important, sophisticated osteological, biochemical, and statistical analytical methods, often borrowed from the biological and physical sciences, can now tell us much more than ever before about skeletal materials.

Of central concern today are issues of ancient population structure and change (paleodemography), health and trauma (paleopathology), and nutrition and diet, all of which involve complex interactions between biological and cultural factors.

Information bearing on all these issues can be derived from the strictly organic remains of humans, such as bones, teeth, and (rarely) other tissues. In this chapter we emphasize the osteological dimensions of burial analysis, along with other kinds of nonhuman biological evidence essential for the reconstruction of diet.

Before turning to the evidence from Copán, however, a cautionary note is necessary. Even as methods for analyzing human organic remains have become more refined and sophisticated, so too has our theoretical understanding of the implications and limitations of the resulting data. Ironically, even as the osteological remains from Copán were being studied, several of our bioanthropological colleagues at Penn State (Wood et al., 1992) demonstrated that what had formerly seemed like straightforward inferences turn out not to be so simple, often for very counterintuitive reasons. For example, in the age-at-death tables constructed from burial populations, the number of people that died at each age is not only a function of the death rate for that age, but also the fertility rate of the population into which they were born. Similarly, skeletons with conspicuous indications of morbidity (ill health or disease) may represent individuals who were more robust in life than those who left behind no such indications. Dead people, in other words, represent a biased sample of the living populations to which they belonged and do not unambiguously inform us about those who survived. And, of course, long before Wood et al. published their critique, bioanthropologists had recognized the difficulty of obtaining representative samples of actual populations—people of all ages and sexes who lived in a locale and mated with each other over a short period of time.

The Copán Burial Sample

No one knows exactly how many burials have been recovered at Copán by archaeologists over the last century or so. Rebecca Storey, who has catalogued and analyzed many of the human remains, estimated in 1992 that the total was probably around 600, but additional ones have since been found. No matter what the exact number, the Copán burial sample is one of the largest in Mesoamerica. It includes remains of royal men and women from the elaborate tombs of the Acropolis (Fash, 1991; G. Stuart, 1997), those of lesser nobles, and hundreds of burials of more common people. Recovery of a large, controlled burial sample was an important objective of the PAC II research design, and the vast majority of all Copán burials derive from the household excavations of this project. Remains of 264 individuals were recovered from Group 9N-8 alone.

Despite the impressive size of the sample and our attempts to be systematic in acquiring it, it is not as representative as we would like. Comparatively few of the burials—probably less than one quarter of the total—date before A.D. 600. Almost all are from sites that have predominantly Coner phase occupation, with a few from Acbi contexts as well. Because the Coner phase spans centuries, we know that all Coner burials do not represent a population in the strict sense of the word, and it is difficult to isolate any large subset of demonstrably contemporary individuals. Most burials are from a few sites in the urban core, (for example, Plate 9-1) and we definitely need more from outlying, small rural sites (although as we saw in Chapter 7 systematic search for burials at many rural sites was unsuccessful). Finally, as almost always is the case, infants are underrepresented.

PALEODEMOGRAPHY AND PALEOPATHOLOGY

Two major preliminary studies have been carried out by Rebecca Storey (1992, 1997) and Stephen Whittington (1989) on large burial samples from the PAC II and related projects. We say preliminary because the laboratory and other analytical work necessary to deal with all the burials will take many more years, especially because of the fragmentary state of most of the skeletal remains. Despite all of the difficulties already noted and the early stage of analysis, we can nonetheless reasonably infer several things from Copán burials that are not

PLATE 9-1   A SAMPLE COPÁN BURIAL FROM URBAN CORE GROUP 8N-11.

only interesting in their own right, but have implications for our simulations of population and agricultural history.

The Children of Group 9N-8

Rebecca Storey decided to begin her study of Copán burials by looking at subadults (i.e., >15 years) from the elite Group 9N-8. Not only was there a very large sample of systematically excavated skeletons from this site, but 122 of these, or about 46% of the total, were subadults (although infants are probably underrepresented). Bones of young people are more delicate than those of adults, and the high proportion of such people in the 9N-8 burial collection reflects in part the attention given to careful retrieval of human remains. The numbers and health status of people who died young have important implications for the larger population of which they were a part. Storey also reasoned that people living at 9N-8, whether of exalted or inferior status, stood better chances of having good nutrition and being buffered from more stresses than people living in groups of lesser rank. In other words, the health status of people in her sample probably provides a best-case scenario because of their increased chances of physiological well-being. Finally, many of these burials unquestionably dated either to the time of the peak Copán polity population beginning in the late 8th century, or the subsequent period of postdynastic demographic decline.

When Storey constructed age-at-death tables for her subadults, she found that 85% of the individuals in her sample died before the age of 5, and that greater than expected numbers of deaths occurred between the ages of 5 and 9 (Storey, 1992, p. 165). While she cautions that it is impossible to tell from these patterns whether the population from which the burials were derived was growing or declining, she does conclude that the subadults are from a high mortality population.

She next searched for pathological conditions preserved on teeth that might indicate what kinds of health problems or stresses affected these subadults. Out of the 83 individuals for whom teeth had been recovered, 76% had hypoplasias, hypocalcifications, or a combination of both. These are defects of enamel that are permanently recorded in a tooth and can be observed macroscopically. Specific ages of occurrence of some defects can be determined, and it is known that they are produced by physiological stresses such as malnutrition or infection. Her sample showed that a high proportion of young Copán individuals had clearly been subjected to such stresses early in life severe enough to have affected the normal development of their deciduous teeth. In fact, some defects had formed *in utero* and during the first year after birth, periods when fetuses or infants are normally buffered from many stresses by the bodies of their mothers and through nursing. Mothers, in other words, seem themselves to have often been sick or in poor condition.

Of course, defects would not show up had the children not survived the episodes of stress, but since these children did die at early ages, a strong inference is that multiple stresses during childhood increased their chances of early death. Storey provides one example of how this might have happened. Many of the children had active caries (cavities) associated with their enamel defects, and these can be pathways to serious infections.

Bones, of course, do not record all instances or kinds of ill-health or bad condition suffered by living individuals, so Storey's Copán young people might have been even more often stressed than evident from their teeth. Because many kinds of stresses can cause the same defects, we cannot pin down exactly what was wrong with these young people—only that they and their mothers were not in good shape. Storey (1997, p. 126) concludes that "The multiple stress episodes suffered by most of the individuals in this population, in spite of their supposed privileged living conditions, indicate that the environment of these children was not buffering them very well, although perhaps it was possible for them to survive more episodes of morbidity than children in nonnoble households." Fortunately, we have a parallel analysis of a large sample of burials from less elite contexts to compare with Storey's.

Health Hazards of the Humble Maya

Stephen Whittington (1989, 1991, 1992; Whittington and Reed, 1997) studied the remains of 148 low status individuals of all ages and sexes. These remains were recovered between 1975 and 1985 by Harvard, PAC I, and PAC II archaeologists during excavations of 22 Copán household groups, plus a handful of salvage efforts. Low status means that all these individuals were associated with, and presumably residents of, sites ranked Type 2 or lower in the settlement hierarchy. About 73% of all burials came from sites in the urban core, and the remainder from more distant peripheral sites, most in the Copán pocket. About 88% of all burials studied dated either from the Coner phase, or from the Acbi/Coner transition.

Whittington (1989, pp. 140–143) used a variety of methods to estimate rough ages-at-death for his sample population. About 54 individuals died before the age of 15 years, and the vast majority of these (n = 43) at or before the age of 5 years. Approximately 32 individuals died in the 16 to 35 year age range, 25 people died at ages of 36 to 50 years of age, and only eight survived more than 50 years. Thirty-six other skeletons could only be classified as "adults." Sex was estimated for 88 individuals, who were roughly split between males (n = 42) and females (n = 46).

In addition to making these paleodemographic estimates, Whittington scrutinized these skeletons for paleopathological markers. Like Storey, he examined teeth for hypoplasias, caries, and tooth loss, but also recorded two kinds of lesions found on skulls and other bones. The first, porotic hyperostosis, is highly associated with anemia. Pre-Columbian New World populations were especially susceptible to iron-deficiency anemias caused by restricted diets. The second kind of lesions, called periosteal reactions, are marks on the bone due to inflammations caused by trauma, infections, and some diseases such as syphilis.

While searching for these specific bone conditions, Whittington also recorded rare types of lesions and any obvious examples of trauma due to injuries. He then applied statistics to determine whether the health hazards he detected were evenly distributed among various subgroups of his burial collection, including people of different sexes and residents of different kinds of residential sites in different parts of the valley.

Whittington, prior to the publication of Wood, et al. (1992), summarized his general conclusions as follows:

1. Individuals in this sample had diets high in carbohydrates.
2. There was a general lack of prenatal stress, but infants and young children experienced extreme stresses.
3. Infants were weaned late—at about 3.5 to 4.5 years of age.
4. There were high frequencies of infection throughout life.
5. Iron deficiency anemia was probably common, and if so would have affected the reproductive capacity of women.
6. Diseases such as tuberculosis and pellagra were probably present.
7. The few signs of trauma seen on some individuals are consistent with low levels of violence or accident, and there are no patterned, war related injuries (Storey came to this same preliminary conclusion on the basis of the approximately 450 Copán burials she has catalogued).

With regard to differences among subgroups, Whittington concluded that there were very few hazard differences associated with sex, rank of residence (i.e., whether Type 1 or 2), or location. The frequency of infection in the urban core subgroup was slightly higher than in the rural areas, possibly because of overcrowding and poorer sanitation. Fertility of the rural population was marginally lower than that of the urban core, and rural childhood stress was greater, but neither in statistically significant amounts. Finally, the earliest burials in the sample suggested that the Acbi population was generally healthier, with lower childhood stress, earlier weaning, and fewer adult infections.

Whittington's conclusions closely resemble Storey's, apart from the different interpretations concerning prenatal stress. Both Storey and Whittington acknowledge the difficulty of interpreting osteological data and generalizing from skeleton samples to the original populations. Both also make the point that such generalizations are most secure when reinforced by evidence from the larger archaeological context. Most of the burials in each sample belonged to populations that we know from other lines of evidence lived during times of high-population density and environmental degradation, or population decline. While we cannot conclude with certainty that most people at Copán suffered from the reduced well-being and frequent stresses evident in the burials, it is very likely that they did. Strong, independent supporting evidence for this conclusion, in fact, comes from recent reconstructions of diet.

RECONSTRUCTING DIET

Determining what ancient people ate provides more than a basic insight into their day-to-day lives. As we just saw, diet has implications for the health and fertility of a population. It can also reflect social status, because in some societies people of rank, wealth, and privilege enjoyed better diets than commoners. Just as important, it can help us understand what ancient environments were like and is essential in assessing carrying capacity and for simulation modeling of agricultural and demographic processes.

Unfortunately, reconstructing diet is not easy. The most direct evidence—organic remains of plant and animal foods—is often not preserved. When such remains are recovered, they may not be representative of what was actually eaten, or in what proportions. For example, bones of large mammals are more obtrusive and more easily recovered than fish bones. When traces of both are found, how does one calculate how much each contributed to the diet?

Faunal Contributions to the Diet

Like all Mesoamerican people, ancient Copañecos had very few species of domestic animals at their disposal. The two primary ones were the dog and the turkey, but the latter is not prolific in the region and is very rarely seen in rural house lots today. Wild animal foods were available, of course, but even pristine tropical forest environments generally support only a low biomass of suitable, large animal species. The list of animals found in archaeological contexts at Copán given in Chapter 8 mainly derives from identifications made by Mary Pohl (1994), who examined the vertebrate fauna from the residential urban core sites excavated by the Harvard project. So far this is the only such analysis carried out at Copán by a trained zooarchaeologist.

Pohl's sample was small, only 750 vertebrate bones representing a minimum of 55 individual animals, all from post-A.D. 600 contexts. She remarks on the low individual count and the low species diversity revealed by her sample, and attributes both to human reduction and disturbance of natural habitats. Aquatic vertebrates, such as turtles (commonly found at other Lowland Maya sites) and fish are not represented.

Some of the identified local species, such as owls and ocelots, were probably used for strictly ritual purposes or for feathers, pelts, and other special products. Virtually all food would have come from just two species, the white-tailed deer and the dog, whose remains dominate Pohl's collections. Deer contributed most significantly to the diet, and deer bones and antlers were found in all excavated groups. Although everyone probably had access to both deer and dogs at Copán, the distribution of the remains shows that "The more elite the group, the higher the number of bones of large animal species" (Pohl, 1994, p. 459). She cites ethnohistoric evidence from the 16th and 17th centuries that Lowland Maya consumption of meat was graded by social rank, and suggests the same pattern for Classic Copán. Ethnographic accounts also show that today's Maya sometimes raise tame deer, another possibility at Copán.

Pohl's study, of course, is heavily weighted toward the most urban parts of the settlement system and the most densely occupied zones of the Copán Valley. Nevertheless, those of us who have worked extensively at smaller and more peripheral sites suspect that their meager faunal collections would yield much the same picture. Nonvertebrates, such as the land snails, or *jutes,* commonly encountered in excavations, probably contributed more to ancient diets than we know (Feldman, 1994), as did fish. Although today the Río Copán does not support abundant fish, fishing and crabbing are favorite activities of contemporary children, and small but predictable catches are routinely made. Pohl does not address the overall importance of animal food to the ancient diet, but obviously it was generally low and predominantly from terrestrial sources.

Plant Remains and Diet

Because of the comparative paucity of wild and domestic animal foods it is extremely important to document the range of available plants that must have collectively contributed very heavily to the ancient diet. Long ago Wilson Popenoe (1919) published a list of plants he saw people use in the valley. These included about 32 domestic, cultivated, or wild edible species that probably would have been available in pre-Columbian times. He also noted 10 other plants that were used for medicine, as dyes, or for other nondietary purposes. Of these, he singled out maize as the most important, asserting that "Maize was undoubtedly the great staple crop of the ancient Maya, as it is today among their descendants" (Popenoe, 1919, p. 128).

More recently, David Lentz (1991) examined 208 archaeobotanical samples from excavated Copán contexts, including the Main Group as well as residential sites in the urban core, the rural Copán pocket, and the eight small peripheral sites summarized in Chapter 7. Some of the samples were macrofossils (i.e., large fragments of plants) while others were tiny fragments recovered from flotation samples.

Lentz identified a wide range of plants (approximately 42 species in all). The most important dietary species included maize, beans, squash, *chayote,* and bottle gourd. These, of course, were full domesticates that originated elsewhere in Mesoamerica and were introduced into the valley. Among food-yielding tree species were two kinds of palms, avocado, nance, and possibly *zapote.* Some of these were essentially wild plants that were cultivated by the Maya, in the sense that they were protected and their growth encouraged because they provided food or other resources. Some such wild plants, such as the *coyol* palm, colonize disturbed ground and probably provided important emergency rations in hard times. Fruits from other minor wild species such as grape, hackberry, and *frijolillo* added variety to the diet. Charcoal fragments from upland pine and oak, and also from deciduous tropical forest trees show that these species were used for fuel or other purposes. Several kinds of minor weeds might have been inadvertently introduced into sites. Lentz's statistical analysis of the distribution of the plant remains led him to conclude that elite-rank sites had significantly richer sets of plant remains than commoner sites. He also listed a number of plants he expected to find but that were missing, including tobacco, cotton, peppers, cacao, and the root crops manioc and sweet potato. Many other plants listed by Popenoe were also missing.

Lentz's list is quite extensive and is consistent with what we know about the Maya from ethnographic studies. Modern Maya consume a wide range of plant foods if they are available and pursue several food-getting strategies.

Extrapolating back into the past, the Copán Maya probably cultivated houselot gardens where orchard crops as well as some vegetables and annuals were grown. Staple annual crops were planted in more distant outfields, and economically important trees may have been encouraged along their edges. Food was systematically obtained from fields that were lying fallow, and the Maya also opportunistically exploited wild plants.

Lentz also studied remains from Ceren, where the extraordinary preservation enabled him to identify a larger, but overlapping, array of 19 plant species there, most of which were eaten (Webster et al., 1997, p. 58). That recent and ancient Maya consumed many plant species does not tell us, however, what we really want to know about Copán. Which plant foods functioned as staples, in the sense that they contributed heavily to the diet in caloric terms? Did the Maya eat nutritionally balanced diets composed of several plant staples, along with many lesser items, or did they focus heavily on just one or two foods, as Popenoe assumed? Could some plants such as manioc and sweet potato have been important staples, but not preserved? Were the diets of the privileged really much different than those of ordinary people?

Applying good common sense and knowledge of Maya ethnography, Lentz himself concluded that maize was by far the most important staple, followed closely by beans. He speculated that root crops could have been staples as well. Fortunately, new lines of independent research provide much more detailed information from Copán on the issues listed above and some surprising quantitative insights about the range of diets.

Bone Chemistry and Diet

During the past decade a series of new biochemical assay methods has been applied to the bones of humans and animals from Mesoamerican archaeological contexts. Foods consumed are cycled through the body, and some of them leave more or less permanent chemical traces in bones and teeth. Some bone structures such as collagen, the principal organic component of bone, are very durable even long after the death of the organisms that produced them. Study of light stable isotope chemistry of ancient bones or teeth, most particularly the stable isotopes of carbon and nitrogen, can yield information not only on the general character of the diet, but in some cases allows reasonable estimates about the contributions of particular plant and animal foods.

Patterns of stable isotopic variation preserved in bones and teeth are partly the products of fractionation that occurs in biochemical or physiological systems during photosynthesis, or during the intake of different element sources. For example, organisms that cycle nitrogen derived from seawater show distinctive concentrations of stable nitrogen isotopes compared to those that intake fresh water. Diets heavy in marine as opposed to terrestrial biota may thus be distinguished. More important, plants with so-called C_3 photosynthetic pathways have stable isotope signatures of carbon different from those with C_4 pathways.

Many of the potential plant foods of Mesoamerica, including beans, squash, manioc, sweet potato, ramon, and cacao, follow the C_3 pathway. Maize, by contrast, is one of the very few C_4 plants likely to have been eaten in bulk, so the contribution of maize to the diet is reflected in the values of C_4-linked carbon isotopes.

Both Gerry (1993) and Reed (1997, 1998) have performed biochemical assays on human and animal skeletal material from Copán. Gerry focused on a sample of 41 human skeletons and deer bones derived from pre-PAC II excavations. Reed analyzed a much larger sample of human remains from 90 individual skeletons unearthed by the PAC II and later projects, along with bones from seven deer and one jaguar. We focus here on Reed's study because it is the most recent and comprehensive and largely confirms Gerry's earlier results. In fact, it is currently the most ambitious such biochemical study yet carried out in Mesoamerica.

The 90 human burials studied by Reed come from 16 sites, ranging from large urban core residences to the smallest excavated rural sites reported in Chapter 7. His sample was not only stratified by site type, but also according to site locale, grave type, age, and sex. Apart from a few that date to the Acbi phase or the Acbi/Coner transition, the burials are all solidly Coner phase and thus postdate A.D. 600–650. Some, from rural site 99A-18-2, plausibly fall as late as the 12th century or even later.

After statistical evaluation of the isotopic patterns he measured, Reed concluded that:

1. Humans showed heavy intake of C_4 plants. Maize is the only locally available plant using this pathway that could contribute so heavily to the diet.
2. Deer had diets predominantly of C_3 plants.
3. Maize contributed about 62 to 78% of all total calories consumed by the individuals in his sample.
4. Social status, if correctly reflected by site rank, had remarkably little effect on diet, as did site locale.
5. Deer and other meat sources were only occasionally eaten by people of all statuses.
6. Male adults show no differences in diet no matter what grave type they were found in.
7. There is a small but significant statistical difference in diet between males from Type 4 sites as opposed to those from lower-rank sites. Counterintuitively, the former seem to eat slightly more maize (this might be a sampling problem).
8. Two subadults showed divergent dietary signatures from adults, probably because of the isotopic composition of their mothers' milk.
9. There were statistically significant differences between the diets of adult males and females, with males apparently consuming a larger percentage of maize.

Not unexpectedly, given its landlocked valley, Copán's population had an overwhelmingly terrestrial diet that was particularly heavy in maize (Figure 9-1). More significant is the extent to which people of all social ranks depended upon maize as a staple. Despite the range of potential plant foods identified from archaeological contexts, maize was either the culturally preferred food or the only one that could be relied upon consistently. We will see in Chapter 11 that this assumption was essential to John Wingard's simulation of Copán's agricultural history, and that his estimate of dietary intake from maize is empirically supported by Reed's later findings. Although reliance on beans cannot be directly calculated, they were almost certainly second only to maize calorically as a food resource. Apparently we can rule out important contributions from other potential staples such as the C₃ root crops manioc and sweet potatoes, which might not have been present. All Copañecos, at least in Coner times, seem to have had remarkably restricted diets.

Compared with all other ancient Mesoamerican populations whose stable isotopes have been studied, Copán's exhibits the most terrestrial, maize-heavy dietary signature. This conclusion supports Whittington's earlier suggestion of a diet dominated by carbohydrates, and both Whittington's and Storey's evidence of nutritionally stressed populations. It also vastly simplifies the simulation of agricultural history and productivity we shall review later.

Also surprising is how standardized the diet was. Disagreeing with Lentz's statistical evaluation of the distribution of plant remains at Copán, Reed feels that there is no significant variation among collections from residences of different ranks. If people of privilege ate more deer, dogs, or a wider array of plant foods than ordinary people, such differences appear more negligible in both nutritional and caloric terms than suggested by Pohl or Lentz. This conclusion about diet does not imply that elites had no dietary advantages. Consumption of even small amounts of prestige foods in ritual contexts might have been socially and politically important. More significant in biological terms is that elite people probably had more assured access to food because they were likely more

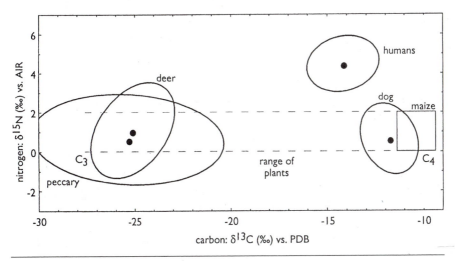

FIGURE 9-1   DIET RANGES (CENTERS AND 95% CONFIDENCE INTERVALS) RECONSTRUCTED FROM STABLE CARBON AND NITROGEN ISOTOPE ANALYSIS OF BONE COLLAGEN FOR HUMANS AND ANIMALS DURING THE LATE CLASSIC PERIOD AT COPÁN, HONDURAS, ARE SHOWN RELATIVE TO THE ISOTOPIC COMPOSITION OF PLANTS. DEER AND PECCARIES ATE SIMILAR, PROBABLY PURELY C₃-BASED (NON-MAIZE) DIETS. DOGS ATE A C₄-BASED (MAIZE) DIET. THE ADULT HUMAN DIET WAS LARGELY MAIZE-BASED AND SHOWS SUPPLEMENTAL INPUT FROM MEAT, OTHERWISE THEY WOULD FALL INTO THE SAME DIETARY RANGE AS DOGS.

buffered against periodic shortfalls. Continuity of supply, in other words, was as important as quality of diet, especially in the 7th and 8th centuries when subsistence crises must have been most pronounced.

Perhaps the most counterintuitive finding of both Gerry and Reed, who collectively analyzed 43 deer bones, is that deer ate little or no maize, a pattern that has implications for the environmental reconstructions made in Chapter 8. Deer are edge browsers and might be expected to thrive when a large amount of the landscape is converted to cropland, so long as patches of forest and secondary growth are left for cover (Carr, 1996, p. 258). In regions where they have been well studied, deer populations are shown to be prolific and able to withstand high rates of culling. For these reasons, Mayanists frequently assume that deer must have been an abundant resource even in Classic times, when human population densities were high.

The data from Copán suggest another interpretation. Because deer ate little or no maize, they might have been effectively eradicated from those parts of the landscape where cultivation was virtually continuous and so lacked secondary growth cover. Some studies suggest, in fact, that if deer are eliminated from very large areas, they recolonize them very slowly even if no threats exists (Carr, 1996, p. 259). Quite possibly deer at Copán are an attractive barometer for the extent of deforestation, which relegated them to the distant boundaries of very extensive cultivated zones. The lack of C_4 pathway foods in the deer diet also makes it unlikely that the animals were tamed and raised around house lots, where presumably they would have been at least fed partly on maize. Another possibility is that deer caught at a distance were briefly kept and fed in house compounds, then used for periodic feasts rather than more regular consumption.

Genetic Analysis

Bioanthropologists are currently developing and refining methods of extracting mitochondrial and nuclear DNA from ancient bones and teeth, and analyzing such samples to assess genetic affinities among ancient and modern populations. Pioneering mitochondrial work of this kind includes the study of nine samples from Copán (Merriwether, Reed, and Ferrell, 1997). Those samples that could be adequately typed in genetic terms relate to two of the four major mitochondrial lineages (lineages C and D) so far identified for ancient New World populations, although greater sample size will probably reveal more variation. Interestingly, the Copán samples show patterns not shared with modern Yucatecan Maya, which might reflect the existence of distinctive populations within the Maya Lowlands.

SUMMARY

Converging lines of evidence from paleodemography, paleopathology, and dietary research all indicate that by the 8th century the inhabitants of the Copán Valley suffered from poor health and nutrition, and possibly from increased mortality and lowered reproductive capacity. To a degree that is surprising in such a hierarchically structured society, people of all social ranks and statuses seem to have broadly shared similar health hazards and diets. Reduction of habitats diminished the reservoir of both wild plant and animal dietary resources. Maize, almost certainly heavily supplemented by beans, was the principal staple, and both the well-being of human individuals and the landscape on which they lived were compromised by a heavy reliance on and production of a few staple crops. All of these factors have profound implications for the decline of the Copán system which we evaluate at the end of the book.

In the future we may expect even more detailed and informative insights from the bioanthropologists who work at Copán, who now include Jane Buikstra and her colleagues and students. We particularly need studies of sizable pre-Coner skeletal samples to contrast with the preliminary conclusions reviewed above, although such samples will be difficult to recover. An exciting prospect is that in the near future evaluation of the biological relationships among subsets of the Copán Valley population might be possible using DNA analysis.

CHAPTER 10
Chronology of Copán Settlement

INTRODUCTION

Nothing in archaeology is more critical or difficult than accurately dating ancient events and processes. Archaeological debates often focus on chronological interpretations because they are so fundamental to our conceptions of culture history and culture change. Despite their significance, chronological methods rarely receive much systematic attention in research design and typically appear in proposals only as minor budget lines of a few hundred dollars for radiocarbon dates. Sometimes, however, chronological issues suddenly and unexpectedly become central to research efforts. This happened to us at Copán.

When we began our settlement and household work in 1981 we gave little thought to how we would sort out things through time. After all, the Maya themselves had left monument dates that could be read in terms of our own calendar, and by 1981 epigraphers had produced a dynastic sequence whose broad outlines already prefigured the one presented in Chapter 2. Viel's first ceramic sequence was also available—its chronology anchored by the calendrical dates and independently checked with data from stratigraphic excavations in the Main Group and urban core and through comparisons with more well-documented sequences elsewhere. The Harvard and PAC I work had begun to reveal the rough chronology of changes in architectural and sculptural forms. We expected that all these lines of evidence, along with a few standard radiocarbon and archaeomagnetic dates, were all we needed.

After our initial seasons of rural survey and test pitting were finished in 1983, we realized that we faced a serious problem. Because almost all sites everywhere were dominated by Coner ceramic assemblages, the only label we could put on most occupations or contexts outside the urban core was "Coner phase," which *then* meant any time between A.D. 700 and 900. Archaeologists, unfortunately, must commonly deal with settlement units based on such lengthy time periods. At some Maya centers such as Tikal, where large populations existed for more than 1,000 years, even such coarse chronological subdivisions provide some sense of long-term demographic changes (Culbert et al., 1990). At Copán, by contrast, the Coner phase population apparently dwarfed that of all previous and subsequent time periods, so understanding its internal dynamics was an essential key to understanding the growth and decline of the Copán polity. The basic problem thus was to acquire a more fine-grained appreciation of how many people were on the landscape, and exactly where they were during the Coner phase. More specifically, could we find a way to refine occupations of particular sites to intervals of less than 200 years?

Excavations in the Las Sepulturas urban core yielded dated monuments, complex stratigraphy, and styles of elite art and architecture that all had such fine-grained chronological implications. At least there one could get a sense of the relative age of Coner contexts, and we had some radiocarbon and archaeomagnetic dates from urban residential excavations, as well as from previous work at the Main Group. The real difficulty was the hundreds of small, outlying sites that were integral to the reconstruction of population and demographic history, and where such clues were lacking. Even if test pitting had routinely produced samples appropriate for radiocarbon dating (which it did not), no project could afford the hundreds of dates necessary to even minimally partition these sites in time. Ceramic seriation might have produced some rough ordering, but sherd collections were often small and very heavily weathered. The prospects seemed discouraging.

The solution materialized in 1982 during one of the "hearts" card games that were so much a part of field life at Copán. Freter knew that obsidian hydration dating, a comparatively untested method, had been partly developed at Penn State University and that the necessary facilities to use it existed in our department. Her tentative proposal to apply obsidian hydration dating at Copán met with considerable skepticism from her fellow card players, who felt it to be a still insufficiently tested method with an unreliable track record. A handful of Copán obsidian samples had, in fact, been dated years earlier, but with mixed results (Meighan and Vanderhoeven, 1978, p. 199). Nevertheless, Freter determined to try it, with unforeseen consequences. Application of the hydration dating method turned out to be one of the most innovative and controversial research initiatives ever carried out at Copán. It has seriously revised our conceptions of Copán's culture history and the nature of the collapse. Nowhere else in the world, moreover, has the method been so rigorously tested on a regional level, so it is essential to understand how it works.

THE COPÁN OBSIDIAN HYDRATION DATING PROJECT

Obsidian is volcanic glass commonly found in igneous deposits in many parts of the world, including the upland regions of Mesoamerica. Because it fractures predictably and has very sharp edges, obsidian was favored as a raw material for cutting tools and was widely traded. Despite the absence of local sources, obsidian in the form of prismatic blades dominated the chipped-stone industry of ancient Copán. Rare is the excavation that fails to produce some obsidian, so apparently all Copañecos, from the humblest to the most exalted, had access to this basic cutting material. Even the small rural sites summarized in Chapter 7 produced hundreds or thousands of blade fragments.

How Obsidian Hydration Dating Works

The potential of the chemical process of obsidian hydration for archaeological dating was first recognized by Friedman and Smith (1960), who noted that a freshly exposed obsidian surface gradually develops a visible layer, or hydration rim, and that the width of this layer, when examined using a microscope, is related to the duration of its exposure (Plate 10-1). What is dated, therefore, is a specific event—the fracture that exposes the new obsidian surface. Subsequent attempts by archaeologists to use this process as a relative dating technique often produced inaccurate results because of a lack of awareness of the chemical processes affecting the hydration time function.

A much better understanding of how hydration occurs now exists. We know that the rate of rim formation depends on at least three variables: (1) the chemical composition of the obsidian, (2) the temperature at which the reaction takes place, and to a much lesser degree (3) the relative humidity and soil pH under which the chemical reaction occurs. If these factors are constant for a data set, obsidian ages can be used to establish relative chronologies among the artifacts and their contexts. If in addition a segment of the relative hydration sequence can be anchored by absolute dates of other kinds (e.g., radiocarbon, archaeomagnetic, Long Count dates, etc.), then the method can be used to determine ages tied into our own calendrical system (at least within the error ranges to which most dating techniques are prone).

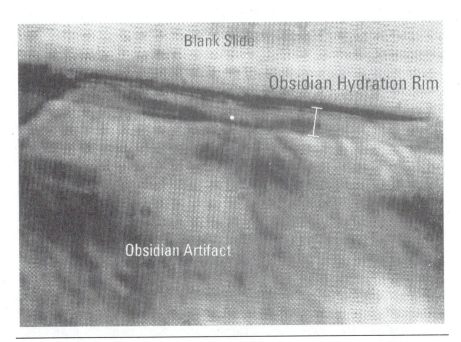

PLATE IO-I   PHOTOGRAPH OF HYDRATION RIM ON EDGE OF AN OBSIDIAN BLADE FRAGMENT.

Apart from the fact that we had the laboratory facilities and that obsidian was ubiquitous at Copán, obsidian hydration had several attractions. First, visual inspection showed that Copán obsidian was rather uniform, suggesting that most of it came from a single source. Second, obsidian hydration dating was cheap, costing only a few dollars per sample, so we could afford thousands of dates. Third, standard radiocarbon determinations from several projects at Copán had produced many anomalous dates for reasons not clearly understood, so we needed an alternative method. Fourth, there is no doubt that the dated events—the fractures—are of human manufacture (something not always clear with radiocarbon samples). Finally, we had enough detailed and reliable chronological information of other kinds to enable us to calibrate a relative sequence of obsidian ages with calendar dates.

One can test the usefulness of a comparatively new chronometric method in two different ways. Research can be designed specifically to assess the nature of the error factors inherent in the method, and these errors can then be experimentally defined and corrected. Alternatively, one can apply the method on a large scale under actual field conditions and examine its utility given other chronometric clues. We chose both of these approaches, and so far the results of the Copán chronology research have been very rewarding.

Developing a Hydration Protocol

Because hydration dating was a relatively untested method we had to create a research protocol that assessed the accuracy and validity of the hydration dates with as much cross-referencing to other chronometric methods as possible. We also had to generate arrays of dates from a large number of tested sites in such a way that they would plausibly capture their occupation spans.

The first step was to determine the location and number of obsidian sources exploited by the Copán Maya. Then the effective hydration temperature for the Copán Valley had to be estimated and corrections for local variations in temperature calculated. Finally, the effects of relative humidity and soil pH variations on the hydration rate time function had to be assessed. Here we discuss only the bare bones of our work; detailed discussions are provided by Freter (1988, 1992, 1997) and Webster, Freter, and Rue (1993).

SOURCING   As we already saw in Chapter 5, compositional analysis fortunately indicated that the obsidian used by the Copán Maya during the Late Classic period came primarily from the Ixtepeque deposits in eastern Guatemala, about 100 km to the south. Without such uniformity, we would have had to source individually each dated sample, undermining our ability to generate the large numbers of dates required for regional settlement analysis.

HYDRATION RATE FOR IXTEPEQUE OBSIDIAN   Next we had to estimate effective hydration temperatures for the Copán Valley. Such estimates were necessary to calculate experimentally specific rim formation rates for Ixtepeque obsidian in the laboratory (Michels, 1986). We could not simply extrapolate back from present climatic conditions in the now-cleared urban core, however. During the past, many sites where the hydration process occurred would have been situationally abandoned and covered with vegetation, and deforestation might have affected local climate. Moreover, we had no long-term weather data from the Copán region prior to the 1970s, when modern deforestation had become intensive. We found two weather station sites in Guatemala where long-term data had been recorded that we felt reasonably approximated ancient Copán conditions. These sites bracketed the Copán Valley in elevation and had multiple-year monthly readings prior to 1970. These measurements were converted into effective hydration temperatures and suitably adjusted to accommodate temperature variations caused by elevation differences.

The Guatemalan data were independently checked against what little early weather data existed for the Copán region, and by data from buried Ambrose thermal cells (small devices that measure annual temperature) at four locations. At best we could hope for reasonable approximations of ancient conditions and acceptable error ranges in our calculations, and cross-check preliminary results against independent chronometric data.

We decided that the effective hydration temperature curve derived from the Guatemalan weather data agreed well with single year measurements from the Copán Valley and was as accurate an estimate of the temperature during the hydration process as was possible given the available data. From it, and from the induced hydration experiments conducted on Ixtepeque obsidian by Joseph Michels (1982), we calculated a hydration rate curve for the Copán Valley, using 50 m elevation increments to correct for differences in altitude.

One potential source of error in hydration dating is variation in temperature caused by differences in the depth at which artifacts were buried. Because of the shallow depositional characteristics of most Copán Valley sites, the vast majority of obsidian samples were recovered from a relatively uniform depth between 40 to 80 cm. In only a very few cases did we date more deeply buried samples, and we excluded obsidian from stone tombs or from deep within large structures. Variations in soil temperature due to the depth of the deposit or insulation by fill did not appear to pose a significant problem anywhere, and certainly not for samples excavated from the all-important rural sites, where deposits were almost invariably shallow and depths comparable from one site to the next.

RELATIVE HUMIDITY AND SOIL pH   The induced hydration experiments used to estimate the hydration rate at Copán were conducted under conditions of 100% relative humidity (RH). Tropical forest ecosystems, as very wet climates, generally maintain 100% soil RH conditions; no correction was deemed necessary for our project. Likewise, while extremes (below 1 or above 12) in pH appear to affect rim formation in studies of glass nuclear waste storage containers, there is no evidence that soil pHs at archaelogical sites have significant impact. Webster et al, (1993) tested the relationship between soil pH and hydration dates at Copán, and found that the small variations in soil pH throughout the valley had no discernable impact on the hydration dates. Thus, a correction for this variable was also deemed unnecessary for Copán.

CHOOSING SAMPLES   Two fundamental sampling errors have hampered some previous hydration research results. Earlier settlement projects elsewhere had sometimes relied exclusively on surface obsidian samples, but because the behavioral contexts of surface artifacts are unclear, interpretations derived from them were limited and often confusing. Another problem is that hydration rims can be affected by exposure to high temperatures caused, for example, by the surface burning that is associated with swidden agriculture. The vast majority (95%) of the artifacts we dated were from known, excavated contexts. Surface samples were only dated for the Río Jila region, for which we lacked test-pitting collections. As it turns out, we did get good results even at sites where artifacts were recovered fairly close to the surface.

Of course we were not interested in the dates of the obsidian events themselves, but rather the dates of the contexts in which samples were found. In the best of all possible worlds a single obsidian artifact would always date its associated context. In a few cases it almost certainly does, such as *in situ* features on floors. Other kinds of associations are much more depositionally complex, such as midden deposits or construction fill beneath floors, where accumulations of mixed material from different time periods are expected.

Obsidian artifacts, unlike potsherds, provide no immediate visual clues even to their rough dates. A prismatic blade made in Preclassic times looks for all practical purposes just the same as one made centuries later. This means that one cannot know for sure whether a blade recovered from an obviously late midden dates even approximately to the time of midden formation. It might well have been redeposited from a much earlier context. This fact makes selection of samples difficult, but in another sense works to the advantage of the archaeologist. There is no way in which the selection of samples might involve conscious or unconscious biases stemming from the formal characteristics of the artifact itself. This means that if enough blades are dated from all contexts, even the "noise" of redeposited samples is informative. For example, if there were massive numbers of redeposited blades of Middle Classic date, a substantial number of them would inadvertently be chosen from Late Classic contexts. In fact, if one simply chose huge numbers of blades randomly from as many contexts as possible in a region such as Copán, the aggregate sample would probably reasonably reflect in a crude way the history and spatial dimensions of obsidian use.

Our own sampling procedures were, of course, more refined than this. Each archaeologist of the PAC II project was asked to list and characterize the deposits she or he had recorded. From each large-scale excavation and tested rural site we selected samples from structure fill, plaza floors, middens, burials, and other primary or controlled secondary deposits in an attempt to include the full range of depositional contexts in our sample of dates. We thus acquired obsidian samples from a wide variety of archaeological contexts, and most importantly from those we judged to be the most secure and informative. Samples consisted of fragments of prismatic blades, so that in each case the surface inspected was known to have been produced by human activity. When sufficient obsidian artifacts were available, we dated multiple blades (3–5) from each context as a control on intradeposit variation. To ensure that the same artifact was not dated

TABLE 10-1A
SITES DATED BY THE OBSIDIAN HYDRATION METHOD
(PERCENTAGE FIGURES INDICATE THE PROPORTION OF DATED
SITES OF A PARTICULAR TYPE IN THE REGION)

Region	NM	SM	Type 1	Type 2	Type 3	Type 4	Type 5*	Totals
Copán Pocket/								
Urban Core	0 (0%)	22 (8%)	49 (11%)	16 (14%)	9 (36%)	7 (43%)	1 (100%)	104 (11.7%)
Main Valley	3 (4%)	7 (6.5%)	44 (32%)	9 (69%)	1 (50%)	—	—	64 (19%)
Sesesmil Valley	5 (9%)	3 (6.5%)	20 (45%)	3 (7%)	1 (50%)	—	—	32 (21%)
Río Jila**	12 (50%)	15 (78%)	10 (52%)	4 (66%)	—	—	—	41 (60%)
Totals	20 (13%)	47 (10%)	123 (19%)	32 (24%)	11 (38%)	7 (41%)	1 (100%)	241

* The only Type 5 site, the Main Group, has very few associated dates.
** The Río Jila region is the least accurately dated, because most samples were from surface collections since no test excavations were carried out in this area. Only the intensively excavated Río Jila site 99A-18-2 yielded subsurface samples.

twice (i.e., two pieces of the same broken blade), only fragments with intact proximal ends were selected whenever possible.

Another consideration was the selection of sites. Our solution was to include all extensively excavated sites in the urban core and rural areas, as well as the test pit sample wherever obsidian was recovered, resulting in the final array of 241 dated sites shown in Tables 10-1a, b.

Most dates came from sites excavated by Penn State archaeologists, but we included 53 samples from the Harvard/PAC I research, and 42 samples from Wendy Ashmore's 1988 excavations of elite Copán pocket residences. All told, about one out of every seven known sites in the Copán Valley has associated hydration dates.

ESTABLISHING ERROR RANGES   In most chronometric methods (except highly precise ones such as tree-ring dating), significant error estimates are associated with the samples and procedures used. In the laboratory, Freter experimentally assessed the errors associated with slide preparation, microscope resolution, and variation among multiple samples from the same context. Multiple derived errors were combined, yielding a general one standard deviation range of ±70 years. Thus, a hydration age listed as A.D. 800 really means that there is a 67% chance

TABLE 10-1B
DISTRIBUTION OF DATED SITES BY RANK

Nonmound	Single mound	Type 1	Type 2	Type 3	Type 4
8 (6.7%)	34 (7.6%)	108 16.6%	27 18.8%	13 43.3%	8 44.6%

Note: Percentages indicate the proportion of dated sites compared to all those recorded for that site classification.

that the obsidian event fell anywhere between A.D. 730 and 870; and a 95% change that it fell between A.D. 560 and 940. In the following discussions we utilize the raw reading for convenience and clarity, but it must constantly be borne in mind that this is simply the mid-point of the error range.

COMPARISON WITH OTHER DATING METHODS   Freter calibrated the sequence of relative dates with other chronological benchmarks, allowing us to express it in absolute calendrical terms. She systematically assessed the reliability of the obsidian hydration dates by cross-checking them against ceramic associations, stratigraphic sequences, radiocarbon dates, and archaeomagnetic dates. This procedure helped determine if there was a significant error in estimating the effective hydration temperature or in the induced hydration experiments. The results of this cross-referencing suggest that our hydration rate curve is, on the whole, a reasonable estimate that fits well with other, more traditional dating techniques. Most convincing of all points of agreement is that the hydration curve nicely puts the Acbi/Coner transition at A.D. 600–650.

CHRONOLOGICAL RESULTS AND REVISIONS

Freter has produced a total of 2,264 obsidian hydration dates for the Copán region. Their general distribution by 50 year intervals is shown in Figure 10-1. As we were gradually amassing all these dates, two encouraging patterns became obvious. First, there was good agreement with independent measures of chronology, including radiocarbon and archaeomagnetic dates, ceramic assemblages, and stratigraphic sequences, for time periods before A.D. 900. In fact, even dated samples from deep deposits dating back to Early and Middle Preclassic times at Las Sepulturas agreed well with stratigraphic and ceramic expectations. Second, collections of dates from individual small sites usually indicated convincingly tight clusters consistent with reasonably short occupations (some examples are displayed in Chapter 7), and those from large sites with complex stratigraphy indicated much longer occupations. All these results suggested that potential error factors in the hydration method were not operating, were minimal, or canceled out one another.

Gratifying and reassuring as these results were, we also saw another very surprising and initially disturbing pattern that is obvious in Figure 10-1. Almost half the dates in our general array fell after A.D. 850–900, the purported end of the Coner phase as envisioned at that time, and some were as late as the 12th and early 13th centuries. Moreover, post-A.D. 900 dates occurred at sites of all ranks and in all parts of the valley, and even the latest dated contexts were associated with Coner ceramic assemblages lacking admixtures of Ejar phase sherds. This distribution was extremely puzzling because we, like all other Copán archaeologists, had long operated on the then conventional wisdom of an abrupt political/demographic collapse in the 9th century.

One possibility was that hydration dating was simply not working well at Copán because there remained many uncontrolled errors in the method. But if

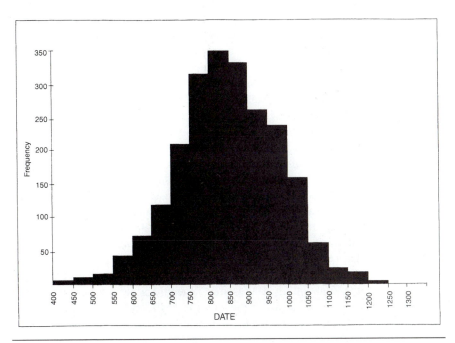

FIGURE 10-1   HISTOGRAM SHOWING 2264 HYDRATION DATES BROKEN DOWN BY 50 YEAR TIME PERIOD.

this was so, why did we find so much convincing agreement with pre-A.D. 900 contexts and other chronometric dates? Why did we get such reassuring clusters of dates from small sites? We concluded that we had not simply incorrectly specified the regional temperature curve, and thus systematically dated all sites too late. If we held the internal relative relationships shown in Figure 10-1 constant and just shifted the whole array backward in time by three centuries to make the late dates fit our expectations of the collapse, the distribution would be at odds with everything else we knew about Copán's culture history from all other sources. The Coner phase, for example, would begin several centuries too early.

Alternatively, the pre-A.D. 900 dates might be working well, but some kind of systematic bias might be affecting the contexts of the apparently late dates, making them appear much too young. This explanation seemed very labored, however, and we could not envision what such a bias might be. The most obvious possibility was that samples from high elevation sites hydrated unusually slowly because of cooler temperatures, and that our temperature adjustments for altitude were wrong. We could easily reject this cause, however, because the estimated ages of sites did not systematically pattern out against elevation. In fact, the opposite was true—sites from the lowest elevations often had some of the latest dates, no doubt because the valley floor was always the most stable, secure, and productive part of the environment. Individual late dates and whole late site arrays came from both high and low elevations, and late dates were stratigraphically consistent with early ones in excavated deposits.

Freter was faced with a startling conclusion. The dates were in fact telling us something new and unexpected. We had been misled about Copán's Late Classic settlement history, the collapse process of the polity, and the timing of the all-important Coner ceramic phase. Corroborating ecological evidence soon materialized in the form of Rue's sediment sequence reviewed in Chapter 8, which showed that much of the Copán Valley was still being cleared of tree species by farmers at least as late as A.D. 1250. An archaeomagnetic date of A.D. 1100 obtained by Daniel Wolfman from Las Sepulturas was no longer an anamoly. Taking this and other much more recent independent evidence into consideration, we now are certain that the chronological implications shown in Figure 10-1 are essentially correct (although any particular hydration date or set of dates might, of course, be contextually wrong and is subject to standard errors).

Even before we began to consider the specific demographic implications of Freter's dates, several things were clear. Not only were many sites occupied after A.D. 850–900, but a significant number of rural sites were actually founded after that time. We also found abundant evidence that occupation continued at some elite rank sites in the urban core for generations after the collapse of the royal dynasty. Until at least about A.D. 1000 some of the inhabitants of these residences still seemed to be carrying on a conspicuously elite lifestyle.

In retrospect these findings should not have surprised us. We had long known that some Maya centers and regions elsewhere, such as Lamanai in Belize, were not abruptly abandoned at the end of the Classic period, thus the so-called "collapse" was not a uniform or predictable process. More to the point, exactly when the Coner ceramic phase ended had always been problematical. Its terminus lay beyond the range of monument dates, Coner materials were in uppermost stratigraphic position, and few Coner sites or materials had been subjected to chronometric evaluations, especially outside the Main Group or urban core. Moreover, the Coner ceramic complex is so different from that at other major Lowland Maya centers that cross-dating gave only rough insights into its duration. Because no royal monuments were erected after the first part of the 9th century, and there were no signs of a widespread, distinctive, "Postclassic" ceramic assemblage that replaced Coner, it was simply assumed that A.D. 850–900 was a good terminus for the effective abandonment of the valley, leaving only a few stragglers or visitors who used imported Ejar vessels for ritual purposes, with no associated domestic assemblage.

Viewing the general date array as a kind of crude proxy for population dynamics, our own original alternative reconstruction of the collapse was far more complicated and protracted. Although the royal dynasty disappeared abruptly near the beginning of the 9th century as previously known, some nobles continued to occupy their residences and maintain some aspects of the elite tradition for about another 200 years. In fact, we found evidence that one impressive Type 3 center in the Río Amarillo region was heavily occupied after A.D. 1000. This site produced Ejar phase sherds. Copán's population peaked at about A.D. 800–900, then began a long decline to about A.D. 1200–1300. In short, there was no precipitous demographic collapse.

As noted at the beginning of this chapter, archaeologists cherish their established chronological schemes, so our findings predictably provoked much controversy, debate, and scrutiny. Some Mayanists (most specifically, Braswell, 1992) were unwilling to accept a gradual demographic decline at Copán instead of a rapid collapse, or the protracted use of Coner phase ceramic types. They objected that obsidian hydration was such a poorly understood dating method and subject to so many potential errors, that it was essentially useless, and that Freter should never have employed it. According to their views, our late dates were wrong, while all the cross-checked dates only coincidentally agreed with other chronological evidence. They maintained that the original collapse scenario was essentially correct and that there were no late inhabitants of the region who used Coner or Coner-like types and assemblages. Coner ceramic forms could not have been used for 400 to 500 years in the region. In short, they maintained that obsidian hydration dating not only provided no useful insights concerning Copán's culture history, but actually distorted and obfuscated chronological relationships.

While many of these objections could be easily dismissed (Webster, Freter, and Rue, 1993), we nevertheless continued to stringently and comprehensively test the hydration results against all more established chronometric methods available. We designed and carried out a particularly important test in 1995–1997.

TESTING THE HYDRATION RESULTS: A CONCORDANCE EXPERIMENT

Radiocarbon dating is the most widely used and trusted chronometric method employed by archaeologists. At Copán, as already noted, applications of the standard radiocarbon method had yielded mixed results (in retrospect, probably because of poor sample selection); this was one reason we turned to obsidian hydration in the first place. By 1995 the accelerator mass spectrometer (AMS) refinement of radiocarbon dating was well developed and had already resolved some important chronological issues in Maya archaeology (Andrews and Hammond, 1990). We accordingly developed a concordance experiment that tested this new, highly accurate method against our hydration dates.

Design of the Experiment

The experiment was logically very simple, focusing on the most crucial arrays of dates—those derived from small individual sites outside the urban core. It was these clusters of dates, typically a century or two long, that we believed captured all or much of each site's occupation span and that were essential in subdividing the Coner phase and calculating population through time (see Chapter 11). Small sites were preferable because they were inhabited for comparatively short periods, and they were less vulnerable than large sites to the introduction of extraneous obsidian (i.e., from other contexts not related to the main occupation). Our basic assumption was that obsidian fragments at small sites were very likely to be from the appropriate systemic contexts—i.e., used and discarded by site occupants.

The most secure source of radiocarbon samples to test against the obsidian spans is burials. A second basic assumption of our experiment is that burials recovered from each site represent deaths that occurred while the site was occupied. Our prediction, therefore, was that the radiocarbon date of each burial recovered from a small site should overlap with some part of the associated hydration array, taking into account the standard error ranges of each method. Essentially we tested one or more death events at each site against a cluster of obsidian events defining an occupation span.

Eleven sites containing burials were selected from all parts of the valley and from elevations ranging from 550 to 900 m asl thus controlling for possible local environmental biases. Their estimated occupation spans are shown in Figure 10-2. Each site selected was associated entirely or overwhelmingly with Coner phase ceramics, and none had produced Ejar phase materials. Ultimately we compared radiocarbon dates from 16 burials at these 11 rural sites against the hydration arrays (total number of dates = 121), adjusting both sets of dates to

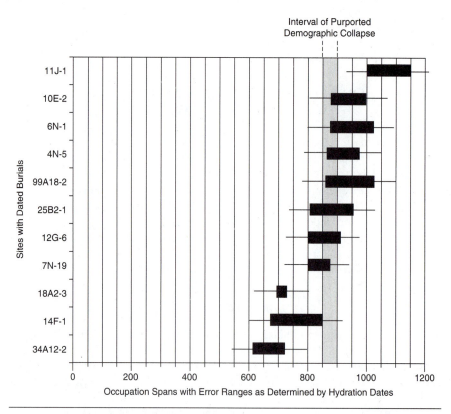

FIGURE 10-2   MINIMAL OCCUPATION SPANS (SHOWN IN HORIZONTAL BLACK BARS) FOR
11 SMALL SITES AS DETERMINED BY OBSIDIAN HYDRATION DATES; EACH HAS A 70-YEAR
(1 SIGMA) ERROR RANGE SHOWN BY HORIZONTAL LINES. THE SHADED VERTICAL
COLUMN REPRESENTS THE PERIOD OF DEMOGRAPHIC COLLAPSE AS ORIGINALLY
ENVISIONED WHEN WE BEGAN THE PAC II PROJECT IN 1980.

the same 1950 baseline. Note that the latest hydration dates fall only as late as the early 12th century, so the experiments have no necessary implications for occupations after that time.

Sources of Error

All experiments are subject to errors, and it is important to briefly specify those associated with ours. First, occupation spans are defined by their earliest and latest dates and are therefore *minimal* spans, because it is doubtful that we chose obsidian samples from either the very earliest or the very latest contexts at any given site. Moreover, given the nature of our test-pit methods, it is likely that we more extensively sampled the late deposits at each site than we did the more deeply buried early ones. For both these reasons we would expect some nonagreement between the two methods, because they were both drawn from two different kinds of artifact samples (burials and tools) with different depositional characteristics. For example, in direct contrast to the obsidian dates, the burial C14 dates are more likely to emphasize the early to middle range of each site's occupation history rather than its final abandonment, since all burial contexts encountered stratigraphically indicated continued post interment site occupation.

In some cases, extraneous obsidian or burials introduced into the sites also might cause some disagreement. Sample size is another important consideration. The radiocarbon method is subject to its own errors and any given AMS date (just as any hydration date) might be wrong. Ideally, we would in each experiment compare many radiocarbon dates against each hydration span, so that aberrant radiocarbon dates could be rejected. Because of the paucity of burials and the cost of AMS determinations ($400 each when we had ours done) only one of our experiments is significantly robust in this regard. If individual radiocarbon dates were obviously highly inconsistent with their contexts, they, of course, were rejected as not relevant to the issue of concordance. Finally, each "date" from each method is really a set of confidence intervals (expressed as one or two sigma ranges) rather than a particular point in time. Thus, partial overlap between a radiocarbon confidence interval and that of one or more hydration dates in the associated span is not necessarily a "better fit" than a more complete overlap, given the uncertainties associated with each method.

Given all these possible sources of error, plus those putatively associated with the hydration method itself, chances for agreement actually seem pretty low. Some disagreement will clearly occur even if both methods are working well and correctly applied. Our goal was simply to show reasonable patterns of consistent agreement.

Results of the Experiments

Archaeologists know that proper evaluation of agreement between two independent kinds of dating methods requires detailed discussion of contexts in each case. We do not have the space to present such a discussion for each experiment here, but general results are shown in Table 10-2.

TABLE 10-2
GENERAL C14 AND OBSIDIAN HYDRATION RATE CONCORDANCE

Agreement at One Sigma Confidence Level	Agreement at Two Sigma Confidence Level	Non Agreement
12 cases	1 case	3 cases*

* includes one rejected radiocarbon date.

In 12 cases there is agreement at the one sigma level or better. One other experiment shows less convincing, but still plausible agreement at the two sigma level. There are three "no fit" outcomes, but one of these is rejected because it is far too early to be compatible with the associated ceramic assemblage. A second no fit outcome from Group 9N-8, as we shall see shortly, is not relevant to agreement. In summary, 13 out of 14 relevant experiments show convincing agreement between the two methods, a surprisingly high level of fit considering the error factors discussed above.

ROBUST EXPERIMENT   One of our experiments is by far the most robust and reliable because it compares five AMS dates against a single hydration-dated occupation span. Contexts are also particularly well known in this case because the burials and artifacts come from one of the completely excavated rural residences discussed in Chapter 7. Figure 10-3 shows how convincingly four of the five

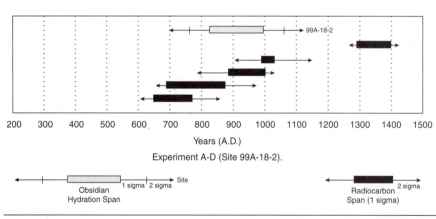

Experiment A-D (Site 99A-18-2).

FIGURE 10-3   TWENTY-SEVEN INDIVIDUAL HYDRATION DATES COMPOSE THE RAW OCCUPATION SPAN FOR SITE 99A-18-2, SHOWN AS THE LIGHT BAR AT THE TOP OF THE CHART. ONE AND TWO SIGMA RANGES OF THE EARLIEST AND LATEST HYDRATION DATES ARE SHOWN AS LINES EXTENDING FROM THE BAR. BELOW, SHOWN AS DARK BARS, ARE ONE SIGMA RANGES OF FIVE AMS RADIOCARBON DATES, WITH TWO SIGMA RANGES SHOWN AS LINES. BOTH SETS OF DATES ARE ARRAYED AGAINST A TIME SCALE FROM 200–1500 A.D. AND HAVE BEEN ADJUSTED TO THE 1950 BASELINE.

radiocarbon dates bracket the estimated hydration span. Note also the late radio-carbon outlier that indicates a burial was probably placed in this site during the 14th century A.D. We cannot reject this non-agreement outlier because we have no independent evidence that it is incompatible with the associated Coner ceram-ics, the duration of which is itself a chronological issue. This date most likely in-dicates (1) that we failed to detect the latest occupation at the site with our sample of obsidian dates, or (2) that a very late burial was made in an abandoned residence. In either case, obviously there still were people in the Copán Valley at this time.

Imagine that we had done this experiment backwards—that we had run the AMS dates first, then the hydration dates. Could one ask for better agreement? In fact, we believe the 27 tightly clustered obsidian dates from Site 99A-18-2 give a better approximation of its occupation span than the radiocarbon dates, given all other lines of archaeological evidence.

Summary

Obsidian hydration dating has been rigorously applied at Copán on an unprece-dented regional scale. It has been successfully and extensively tested against many other independent chronological data and shown to be a remarkably reli-able and consistent chronometric method. The overall patterning of dates indi-cates a much more protracted and complex collapse process for the polity than previously envisioned. More important than this insight about Copán's culture history is a methodological payoff—we can now reasonably partition in time hundreds of tested archaeological sites that otherwise could only be dated to the Coner phase.

Viel's ceramic sequence shown in Chapter 2 is a revision of his 1983 ver-sion, most *important* is his presentation of the Coner and Ejar ceramic phases. He begins Coner at A.D. 600–650. With respect to the end of the complex, he noted that "The fall of the centralized order does not necessarily mean the end of life at Copan. A progressive decline is a more likely model than a sudden death" (Viel, 1993, p. 17). He suggests that between A.D. 800 and 950 Coner forms continued to be used, but mixed with some early Ejar forms. After A.D. 950 Coner ceramics entirely disappeared, and Ejar is represented only by an ex-tremely small collection of imported or rare types mainly deposited in ritual contexts until about A.D. 1000. Although Viel does not say this in so many words, the implication of his 1993 sequence is that the Copán Valley was essen-tially depopulated by A.D. 950—not a significantly different date than that given in his 1983 sequence, in which he envisioned the valley as almost com-pletely depopulated by A.D. 900.

Both hydration and radiocarbon dates support the Acbi/Coner transition at about A.D. 600–650. Both methods, and the new radiocarbon dates by them-selves, indicate the protracted occupation of the valley. Taken together, both methods tell us that Coner ceramics, or at least ceramics that are Coner-derived, were used at least until the 13th century and possibly later. No doubt there were many changes in the ceramic tradition during this time that fine-grained studies might reveal, and subdividing this long interval would be very desirable. As now defined, however, Coner-like assemblages were used far longer than originally suspected.

One other interesting pattern is quite clear—obsidian blades were used by people from all social levels until very late, at least through the 12th century. We know that they were not simply reusing old blades scavenged from dynastic contexts because then the obsidian events would date to the time of manufacture, not later use (and, of course, would unduly inflate estimates of the Classic population). Apparently access to raw obsidian or rough prismatic cores continued long after the demise of Copán's rulers, and even after the nobles were effectively gone, indicating that the degree of social ranking and political centralization was not a necessary component of obsidian procurement.

Our chronology is not a new chronology. In fact, its strength is precisely that in most respects it supports the traditional Copán sequence as known from many other lines of evidence. The only part that is new is the extended post-A.D. 900 occupation of both elite and non-elite sites.

Successful application of hydration dating at Copán does not necessarily mean that the method will always yield comparable results elsewhere. We had the advantage that almost all the pre-A.D. 600 raw material came from a single source, and Ixtepeque obsidian is comparatively easy to process and "read" in the laboratory. Just as important, all samples were prepared and examined by a single researcher (Freter), thus ensuring comparability and eliminating the inevitable bias produced by multiple observers. We had access to a wide range of well-controlled, excavated archaeological contexts in which obsidian artifacts were very numerous and depositional contexts reasonably uniform. Finally, many years of work by other archaeologists provided a rich framework within which to evaluate the hydration method and the results of our field and laboratory research. Few other projects will be as fortunate as ours in all these respects.

It is sometimes said that archaeologists find what they expect to find or can read what they wish into their data. Of course, if this were so we would never learn anything new. In our experience being wrong can be very gratifying. We were wrong about the nature of the Coner phase and the Copán collapse, and only found out how wrong we were by experimentally applying a comparatively untested chronological method. As we shall see in the following chapter, obsidian hydration supplied the key to reconstructing the scale, distribution, and dynamics of the regional population for all time periods, but especially those falling after A.D. 600–650.

CHAPTER 11

Population and Agricultural History

of the Copán Kingdom

INTRODUCTION

How many people supported great Classic Maya centers such as Copán? How were they distributed on the landscape, and how did they derive a living from it? These questions have long been central concerns of archaeologists. Early reconstructions of Classic period population sizes and distributions derived heavily from ethnohistoric information about the 16th-century Maya of northern Yucatán. At that time, overall densities even in the most centralized polities were apparently less than 15 people per sq km, and Spanish descriptions suggest that most farmers practiced extensive forms of swidden agriculture commensurate with low populations (but see McAnany, 1995, for another interpretation).

Beginning in the 1930s surveys around sites such as Uaxactun, and later Tikal, indicated much heavier concentrations of small residential structures than previously expected. Population estimates derived from these surveys exceeded those supportable by long-fallow swidden agriculture and consequently stimulated the search for evidence of more intensive agricultural strategies such as hillside terracing and drained fields (Flannery, 1982; Harrison and Turner, 1978; Fedick, 1996). Recent estimates of population densities for huge regions around some Classic centers now are on the order of 200 to 300 people per sq km (Culbert and Rice, 1990).

Accurate reconstructions of population are not only keys to understanding the ancient Maya subsistence economy but also the political economy and, more generally, the sociopolitical organization. Were processes of population growth related to increasing social and cultural complexity? How were Maya of high rank supported by common producers? How much labor could kings and elites command for construction of their palaces, temples, and monuments? On what scale was warfare carried out in the Maya Lowlands? Did demographic stress contribute to the decline or collapse of some centers? In short, our conceptions of many important features of Maya society and culture historic episodes are heavily dependent on our assessments of the demographic sizes of polities.

These questions were also fundamental, of course, to understanding the development and character of ancient Copán. Prior to the PAC I project one could only guess at how many people lived in the Copán region at any particular time. After the PAC I surveys it was evident that the Copán pocket was the demographic core of the kingdom, and that population densities there were very high. William Fash (1983a, p. 187) estimated that maximally about 17,000 people lived in the Copán pocket. This was an accurate, informed estimate, but it referred only to the peak Coner phase population and to only part of the total region. After the PAC II surveys and test pitting in the outlying zones of the valley were we in a position to estimate more systematically the whole population of the kingdom for various time periods because of chronological insights derived from our obsidian hydration research.

We are now able to compare the results of two separate reconstructions of population and agricultural history in the Copán region. The first is called the *settlement model,* and derives from survey data. The second, largely independent *soil model* derives from landscape archaeology.

Reconstructing Population History at Copán: The Settlement Model

Archaeologists depend most heavily on the results of settlement surveys to reconstruct population. Fortunately, as we have already seen, remains of individual structures are visible on the landscapes of the Maya Lowlands. The general strategy is therefore to estimate how many such structures were residential, how many were occupied at any particular time, and assign some number of people to each inhabited structure. Straightforward as this approach sounds, it is both conceptually very complicated and fraught with many potential errors. How large and representative is the sample of available structures of a whole region? How can one reasonably extrapolate for settlement units that have not been recorded, or partition the sample in time? Finally, how does one decide what number of residents to assign to some set of settlement features? Given all these uncertainties, the best we can hope for are reliable order of magnitude estimates, not precise ones.

Any kind of attempt at estimating ancient archaeological populations takes the form of a simulation model in which what is known about the ancient system is supplemented with reasonable assumptions about what is not known. For example, the numbers and locations of recorded sites are supplemented by extrapolations for sites not found, and numbers of residents assigned to particular settlement components are educated guesses. Every archaeologist engaged in such a simulation must make assumptions, and the objective is to make them as reasonable and explicit as possible.

Much of our settlement research at Copán was specifically designed to provide information concerning the assumptions that we eventually incorporated into our calculations. For example, Freter's test pitting was partly concerned with documenting the percentage of residential sites recorded on the landscape, as well as the presence of hidden structures. Webster's and Gonlin's follow-up large-scale excavations of small rural sites in turn checked her findings, and, of course, we had other reliable information from the extensive Las Sepulturas work. Most important, the obsidian hydration research allowed us to control occupation intervals at a large sample of specific sites of all ranks.

Estimating Copán Population Dynamics

We developed a complex set of procedures for estimating Copán's population history based on the many lines of settlement research reviewed in previous chapters. Our approach broadly parallels that used by most other Maya archaeologists but has adjustments suitable to the Copán situation. The basic logic of our procedures and the components and values used in our simulation models are briefly summarized below but are far too complex to review in detail here. Those interested in more complete discussions should consult Freter (1988, 1992, 1994); Webster and Freter (1990a, 1990b); Webster, Sanders, and van Rossum (1992); van Rossum (1998); Webster, Gonlin, and Sheets (1997); Paine (1996); Paine and Freter (1996); Paine, Freter, and Webster (1996).

ESTABLISHING A BASELINE SETTLEMENT SAMPLE   The initial problem faced by all archaeologists attempting to reconstruct population from settlement data is to acquire a regional settlement sample that is sufficiently large and representative to yield reliable inferences. The surveys of our predecessors, along with our own PAC II work, completed this essential phase of research by 1984. The Copán settlement sample of 1,425 sites of all ranks with 4,507 associated buildings was then, and remains, one of the most extensive available for any Maya polity.

ESTABLISHING THE CHARACTER OF MAPPED SITES   By 1988 both large-scale excavations and test pitting had abundantly documented the essential functions, sizes, and features of sites and their individual component buildings. No comparably detailed information existed for any other large Maya polity.

Three kinds of information were crucial. First, we had an excellent grasp of the functional variation of structures within sites of all ranks, and could reasonably distinguish special purpose buildings from domiciles. Second, we understood room arrangements very well for domiciles in sites of all ranks. Third, we had quantitative data about the numbers of hidden structures unrecorded on the surface, and the degree to which surface mapping correctly reflected the numbers and arrangements of visible structures.

CHOOSING A SETTLEMENT COMPONENT   There are several ways to estimate population on the basis of Maya settlement features. All depend on some presumed correlation between a documented settlement component and some kind of demographic measure.

A commonly used approach is to assume that there is a reasonably tight relationship between the number of occupants of a building and its associated roofed-over floor space (Narrol, 1962). Here the component is a spatial calculation. This method is widely used in places like the American Southwest, where buildings and rooms are very well preserved so that floor space can usually be determined even from surface indications. We rejected this method at Copán for two reasons. First, our test-pitting program was not focused on buildings and thus did not provide the required detailed evidence concerning room sizes, which are difficult to estimate accurately from unexcavated buildings. Second, we doubt whether there was a consistent relationship between floor space and the number of occupants at Copán. Many domiciles were occupied for a generation or more, and rebuilding efforts used the old basal platforms, which in a sense dictated house and room size. A one-room structure originally built or renovated to house a young husband and wife with several children might have a very different occupant to floor space ratio when the children later reached adulthood, leaving only the two old adults behind—a situation familiar from our own society. Similarly, houses occupied by big families during a period of overall population increase during one generation might have had fewer occupants a couple of generations later when population was declining and families were smaller.

An alternate method is to identify a basic form of residential organizational unit (for the Maya this is usually an extended family), estimate its average size, and assign this constant value to residential sites or groups of structures within sites, which then are the basic settlement components.

Because of our excellent understanding of site and structure configuration, we decided to use a strategy different from either of these, one that emphasized individual rooms. From our excavations we knew the mean number of rooms associated with domicile structures in sites of various ranks. For example, excavated rural Type 1 structures had only one room each, so this number was attributed to all domiciles associated with such sites. Rooms in Copán structures are generally small, and most of them probably could not have housed a social group much larger than a nuclear family. Because mean room numbers per domicile, and to some degree room size, varied with site rank, we made appropriate adjustments at each level. We also assumed that residents of the large domiciles in groups of elite rank had fewer people per room, both because this was a prerogative of high status and because elite Maya men were probably polygynous, occupying their own private rooms while others were used by their wives and children (these possibilities also, of course, are at odds with the assumption of a consistent relationship between occupants and floor space).

We assigned specific numbers of people (see below) to known or extrapolated rooms in structures of all ranks thought to represent domiciles (as opposed to ritual buildings, kitchens, storerooms, or other special purpose buildings).

DETERMINATION OF OCCUPATION LENGTH   As we already discussed, perhaps the most intransigent source of error in demographic reconstructions is the issue of how long any particular site was occupied. Our large suite of hydration dates provided a solution to this problem. For each site with multiple dates we assumed a constant occupation between the earliest and the latest hydration dates (using as the date the actual hydration reading expressed as a single calendar year). This we call the *raw site occupation span*. Some sites had only single dates. Using a subset of 93 sites with five or more dates, we determined the average length of occupation for sites of each rank, then centered this interval on the single dates from sites of the appropriate rank.

After dividing the Copán chronological sequence into 50-year intervals from A.D. 400 to 1299, we scored each dated site as *occupied* during any such interval that had at least one date. The same logic would apply no matter what chronological method provided the dates. Scoring was not dependent on the number of dates that fell into a particular 50-year interval (i.e., one date for a site gave the same result as multiple dates) and so was not directly dependent on the raw distribution of hydration dates displayed in Figure 10-1. Our scoring procedure allowed fine-tuning of the settlement chronology, especially within the all-important Coner phase.

Obviously this calculation is itself prone to errors even if all the obsidian dates are accurate. For one thing, occupation spans are minimal estimates when determined in this way because we might not have sampled the earliest or latest contexts. If there were consistent errors of this kind (if occupations were systematically longer) then we would underestimate population. This is especially a problem for small sites with short spans. To compensate for it, we extended the estimated population span of each site to include the one sigma 70 year error ranges associated with the earliest and latest known associated dates (i.e., we extended the "raw" spans by 70 years in each direction).

Another source of error is that sites might have been periodically abandoned during the presumed occupation span, resulting in excessive demographic estimates if we inappropriately designated it as occupied during that period of time. We have no statistically valid way of correcting for this possibility, so we were forced to ignore it.

It is important to note that having large numbers of dated sites helps negate certain kinds of errors. Any given short occupation span might well be skewed inappropriately early or late. Although we could not detect such skewing, this bias would probably not be systematic, so there is an excellent chance that these errors cancel out one another. For example, if a particular Type 1 site was occupied 50 years later than we concluded, and another one 50 years earlier, these two errors would correct each other in the aggregate demographic calculation even though each individual occupation span was inaccurate.

Because of the nature of our chronological adjustments, the simulation reviewed below almost certainly overestimates population for any particular 50-year interval—it yields *maximal* estimates. We chose to skew our errors in this direction because maximal rather than minimal population sizes and densities are currently the critical issues with respect to regional Maya polities.

EXTRAPOLATIONS AND CORRECTION FACTORS   Any simulation of regional population from settlement data requires several kinds of extrapolations from what is known to what is not known and also has some other problems that must be addressed.

On the most basic level, we obviously could not hope to recover data on all residential sites the Maya had built on the Copán landscape. Some were situated in areas we could not or did not survey. Others had been destroyed, buried by eroded soil, or obscured by later constructions, and of course, the urban core, where such a large proportion of people obviously lived, was most troublesome in this regard. Initial extrapolations had to be made to account for these missing sites, and again we tried to make generous ones. Once these calculations had been made, we also had to extrapolate for critical site features. Most important, the information from excavated sites was used to calculate how many domicile rooms existed in the universe of other sites known or projected to exist in the region.

In each quadrant of our survey, as well as the urban core, we extrapolated for the occupation spans of sites that had not been dated from those that had. For example, if 50% of the dated Type 1 sites in a survey zone had occupations falling into a particular 50-year interval, we scored 50% of the residual (i.e, undated) Type 1 sites known or presumed to exist in that region as also occupied during that interval.

Another correction had to be added to accommodate potential room disuse. At any given time some domiciles at a particular site might have been abandoned even though the site as a whole still was occupied. This would most likely be a problem under two interrelated sets of circumstances: (1) as the number of people at a particular residential site declined from an earlier peak size (see below), and/or (2) as the total population of the Copán Valley gradually declined after its regional peak. We introduced correction factors to account for such disuse, applying different values for periods during which the numbers of occupation spans were increasing, the period when they peaked in number, and the long period of their decline (see below)..

Large elite sites pose another occupancy dilemma. Many of them were inhabited for hundreds of years, and of course, their final expression in the archaeological record most directly reflects the period of largest resident population (generally the 8th century). Despite extensive excavation in such sites we lack a firm grasp of what their earlier, and especially pre-Coner, architectural arrangements were like. Many 8th-century Type 3 and 4 sites would have had the configurations of Type 1 or 2 sites a couple of centuries earlier. On the other extreme, rooms were undoubtedly gradually abandoned as resident populations declined after the population peak was reached. Even though we have the dates to score sites as occupied or not, it is currently impossible to know how the associated numbers of domicile rooms fluctuated through time. We accordingly used the mature site configurations for the period from A.D. 750 to 900, then scaled back in-use domicile estimates for periods when fewer were used. While this scale-back of in-use domicile estimates post A.D. 900 is a realistic correction given what we know about the culture history of the Copán valley, it does create a sharper, more sudden population decline profile than likely existed right at the A.D. 900 interval.

ASSIGNING POPULATION UNITS   This is in many ways the most crucial step of all, because assigning too many people to domicile rooms seriously overestimates population. Archaeologists often assume, based on ethnohistoric and ethnographic descriptions, that the ancient Maya usually lived in extended or joint family households. We also make this assumption, with the caveat that such families themselves go through developmental stages and that these have implications for settlement components. Thus, a married couple might establish a small new household. Later their own married offspring and grandchildren might continue to reside there, along with unmarried siblings, resulting in enlarged or more numerous residential facilities. At some later time, the original founders die and some individual nuclear families of the younger generation fission off to start spatially distinct new households, beginning the process all over again. The whole cycle might take two to four generations. Many residential sites such as the larger ones described in Chapter 7 are the architectural residues of this kind of completed process, while small sites reflect developmental cycles that for some reason were interrupted or attenuated.

When archaeologists attempt to estimate population for a particular time they essentially ask the same question as census takers. To express this idea more concretely, imagine being able to go back to Copán at, for example, a day in A.D. 750, find everyone at home, and simply make the rounds of all the households, counting the people associated with each domicile building. If we did this, we would obviously encounter great variability in the number of occupants of any particular residence depending on the idiosyncratic domestic history of each household. Because such a census is impossible, we cannot possibly know at what stage of its cycle any particular ancient Copán household was at any given time, and so we cannot assign time-specific residential figures to each one. We have to choose some sort of average figure and apply it across the board to domiciles as a whole for a particular time period.

Our solution to this problem emphasizes the reproductively active *nuclear families* (monogamous married pairs and offspring) that formed the cores of extended or joint families. It is reasonable to assume, judging from structure layout and the average size of rooms, that domiciles in most sites of Type 2 rank and lower were occupied by small numbers of people. Many rooms in elite rank sites are also small. The question is, what is a reasonable average population size for a nuclear family?

Maya archaeologists have frequently used statistics derived from observations of the rural Maya Yucatecan community of Chan Kom in the 1930s (Redfield & Villa Rojas, 1934). Nuclear families (spouses and children) with a mean size of 5.1 people comprised the core components of Chan Kom's households, and mean total household size was only slightly larger—5.6 people. In fact, neither of these numbers should be used as an analog for the ancient Maya at Copán or elsewhere because of the special nature of the Chan Kom population. The village was a pioneer community with abundant resources and many fertile young adults, and its population was reproducing itself far faster (at a doubling rate of about 17 years) than we can reasonably expect happened in prehistoric times. Both household and demographic research suggest alternative reasonable solutions.

John Hajnal (1982) surveyed household sizes in societies with strongly contrasting traditions of household organization. He unexpectedly found that households (defined as residential "housekeeping" units that eat from a common store of food) are generally composed of about 5 people, whether the tradition of household formation emphasizes nuclear families or joint families.

Unfortunately there is no information on how people in joint or extended families were apportioned among household domicile structures. Hajnal's study suggests that assigning a resident group of about five people to sites with a single domicile building is reasonable. Where more domiciles exist, this figure might still be appropriate for the group as a whole, assuming it constitutes the household facility. On the other hand, one could assign about 5 people to each domicile, assuming that these were effective household segments.

Comparative demographic data offer a related perspective. Campbell and Wood (1988) studied the fertility of 70 traditional societies and found that in 90% of them the range of live births during each woman's reproductive span ranged from four to eight, with an average of about six live offspring. These figures remained remarkably constant no matter how this sample was subdivided (e.g., foragers vs. horticulturists, etc.). In terms of our census exercise this means that at any point in time we might find some nuclear families with as few as two members (no children born yet or all children gone from the domicile) or as high as 10, assuming that all children had survived. But, of course, we cannot assume such survival because in such traditional societies roughly 50% of children die before reaching reproductive maturity, with most mortality concentrated in the first year after birth (a pattern consistent with Rebecca Storey's and Stephen Whittington's paleodemographic studies of Copán skeletons). Not only would many children have thus been eliminated and so not counted, but some would not yet have been born and others would have left the household. Mean numbers in the range of four to five people per nuclear family *at any given time* are reasonable estimates, and such figures are large enough to account also for other household members not part of the nuclear or joint family per se (old surviving grandparents, unmarried siblings, etc).

One further modification is necessary because nuclear or joint family size would be on average larger when the total population was increasing than when it was stable or decreasing. Fortunately the total array of obsidian dates shown in Figure 10-1 is a rough proxy for population trends (and it is in agreement with many other lines of evidence).

Based on all these considerations, we simulated population using a nuclear family size of five per domicile for the period of population growth (A.D. 400–799), four people for the period of comparative stability between A.D. 750 and 899, and 3.5 people for the subsequent period of decline. For all time periods until A.D. 850 we included a Main Group population of 250 people. These figures are generous and tend to overestimate population (see Freter, 1994, for a simulation that applies a constant population figure for all time periods but yields very similar results to the one summarized here).

COPÁN POPULATION HISTORY

The components and values reviewed above were combined into a long equation that was then run on a Quattro Pro (Version 1) computer program devised by Peter van Rossum (1998). The results of the simulation are shown in Figure 11-1. As already noted, there are some abrupt "jumps" in the sequence caused by the mechanics of the simulation itself. For example, the sharp drop between the A.D. 850–899 and the A.D. 900–949 intervals is partly caused by the fact that the shift from four to 3.5 occupants is programmed to happen at this point as is

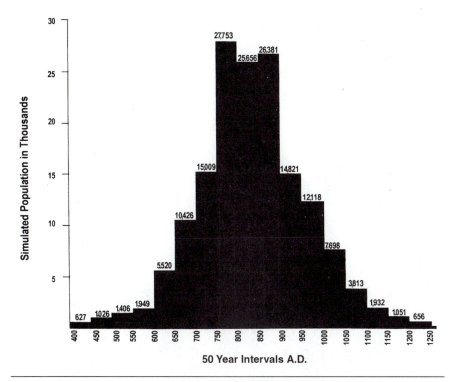

FIGURE 11-1 RAW POPULATION ESTIMATES FROM SETTLEMENT SIMULATION, BROKEN DOWN BY 50-YEAR INTERVALS FOR ALL TIME PERIODS BETWEEN A.D. 400–1300.

our reduced in-use domicile estimate (i.e., the decline was probably really less steep, and population higher than shown at A.D. 900–949). These shifts, however, do not obscure overall trends. Table 11-1 shows how these estimates break down according to subregions of the Copán Valley while Table 11-2 gives distribution by site type. As already noted, we do not expect precision in these figures, only rough order-of-magnitude accuracy. Remember too that our simulation here is geared in several respects to produce *maximal* population figures.

The Period of Growth (A.D. 400–750)

We do not attempt to simulate population before A.D. 400 because of the lack of settlement data, and results are most reliable after A.D. 600. The simulation shows only 627 people in the whole polity at A.D. 400, and 5,520 as late as A.D. 650, about the time that the Acbi/Coner transition is completed. We think our reconstruction of the pre-Coner phase population is clearly too low, especially because of the difficulty of sampling early settlement on the floor of the Copán pocket. Our educated hunch is that between A.D. 400 and 450 the actual population of the

TABLE 11-1
Raw Simulation of Population Distribution Through Time in Various Subregions

Time Period	Urban Core	Copán Pocket	Upper Main Valley	Lower Main Valley	Sesesmil Valley	Jila/Mirasol Valleys
400–449 A.D.	627 (100%)	0 (0%)	0 (0%)	0 (0%)	0 (0%)	0 (0%)
450–499	683 (66.6%)	38 (3.7%)	0 (0%)	0 (0%)	105 (10.2%)	200 (19.4%)
500–549	968 (69.8%)	38 (2.7%)	0 (0%)	0 (0%)	200 (14.2%)	200 (14.2%)
550–599	1,024 (52.5%)	38 (1.9%)	83 (4.3%)	0 (0%)	380 (19.5%)	424 (21.8%)
600–649	2,519 (45.6%)	1,312 (23.8%)	393 (7.1%)	48 (0.9%)	452 (8.2%)	796 (14.4%)
650–699	4,368 (41.9%)	2,973 (28.5%)	1,028 (9.9%)	48 (0.5%)	593 (5.7%)	1,416 (13.6%)
700–749	5,910 (39.4%)	5,642 (37.6%)	1,158 (7.7%)	150 (1%)	629 (4.2%)	1,520 (10.2%)
750–799	11,828 (42.6%)	10,627 (38.3%)	1,739 (6.3%)	341 (1.2%)	902 (3.3%)	2,316 (8.4%)
800–849	10,261 (40%)	10,159 (39.6%)	2,021 (7.9%)	436 (1.7%)	885 (3.4%)	1,894 (7.4%)
850–899	9,736 (36.9%)	10,227 (38.8%)	3,050 (11.6%)	534 (2%)	780 (3%)	2,054 (7.8%)
900–949	4,276 (28.9%)	6,031 (40%)	2,240 (15.1%)	414 (2.8%)	622 (4.2%)	1,238 (8.4%)
950–999	3,262 (26.9%)	4,939 (40.8%)	2,239 (18.5%)	328 (2.7%)	424 (3.5%)	924 (7.6%)
1000–1049	1,679 (21.8%)	3,069 (39.9%)	2,037 (26.5%)	243 (3.2%)	260 (3.4%)	410 (3.4%)

TABLE 11-2
SIMULATION OF NUMBERS AND PERCENTAGES OF PEOPLE LIVING IN COPÁN HOUSEHOLD GROUPS OF DIFFERENT RANKS

Time Period	Single Mound	Type 1	Type 2	Type 3	Type 4
400–449 A.D.	0 (0%)	0 (0%)	92 (14.7%)	0 (0%)	535 (85.3%)
450–499	58 (5.7%)	247 (24.1%)	92 (9%)	94 (9.2%)	535 (52.1%)
500–549	58 (4.1%)	342 (24.3%)	92 (6.5%)	94 (6.7%)	820 (58.3%)
550–599	141 (7.2%)	718 (36.8%)	120 (6.2%)	150 (7.7%)	820 (42.1%)
600–649	275 (5%)	2,231 (40%)	913 (16.5%)	387 (7%)	1,714 (31.1%)
650–699	380 (3.6%)	4,732 (45.4%)	1,691 (16.2%)	958 (9.2%)	2,665 (25.6%)
700–749	654 (4.4%)	7,083 (47.2%)	3,132 (20.9%)	1,386 (9.2%)	2,754 (18.3%)
750–799	877 (3.2%)	10,546 (38%)	8,029 (28.9%)	2,868 (10.3%)	5,433 (19.6%)
800–849	970 (3.8%)	10,551 (41.1%)	7,674 (29.9%)	2,065 (8%)	4,396 (17.1%)
850–899	1,225 (4.6%)	11,723 (44.4%)	7,222 (27.4%)	2,065 (7.8%)	4,146 (15.7%)
900–949	948 (6.4%)	9,265 (62.5%)	2,421 (16.3%)	793 (5.4%)	1,394 (9.4%)
950–999	919 (7.6%)	8,055 (66.5%)	1,486 (12.3%)	625 (5.2%)	1,031 (8.5%)
1000–1049	677 (8.8%)	5,773 (75%)	594 (7.7%)	214 (2.8%)	440 (5.7%)

polity was several thousand people, as shown in the smoothed population profile in Figure 11-2. As an aside, however, a statistical analysis of population trends by Richard Paine et al. (1996) shows that our pre-A.D. 600 population estimates are consistent in terms of scale and rates of change, with the later, more well documented parts of the sequence.

Beginning in the 7th century there is a steep increase culminating in a peak of 27,753 people at A.D. 750. The general profile of this trend is supported by what we know about the amounts and distributions of Acbi as opposed to Coner ceramics and is in accordance with the recognition by the PAC I archaeologists (Fash, 1983a, 1983b) that Coner phase sites are overwhelmingly preponderant on the Copán landscape.

Population was very heavily concentrated in the urban core and the Copán pocket for the period of growth (over 80% as late as A.D. 750)—just what we would expect because these are the most attractive parts of the landscape and among the earliest colonized. The residual population is scattered in other parts of the main valley, and also in the Sesesmil and Río Jila tributary valleys (Figure 11-3).

The rapid rise in population after A.D. 600–650 initially led us to suspect that the increasingly powerful Copán kingdom, especially under its vigorous 12th and 13th rulers, had attracted outside migrants. Statistical analysis, however, showed that this need not be assumed and that the pattern can be accounted for by the intrinsic increase in the local population (Paine, 1996; Paine, et al., 1996).

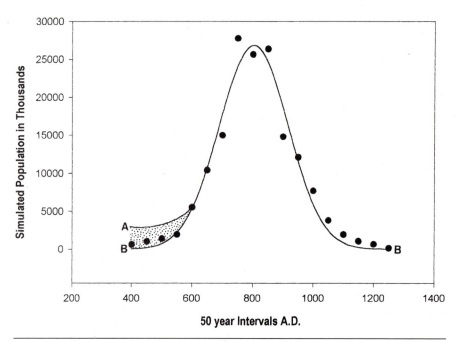

FIGURE 11-2   LINE B-B REPRESENTS A COMPUTER-SMOOTHED COPÁN POPULATION
DISTRIBUTION BASED ON THE RAW SIMULATION FIGURES (BLACK DOTS); NOTE
INFLATION OF PRE-A.D. 600 FIGURES. WE SUSPECT THAT THE PRE-A.D. 600 ESTIMATES
ARE TOO LOW, AND THAT A MORE REASONABLE PROFILE IS INDICATED BY LINE A-B,
WHICH ALLOWS FOR AN INFLATED EARLY POPULATION (SHADED ZONE).

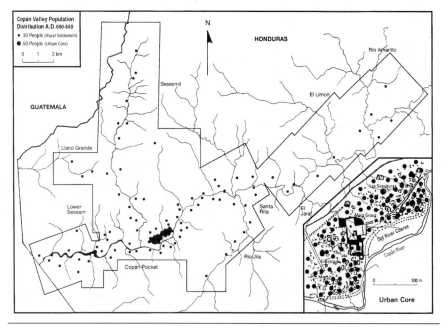

FIGURE 11-3   ESTIMATED DISTRIBUTION OF COPÁN POPULATION AT A.D. 600–650.
MODIFIED FROM FRETER 1992: 126, FIGURE 3.

The Peak Population (A.D. 750–900)

The population peak of the Copán polity occurs between A.D. 750 and 900, reaching a maximum of 27,753 people at the beginning of this interval, during the final dynastic reigns. At this time the population of the Copán pocket is only slightly higher than that estimated earlier by William Fash (1983a) on the basis of the PAC I surveys. This is a far smaller peak figure for the kingdom as a whole than previously estimated and in fact is much lower than our own educated guesses prior to completion of the PAC II surveys, which then were as high as 40,000–50,000 people (Webster, 1985).

One surprise was the large proportion of the whole population—75 to 80%— still concentrated in the Copán pocket during this interval (Figure 11-4). Of these people, an estimated 11,827 lived in the urban core alone in an area of roughly about one sq km. This is the densest concentration known for any Classic Maya center and gives this zone a distinct urban character in terms of sheer density. Because Type 3 and 4 sites dominate the urban core, about 25 to 30% of all people in the polity lived in them at this time. It is impossible that all such residents were themselves of high rank in terms of their wealth or social and political positions; elites in the strict sense probably comprised 10% or fewer of the total population. It follows that many occupants were of modest status, and in fact elite groups include many small, poorly made structures and rooms, and also yield simple burials, both consistent with this interpretation.

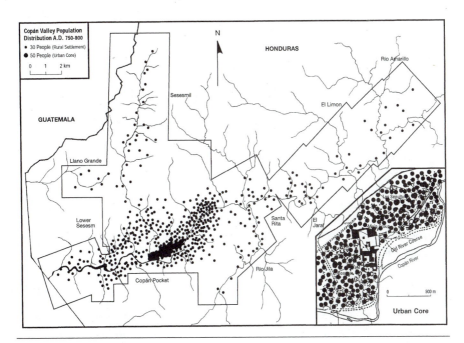

FIGURE 11-4 ESTIMATED DISTRIBUTION OF COPÁN POPULATION AT A.D. 750–800. MODIFIED FROM FRETER 1992: 127, FIGURE 4.

Outside the Copán pocket population was much lower, but the tributary valleys appear to have had fewer people than the occupants of the upper main valley. Because there were comparatively few elite rank residences outside the Copán pocket the peripheral elite population was small, amounting to a few hundred people. For several reasons, people of rank and prestige overwhelmingly resided close to the royal court at the Main Group. An implication of the heavy concentration of people in the Copán pocket, as we shall see later, is that the population was not distributed rationally in terms of food production.

Assuming that the whole Copán drainage in Honduras measures roughly 500 sq km, overall peak population density would be about 55 people per sq km. If we consider only those zones reasonably attractive for habitation and agriculture, then densities were much higher—briefly reaching concentrations of 370 to 452 people per sq km if our maximal population rates are accepted. But these overall figures are deceiving because most people lived in the Copán pocket, which achieved a maximal density of 935 people per sq km. Taking this concentration of people into account, the more distant, outlying parts of the valley had an overall peak density of only about 11 people per sq km.

The Period of Decline (after A.D. 900)

Of all the periods of Copán's population history, that falling after the demise of the royal dynasty is the most controversial. The raw hydration date distribution offered convincing evidence that there were still people in the valley after A.D. 900, and that population was generally starting to decline, but no direct implications about how many people there were nor where they lived. Our simulation now provides that information, and the post-A.D. 900 period is the best controlled interval from the point of view of the hydration sample. We will examine the implications of the demographic decline in Chapter 13, and describe here only the basic patterns.

After maintaining itself at an average level of about 26,000 people for a century and a half, population began to decline, but not at the precipitous rates originally imagined. During the first 75 years after A.D. 900 about half the population disappeared, but 30% were still present at A.D. 1000. (Figure 11-5). By A.D. 1150–1200 only a few more than 1,000 people were left, and thereafter the region appears effectively depopulated. Remember, however, that a burial recovered from one rural site was radiocarbon dated as late as the 14th century. In all probability the Copán region was never entirely abandoned and always had a few hundred people in residence. Even if they still used obsidian we would have a difficult time detecting them.

Some strong spatial patterns are also associated with the period of decline. After A.D. 900 the proportion of people in the peripheral regions outside the Copán pocket began to increase, a process of decentralization that reached its apogee at A.D. 1050–1100 when the pocket population fell to just 51.4% of the total. People abandoned the steeper Sesesmil Valley more rapidly than they did the upper main valley or the southern tributary valleys.

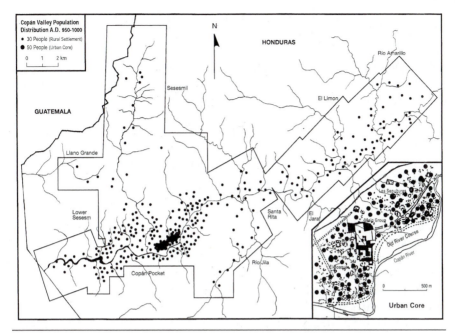

FIGURE 11-5   ESTIMATED DISTRIBUTION OF COPÁN VALLEY POPULATION AT A.D. 950–1000. MODIFIED FROM FRETER 1992: 129, FIGURE 6.

Also significant is the pattern of abandonment of elite rank sites. As late as A.D. 950–1000 an estimated 14% of all Copañecos still resided in some elite Type 3 or Type 4 groups, although others appear to have been abandoned. In fact, a sizable proportion of the population continued to inhabit such sites (almost all in the urban core) through A.D. 1200–1250. Construction and other activities that we can reasonably interpret as elite in nature continued through the 10th century. After about A.D. 1000 occupants of these groups probably were no longer carrying on in any sort of elite fashion, but instead squatting in or around increasingly dilapidated structures built long before.

One possible exception to this elite decline is a Type 3 site in the Río Amarillo zone locally known as Piedras Negras, which seems to have a short resurgent occupation span beginning just after A.D. 1000. Our hunch, still to be tested by extensive excavations, is that some sort of small, local polity of a thousand people or so briefly reconstituted itself there—its elites displaying a more limited set of political symbols than in earlier times. The outlying centers of Río Amarillo itself and the large site under the modern town of Santa Rita might also prove to have late populations when more data are available.

In summary, Copán's population was not effectively gone by A.D. 900 as previously supposed, but rather dwindled away over about 400 years after the dynasty fell. Evidence of continued activities of some elites, moreover, profoundly changes our conceptions of the political demise of the kingdom. Certainly there was no abrupt collapse, either in political or demographic terms.

AGRICULTURAL HISTORY OF THE COPÁN KINGDOM: THE SOIL MODEL

Simulations prove nothing. Their results are only as useful or plausible as the assumptions, components, and values built into them. All these, of course, are debatable, or at least have wide ranges. One way to assess a simulation is to repeat it many times, subtly altering it on each occasion to see how the outcomes are affected. In this manner we could test both the robusticity of particular parts of the model (i.e., find out which changes have the greatest effects) and its tolerance (the range of its varied outputs). We have not yet made multiple runs of our Copán population simulation.

Another way of exploring the plausibility of our simulation is to compare its results against those of a totally independent method of estimating population. Fortunately, we have just such an effort by John Wingard, who developed a complex model of agricultural history of the Copán Valley (Wingard, 1992, 1996). Wingard, trained both as an anthropologist and an agricultural economist, participated in the PAC II surveys and so knew the Copán Valley well, but his simulation was largely carried out separately from our own and without knowledge of our procedures or results. His own interests were the changing relationships among agricultural strategies, population levels, and environmental change during the evolution of the Copán polity.

Wingard's work is an example of landscape archaeology because it is not site-centric but rather assesses variations in landscape features—namely soils and their productive capacities. Because his simulation yields population figures based on a different data set than we used, it constitutes a fair test of our conclusions. More significant, it provides sophisticated reconstructions of the agricultural history of the region.

Simulating Agriculture and Population at Copán

Wingard's research was built on earlier Copán ecological studies and his own interviews with modern Copán farmers. His most basic data set consisted of 200 soil samples that he systematically collected and analyzed from a region of 200.7 sq km centered on the main Copán Valley and the Sesesmil tributary valley. Both zones were heavily represented in our PAC II surveys and test pitting.

Wingard's simulation used a complex EPIC (Erosion/Productivity Impact Calculator) model developed and widely used by the U.S. Department of Agriculture. Because this model uses so many variables, particularly those pertaining to climatic factors, bedrock, soil types and nutrients, and physiological requirements of different kinds of crops, it is very robust and capable of modeling long-term processes. Only the bare bones of Wingard's simulation are summarized here, so interested readers should consult his own detailed presentations, which include rationales for the components, attached values, and possible error factors and their output consequences.

AGRICULTURAL MODEL INPUTS   Basic elements of Wingard's simulation are:

1. Measures of productivity and sustainabilty (i.e., fertility and erodibility) for each soil type in terms of maize production.
2. Six soil slope classes (from 0.0001% to greater than 30%).
3. Dietary intake from maize equal to 60% of total caloric intake, or 120 kg per individual per year.
4. A seed population of 1,000 people on the floor of the Copán pocket at A.D. 0.
5. Five agricultural management strategies involving increasing levels of intensification, beginning with long-fallow swidden and progressing to continuous use, with irrigation in some zones.
6. A range of maize production estimates of 813 to 1834 kg/ha, depending upon soils and management strategy.
7. Annual rates of population change: +.28% for A.D. 1–700; +.85% for A.D. 700–850; –.31% for A.D. 800–1050.
8. Recovery periods for situationally abandoned soils.

Note that our own settlement data, population estimates or hydration chronology did not contribute to his simulation, and in fact, some of Wingard's assumptions, such as the size of his seed population, differed markedly from our own demographic conclusions. Most important, his population thresholds are generated by maize production limits.

Wingard's soil model basically reflects choices that maize farmers would optimally have made, given previous constraints on land occupied and degraded under successive management strategies. No influences on their choices by political or social factors are assumed, although they undoubtedly existed.

Results: A Profile of Agricultural History

Wingard's main conclusions (see his population estimates in Figure 11-6) are as follows:

1. The seed population initially used a long-fallow strategy on the alluvial/foothill soils of the Copán pocket, which filled in to capacity at 3,000 people by the end of the 4th century. By about A.D. 575 this strategy had been extended over all other alluvial pockets, reaching capacity at about 5,000 people and necessitating a switch to a medium-term fallow system.
2. The medium-term fallow strategy on the alluvial/foothill soils reached its capacity by about A.D. 650 throughout the survey zone at a population level of just over 6,000 people.
3. An annual (permanent) wet-season cropping strategy was then established on the valley floor, supporting at capacity 6,400 people by A.D. 675.
4. Hillside soils were colonized at about A.D. 650–675 and then went through the same processes of extension and intensification outlined for the valley floor. About 120 sq km of uplands were deforested between A.D. 675 and 800 and around A.D. 700–800 "... the Copán Valley probably experienced a rather massive erosional event ..." (Wingard, 1992, p. 182). Sometime around A.D. 700–750 maize production outside the Copán pocket exceeded that within it. By A.D. 800 the valley had a

total population of about 14,000 people, and all soils were either in permanent cultivation or exhausted and lying fallow.

5. Land throughout the alluvial/foothill zones was then double-cropped annually, supporting 20,000 people by A.D. 850–900. Irrigation was applied to areas of less than 5% slope in the Copán pocket, allowing the peak population to reach about 22,000. Neither of these levels was sustainable, however, and population declined after A.D. 900.

6. By A.D. 1000 population had fallen to A.D. 800 levels, with some soils recovering lost fertility. Reasonable levels of productivity would always support some occupation.

Not surprisingly, given the topography of the Copán region, Wingard found erodibility to be the single greatest cause of decline in agricultural productivity.

COMPARISON OF THE SOIL AND SETTLEMENT MODELS

The two independent methods of calculating population produced remarkably similar peak figures—22,000 (soil model) and 27,753 (settlement model). Because our settlement-based simulation was geared to produce maximal figures, we believe that Wingard's lower estimate is the more plausible of the two.

Wingard's population peaks at A.D. 850–900; the settlement derived peak is shown at A.D. 750 (see Figures 11-2 and 11-6). Note, however, that there are three very similar high estimates in the latter extending to A.D. 900. In effect, the settlement peak could have occurred at any time between A.D. 750 and 850. Again, agreement is good.

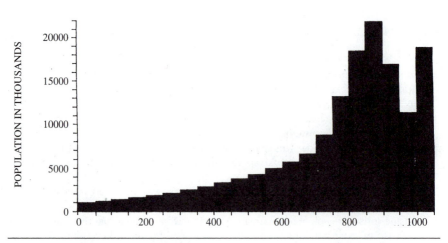

FIGURE 11-6   HUMAN CARRYING CAPACITY THROUGH TIME IN TERMS OF THE STAPLE CROP, MAIZE, WHICH IS ASSUMED TO MAKE UP 60% OF THE DIET IN WINGARD'S AGRICULTURAL PRODUCTION SIMULATION. THE "JUMP" OF POPULATION FOR THE LAST INTERVAL IS DEBATABLE, AND IS CAUSED BY THE ASSUMPTION IN THE SIMULATION THAT AT THIS TIME MUCH PREVIOUSLY ABANDONED LAND BECAME PRODUCTIVE AGAIN.

In the soil model the highest population estimate corresponds to an *overall* density of 110 people per sq km for the region Wingard sampled.[1] Densities of this magnitude are far more convincing than similar densities in the 200 to 300 person per sq km range projected for other parts of the Maya Lowlands, which we feel were neither reachable nor sustainable. The densities cited above from our settlement simulation are much higher because they apportion the population only to those areas of the landscape with reasonable agricultural potential.

Close agreement between the two models suggests that Wingard's assumed rapid rates of increase are accurate in order of magnitude terms. Processes of environmental transformation would be slowed down by greatly decreasing his seed population, or by decreasing the rates of growth. The seed population estimate of 1,000 people at A.D. 0 is certainly reasonable, however, given available archaeological evidence. Decreasing growth rates would produce a much later peak, but this is unacceptable—all previous estimates of the timing of the Copán population peak from all lines of evidence place it in the A.D. 750–900 range. No one, so far as we know, thinks that 22,000 people is an unreasonably high peak estimate (in fact the contrary is the case).

Wingard predicts the rapid colonization of upland areas during the last half of the 7th century. In the settlement model this process begins about 50 years earlier, and uplands fill in faster because population increases more rapidly. Large-scale erosion certainly occurred at Copán as a result of upland cultivation. As we saw in Chapter 8, excavations strongly suggest major erosion events at or about the time predicted by Wingard's simulation. Both models agree that population decline begins at about A.D. 900, but in the soil model there is no population plateau as shown for the period between A.D. 800 and 900 by the settlement model. The rate of decline is also less steep in the soil model (although remember this is partly a result of the mechanical way in which changes are factored into the settlement-based simulation). Wingard terminated his simulation at A.D. 1050, with an estimate for the valley as a whole of about 14,000 people. Only 3,000 are calculated for that time by the settlement model, which also shows that until A.D. 1150 population remained respectable outside the Copán pocket, then quickly decreased. The jump in population between A.D. 1100–1150 might not be realistic; it is based on the assumption that previously depleted lands became productive once again.

Had Wingard's simulation continued beyond A.D. 1050 the decline would have been interrupted and population stabilized, at least for a time, and a population of some reasonable size would remain present. There would never be a complete demographic collapse as the settlement model shows. Interestingly, Wingard's model predicts an even larger and more extended post-A.D. 900 population than that derived from settlement predictions.

There are two spatial dimensions of the soil model. One is extension beyond the alluvial/foothill zone of the Copán pocket to other parts of the valley. The

---

[1] By overall density we mean simply the relationship between population and the entire region considered, regardless of any internal variations in agricultural potential and hence population concentrations.

second and partly overlapping dimension is vertical—colonization of upland zones where soils are generally less fertile and stable. Wingard placed his seed population in the Copán pocket based on existing archaeological evidence and assumptions about the choices early agriculturists would have made. Had he planted his seed population elsewhere, say in intermontane alluvial pockets of the Sesesmil Valley, it would quickly have overrun the productive capacities of these small zones and colonized the Copán pocket, which thereafter would have rapidly developed the greatest demographic and productive weight in the system anyway. Overall, the simulation would not look very different.

According to Wingard's model all alluvial/foothill soils in the valley were utilized on a long fallow basis by A.D. 575. The settlement model should consequently show expansion into non-pocket zones between A.D. 400 (when the Copán pocket is filled to capacity) and A.D. 575. In fact it does. Thirty percent of the population is in these areas as early as A.D. 450–499, and rises to 41% by A.D. 575. By A.D. 675 settlement should be even heavier throughout all the alluvial/foothill lands under a permanent cultivation regime. The settlement model does show an absolute increase in nonpocket areas, but a percentage reduction vis-à-vis the pocket to 24% from the earlier 41%, indicating more concentration of population there than predicted.

Hillside cultivation begins in the soil model about A.D. 650 and uplands throughout the valley were heavily utilized by A.D. 700–750. By the latter date maize production outside the Copán pocket exceeds that within, so outlying populations should be greater than 50% of the total if people are living near the lands they cultivate. The settlement model (optimally reliable at this point) does not conform to this spatial expectation. Growth in the pocket outstrips all other regions combined, which collectively have only 23% of the population. We will explore the implications of this imbalance later.

Spatial patterning of the hydration dates shows that a few upland sites were occupied earlier than assumed by Wingard, but of course, there are upland pockets of good alluvial/foothill land. According to our dates colonization of zones at elevations of >750 m occurs just when Wingard predicts it should— roughly between A.D. 600 and 700. Widespread erosion of upland zones in the soil model results in population declines at higher elevations at about A.D. 750–800. The settlement model conforms reasonably well to this expectation at 900 m asl and above, but at intermediate elevations population declines later than predicted—about A.D. 900–950. On the other hand, the expectation that upland sites were generally founded later, had shorter occupations, and were abandoned earlier than valley floor sites, is strongly supported by Paine's and Freter's (1996) statistical study of occupational life spans of sites with five or more dates.

Although there are differences between the soil and settlement models, the degree of fit between them is really quite remarkable given the essential independence of the data sets and the many errors and simulation distortions to which each is prone. General population profiles are reassuringly similar, exhibiting a single accelerating growth curve with a downturn at the end of the Late Classic.

The settlement model predicts much greater demographic concentration in the Copán pocket population and a faster decline than the soil model, and population does not stabilize at some reasonable level after A.D. 1050 as the soil model predicts. We nevertheless believe that the demographic decline shown by the settlement model accurately captures the general trend.

Behind these abstractly modeled processes we must remember that there were real people, and that the consequences of changing populations and agricultural strategies immediately affected both their day-to-day lives, their long-term adaptive choices, and consequently their well-being. As time went by, some people had to work harder for less by farming on hillsides rather than cultivating the deep soils of the valley floor. Farmers forced to shift to shorter fallow periods, and ultimately permanent cultivation, also experienced declining yields. Some people, in short, were advantaged over others. Moreover, some of these changes occurred extremely rapidly over only one or two generations and must have been socially and economically disruptive. Later on we will examine the effects of such changes in detail when we consider the mature Copán polity and its collapse.

SUMMARY

Our two independent simulations of population and agricultural history plausibly reinforce one another and yield the following general conclusions:

1. After a very long interval of low population (i.e., before A.D. 400), there was a rapid increase of population, a period of relative stability, and then a gradual decline.
2. Peak population size of the polity might have reached 28,000 people but was more realistically in the 22,000 range. Demographically speaking, the Copán polity was much smaller than previously envisioned.
3. During almost all periods, population was heavily concentrated in the Copán pocket, and by about A.D. 700–750, settlement distribution was no longer congruent with the distribution of productive land.
4. The nature of Copán's agricultural landscape and the human modifications of it heavily affected patterns of land use and the distribution and character of settlements through time.
5. Human-induced processes of environmental degradation were especially pronounced after A.D. 600.
6. There was no catastrophic elite or general demographic collapse at or just after the demise of Copán's royal dynasty, but rather a protracted process of political and population decline.

In Chapter 1 we described the Copán agricultural landscape using the image of islands of high quality land floating in a sea of comparatively infertile and unstable uplands. Our description was not merely a useful visual one but has larger implications as well. Due to their environmental and social conscription, island environments have been singled out by many anthropologists as ideal natural laboratories for examining the interrelationships between population, resources, and sociopolitical complexity.

Although obviously not an island in the strict sense of the word, the Copán polity is about the best approximation of such a circumscribed situation we can find in the Maya Lowlands. The agricultural history of the polity and its environmental consequences described above are generally similar to those summarized for Hawai'i by Kirch (1990). Histograms of occupations derived from dated household clusters in one of the most powerful Hawai'ian chiefdoms (Kirch, 1990, pp. 324–325) closely resemble those from Copán, suggesting that the processes that we have detected are far from unusual in a larger comparative perspective.

We now have provided answers to some of the questions posed at the beginning of this chapter. We make no claims for precision in the results of our simulations. They are our best efforts given what we know to date about Copán's archaeological record and comparative demography. Future work probably will necessitate some changes in various details. Our results are, however, based on extensive and methodologically sound settlement and landscape research, including an unprecedented grasp of settlement chronology, and we believe the general conclusions will stand. We predict that despite future tinkering (which we ourselves will undoubtedly do), order of magnitude estimates for the peak population of the Copán polity will hover in the 20,000–30,000 person range, and that the general trends will remain as we have identified them. Perhaps most important of all, we have tried to be explicit about how we came to our conclusions so that others can use or modify our simulations to suit their own data sets and assumptions, or can derive test implications from them to structure future research.

CHAPTER 12

Eighth-Century Copán:
The Kingdom at Its Height

INTRODUCTION

Yax Pasah, the 16th ruler of Copán, had much to feel complacent about as he surveyed his kingdom at the end of the 8th century. From his vantage point high on the Acropolis he could see, within a few km of his ancestral palaces and temples, the houses of thousands of his subjects. No Copán king before him had ever ruled so many people. Clustered within a radius of a few hundred yards on the valley floor were the impressive household compounds of many noble families, some of them his relatives by marriage and members of his royal court. Farther up the hillsides were visible the farmsteads and gardens of the common families whose labor and devotion were central to the vigor of his dynasty. On a clear day scores of people could be seen working in the quarries on the northern edge of the Copán pocket, from which a steady stream of porters carried building stone for the great royal projects *Yax Pasah* had initiated. The final stages of the great Structure 11 were being completed, as were the upper portions of the immense pyramid-temple Structure 16. Dwarfed by these huge projects, but of great personal importance to the king, was Structure 18, the tomb being prepared as his final resting place in the heart of the Acropolis.

Royal artisans were busy executing the sculptural programs essential to all these buildings—depictions in eternal stone of gods, earlier rulers of the dynasty, and other great notables of the kingdom. *Yax Pasah* himself had carefully overseen the designs and inscriptions for all this sculpture, in which he prominently figured as the great ruler, guarantor of prosperity and order, and the last and greatest dynast in a line of Copán kings stretching back 400 years. The king was also featured in the splendid rituals associated with the dedication of all these buildings and monuments, in which he exhibited his royal person to his subjects of all ranks.

Only the oldest of his people, fortunately, could remember the embarrassing capture and sacrifice of the 13th ruler, *18 Rabbit,* by the upstart ruler of Quiriguá 60 years before. Since then tangible reassertions of the power of Copán's kings, most notably embodied in the great Hieroglyphic Stairway, had largely erased the memory of this political embarrassment, and skilled diplomacy had reestablished

Yax Pasah's relations with that nearby kingdom. Just to make sure that no one misjudged his authority, however, *Yax Pasah* dictated that many of his monuments portray him as a mighty warrior, and that themes of war, sacrifice, and death were prominently displayed at the Main Group to impress both his own subjects and visitors from distant realms.

Much of this we could reasonably have inferred more than 20 years ago. The research reviewed in earlier chapters that has been completed since that time now enables us to step back and take a more detailed, analytical, anthropological look at the political, social, and economic underpinnings of the mature Copán polity. The picture that emerges shows that, for all his kingdom's apparent prosperity and splendor, *Yax Pasah's* complacency was not so well deserved. In the following sections we provide our own concept of the polity during the 8th century and also discuss major issues and debates among archaeologists that remain unresolved.

The Urban Status of Copán

The Copán Main Group achieved its final form late in the 8th century, as did the surrounding urban core. We now understand this great concentration of structures much more completely than ever before and can relate it to a central issue in Maya archaeology—were Classic Maya centers urban in character? If urban places are defined as the largest and most complex settlements in a network of communities, or as political capitals, then the answer is yes. Tikal, Palenque, Copán, and scores of other centers were cities. If we take a more broadly comparative perspective, the answer is not so simple. Clearly even the largest Classic Maya centers were much different from great central Mexican Mesoamerican cities such as Teotihuacán or the Aztec capital, Tenochtitlán. The latter were spatially more extensive, had much larger, denser, and heterogeneous populations, and a wider variety of functions, particularly economic ones.

We believe that Copán conforms to another distinctive model of central place characteristic of Lowland Maya civilization called the *regal-ritual city* (Fox, 1977; Sanders and Webster, 1988). Such places essentially consist of the households of kings, along with the associated political, ritual, and ideological apparatus essential to dynastic rule. The Tulane University excavations at Copán have revealed that the royal residential or "palace" facilities in the strict sense were at Group 10L-2, located just off the southern end of the Acropolis. Although extremely well constructed and embellished with sculpture, this group by itself strongly resembles other impressive elite compounds in Las Sepulturas. There may be older palace facilities buried beneath the late architecture of the Main Group, but by the 8th century its temples, ball court, courtyards, and carved monuments constituted the hypertrophied political/ritual apparatus of the kingdom that immensely overshadowed the attached royal residence. The Main Group is less a construction than an accretion—400 years of superimposed buildings, many of which symbolized cosmic order and centrality, commemorated royal ancestors (and in some cases contained their tombs), communicated the power of the king, and served as the setting for his ritual and political acts.

Permanent residents of the regal-ritual core of Copán (the Main Group and Group 10L-2 together) were probably few in number—we estimated 250 people in our population simulation—and included the king, other members of the royal lineage, various retainers and officials, and elite young men in their special dormitory. These, plus situationally present outsiders, constituted the royal court.

Copán takes on a decidedly more conventional city-like aspect if we expand our perspective to include the whole urban core. In fact, the reason we use the term "urban" for this zone is because its population was so dense and nucleated. With perhaps as many as 12,000 people in just 1 sq km, the urban core falls well within the range of preindustrial cities in many parts of the world in terms of population size and density. Of course, the Copán urban enclave is spatially much more limited than those in many other Mesoamerican cities. Nonetheless, Copán's population concentration is impressive and in fact greater than that yet found at other Classic Maya centers.

As in ancient cities elsewhere, population was not only dense but included people of all ranks from kings and nobles to the very humble commoners, thus reflecting the larger composition of the society. We now recognize that the urban core was essentially a huge residential enclave dominated by elite compounds. Even inhabitants of its smaller groups probably had close connections to nobles living nearby. Most of the nobles in the Copán political system lived so close to the Main Group that they could easily have participated in court functions.

One surprising result of our population simulations was the imbalance between urban core and outlying populations. Roughly half the people in the Copán kingdom lived in the core, and we will shortly investigate some implications of this unusual pattern.

An important characteristic of regal-ritual centers is that they have very limited productive or redistributive functions in economic terms but rather are generally places of consumption, supported by the goods and services provided by others. Because of their strongly residential character, they are not strikingly differentiated from other settlements in the system, which also consist of households, albeit ones that are much more modest and short lived. Distinctions between the "urban" population and people living in the countryside are therefore not sharply developed. Cities such as Tenochtitlán and Teotihuacán, of course, consumed goods from the rural areas but also were places of production for both local and long distance exchange. In part, such economic complexity is stimulated by large, dense populations, and we thought that evidence of specialized production might be found at Las Sepulturas. None of our excavations, however, revealed much convincing evidence for such large-scale, specialized production or for market exchange.

In summary, while the Copán urban core is city-like in demographic terms, it seems to lack the range of economic and other functions characteristic of more well-developed urban places. It conforms much better to the regal-ritual model in that it is primarily a ruling place dominated by residences of kings and lords.

POLITICAL AND SOCIAL ORGANIZATION

As elsewhere in the Classic Maya Lowlands, kingship is the most obtrusive political role expressed in art and inscriptions at Copán, and we have already reviewed the main outlines of the Copán dynastic sequence. Because Copán's epigraphic tradition emphasized comparatively ahistorical themes, there are many details of kingship that remain uncertain. For example, because kinship expressions are few, we cannot clearly reconstruct patterns of royal succession, which might have been more complex than simple unilineal transmission from father to son or other patrilateral relative (e.g., brothers, grandsons, nephews). Rene Viel (in press) suggests that several court factions contributed rulers at different times, and that succession was not always smooth. However it was transmitted, kingship was the central institution of the Copán polity, and kings were continuously in office, although not necessarily continually in effective control over political events. What seems certain, though, is that despite their assertions of authority and ritual centrality, Classic Maya kings, *Yax Pasah* included, were not autocrats but had to negotiate power-sharing with other highborn, notable people.

Epigraphers working with texts from other Maya centers have begun to identify many other nonroyal official or court titles that flesh out details of political organization (see Stuart, 1995, for a summary). Insights from Copán's inscriptions are unfortunately limited. There are hints that from the very beginning of his reign *Yax Pasah's* royal power might have been circumscribed by other nobles of quasi-royal status. Chief among these was a mysterious individual called Personage A (Stuart 1992). Personage A was closely related in some way to *Yax Pasah,* was "seated" in his office on the same day that *Yax Pasah* became king, and most unexpectedly sported the *k'ul ahaw* (holy lord) title normally reserved for rulers. Assuming that Personage A was a real person and not a deity (a distinct possibility), several questions arise. Did this individual in some way share power with *Yax Pasah* as a co-ruler? Was he an heir-apparent, or even eventually a 17th ruler? We cannot answer these questions, but *Yax Pasah* probably did not reign supreme. Quite possibly the Sepulturas elite group 8N-11, which contains a skyband bench with imagery normally associated with kings, was the home of a co-ruler.

We also saw in Chapter 4 that during *Yax Pasah's* time some other great nobles were able to employ labor on an unprecedented scale, building themselves residential compounds in the urban core that favorably compared in many ways with the royal residence. They also began to exhibit their own façade sculpture, carved benches, and public altars, and the impressive outlying Type 4 center of Río Amarillo even had its own emblem glyph. Some archaeologists (Fash et al., 1992) believe that after the dynasty's loss of face in A.D. 738, a special *popol nah* (mat house) was erected on the Acropolis by the weak 14th king as a place where rulers had to negotiate with increasingly assertive nobles. *Yax Pasah* seems to have built little during the last half of his reign, and all of this evidence together suggests a weakened dynasty in which rulers increasingly had to defer to other powerful individuals and factions.

Part of the rapprochement between kings and nobles may have involved inter-marriage among their families. Although we have no direct proof of such relationships, some Las Sepulturas nobles did commission inscriptions that include titles, such as "scribe," linking them to *Yax Pasah* and his royal court (such titles might have been more honorific than functional). We have no good evidence of any kind of complex, professional bureaucracy. Important affairs of the kingdom were probably in large part handled by royal relatives and other courtiers close to the king, as an extension of the management of the royal household, or of those of lesser noble-courtiers. Quite possibly there was very little specialized decision-making or authority, with much administration carried out on a case-by-case basis by the most appropriate and experienced royal relative or courtier.

Most people at Copán, of course, were commoners. Archaeologists routinely apply a rule of thumb to ancient agrarian societies with simple technologies: something on the order of 80 to 90% of all people had to be food producers. Although a convincing logical deduction, this assumption is seldom rigorously tested for particular prehistoric societies. Our settlement surveys and demographic reconstructions suggest that the ratio is just about right for late 8th-century Copán, when about 70% of all Copañecos lived in unimposing residential groups. Many of the residual 30% of the population who lived in Type 3 and 4 elite residences were undoubtedly themselves of low social standing, thus bringing the estimate close to the cross-cultural expectation. We suspect that titled people and their immediate families were a tiny proportion of the total population—say 5% or less.

If we were able to visit 8th-century Copán as experienced anthropologists, our initial impression would probably be that there were two conspicuous categories of people: a vast number who produced food or were otherwise engaged in nonspecialized, unskilled labor (the commoners or basic producers discussed in Chapter 7) and a much smaller number who were supported by such efforts (consumers or nobles). Closer inspection would reveal many gradations of wealth, prestige, and status within these broad categories, and perhaps a few anomalies, such as artisan-nobles, perhaps even the sons of kings, who produced such things as sculpture and other elite items. On analogy with the 16th-century Maya, there might also have been some slaves attached to rich households, although there is no direct evidence for them.

At the risk of overgeneralization, we believe it is useful to conceive of Copán social organization in this dualistic way because it emphasizes what we would *not* see—a vigorous middle social level made up of professional merchants, full-time craftspeople, or other nonfarmers, a pattern found (albeit comprising a comparatively small proportion of the populace) among later Mesoamerican peoples such as the Aztecs. This is an important point because archaeologists often use the presence of full-time economic specialization as a barometer of general social complexity.

Our assertion that Copán had a comparatively simple economic system in terms of specialization is not just a guess but based on sound analyses. Two examples involve sculpture and obsidian, both very obtrusive classes of artifacts at Copán. Visitors to Copán today are properly impressed by the ancient output of sculpture. One easily jumps to the conclusion that there must have been many full-time, professional sculptors. Archaeological experiments carried out at Copán by Elliot Abrams (1984b, 1987, 1994), however, show that ordinary people can rapidly master the carving of complex iconographic elements, and that very small numbers of sculptors could quickly carve large monuments such as the stelae in the Main Group, provided that they are given patterns showing the required themes and symbols.

John Mallory's (1984) analysis of obsidian production and consumption similarly points out the small number of people necessary to procure the raw material, make, and distribute finished obsidian tools. Along with the paucity of obvious evidence for specialized production found in our rural surveys and excavations, such studies indicate comparatively little economic specialization in the Copán economic system.

We now must face two critical questions with regard to the overall structure of sociopolitical organization at Copán. How did powerful, titled people relate to the king? How did rulers and political elites together relate to common people? Classic Maya inscriptions, whether at Copán or anywhere else, provide few definite answers to the first question, and none at all to the second.

There are two main ways to account for most of the wealthy, privileged people who lived in Copán's impressive elite residences. They might have been lesser relatives of the royal line (i.e., descendants of earlier kings) who were not directly eligible to occupy the throne because of genealogical distance from the central royal family. Alternatively, they might have been families that enjoyed independent high rank and wealth, with very deep genealogical identities of their own. Nor are these two possibilities mutually distinct. Both kinds of aristocrats were probably present at Copán, and in any case independent noble families, if present, probably would have tried, in good Mesoamerican fashion, to establish marriage links to the family of the ruler (and vice versa), as already noted. We currently have no direct evidence concerning these relationships. Perhaps new evidence in the form of additional inscriptions or sophisticated genetic studies will shed light on them in the future.

Even more intransigent is the nature of the social, economic, and political relations between commoners on the one hand, and nobles and kings on the other, and this issue is fundamental to understanding the specific political structure and political economy of 8th-century Copán. So far we have used the rather vague terms "polity" or "kingdom" when referring to Copán, rather than "chiefdom" or "state," which are particular kinds of political societies. As William Sanders (1992, p. 279) has pointed out, terms such as "stratification" and "ranking" refer to forms of sociopolitical organization and only loosely relate to such political types as chiefdoms or states, and it is the organizational principles that we wish to emphasize here.

Our conscious avoidance of loaded terminology with respect to the political categorization of whole polities reflects the difficulty, despite all of our research and that of Mayanists elsewhere, in reconstructing sociopolitical relations in the absence of detailed historical information. The basic issue for Copán is whether political elites were effectively separated from commoners by a distinct social gulf—*the stratified model*—or whether kin relationships connected people of all social ranks—*the kinship model*.

Because of Copán's location on the margins of the Maya culture zone, a complicating dimension in reconstructing relationships between nobles and commoners is an ethnic one. People inhabited the Copán region for hundreds or even thousands of years before Classic Maya cultural patterns appeared in the 5th century, and throughout the whole history of the polity its ceramic traditions were different from those of the Maya Lowlands proper. Our excavations of some rural residential groups, moreover, failed to turn up the patterns of household burials anticipated for Maya commoners. On the basis of present evidence we cannot know whether the commoner segment of society had non-Maya ethnic origins that differentiated them from intrusive Maya elites. If they did, the kings and nobles who were the bearers of the larger Lowland Maya Great Tradition might have considered themselves to be largely of different descent than their subjects.

Leaving the ethnic question aside, the stratified model posits well-developed social gulfs or classlike differences between nobles and commoners. We have many ethnographic examples of such arrangements from other parts of the world. For example, 18th-century native kingdoms in Hawai'i were dominated by a small class of hereditary rulers and elites who had exalted lines of descent, who conceived themselves to be unrelated to commoners for all practical purposes, who dominated all positions of political importance, and who claimed outright ownership of all productive resources. Commoners lived in small family groups that lacked broader, corporate kinship organization, worked the land under the direction of managers representing the elite proprietors, and provided labor for elite enterprises and war. Essentially they were marginalized political and economic clients who served elite patrons not related to them by kinship in any meaningful way. In such highly centralized societies elites could, with comparative impunity, disenfranchise commoner families or communities from their agricultural landscapes—an extremely potent dimension of political power.

Nor must we look very far afield from Copán to find this kind of system—a rather similar one characterized the early 16th-century Quiché kingdom in the Maya highlands of Guatemala. The obtrusiveness of royal and elite people in the art and inscriptions of Copán is consistent with such stratification.

Alternatively, the kinship model links even the most humble Copán Maya with lords and rulers. Such a model still allows for pronounced differences among individuals or families in terms of social rank, power, prestige, wealth, and access to offices and titles, because individuals are differentiated through their respective positions in descent groups. But it also emphasizes the vertical ties and reciprocal responsibilities of kinspeople of different ranks vis-à-vis one another, and the existence of large, corporate kinship groups (lineages) that had their own strong traditional identities, resources, leaders, and political agendas. The highest ranking of all such corporate kin groups would have been the royal lineage, and to the extent that the actual royal family was conceptually separated from other people of rank, this model includes some elements of stratification.

Note that in this politically less centralized kinship model, nonroyal nobles are in somewhat ambivalent political positions. On the one hand, they derive their high status, prestige, and leadership roles from genealogical ranking within their kin groups, and lesser kinspeople are their natural political supporters, whose interests they must represent and protect, and who may not easily be disenfranchised from their agricultural holdings. On the other hand, such highly ranked nobles have more in common, in terms of their elite lifestyles and sensibilities, with other highly ranked lineage elites and members of the royal family, with whom they might intermarry.

The first, or class-like model is more politically centralized in the sense that rulers had direct, or unimpeded, access to the labor and products of commoners. In the second kin-based model there was less centralization, because rulers had to work through lesser nobles to acquire such access.

The two models have some things in common. In both, most people were food producers. In both, elites were few in number and had privileged political roles, held high offices or titles, and enjoyed considerable wealth. Kinship was very important in both models, but in the stratified model only among elites, whereas it pervaded all social ranks in the second kin-based case. In both kinds of systems there was considerable potential for internal status rivalry among political elites (see Webster, 1998). A major difference is that in the kinship model elites had direct kin connections and strong reciprocal obligations to ordinary people, who were thus not politically marginalized, who were buffered to some degree from royal demands, and who formed the natural political constituencies of their lordly senior relatives.

These models are, of course, part of our etic or "outside observers" view of Maya society. No matter which one is most appropriate for Copán, the Classic Maya themselves, from their emic viewpoint, no doubt thought about their social and political relationships rather differently than we do. Nevertheless, the models do focus our attention on some very important kinds of relationships, and our conceptions of Copán's 8th-century sociopolitical organization and the subsequent decline of the kingdom depend to a large degree on which one we choose to apply. While we cannot confidently discriminate between the stratified and kinship models (and of course, there are others we could discuss as well), we do have some suggestive lines of evidence.

Settlement Patterns and Energetic Expenditures on Architecture

By the mid-8th century there were many discrete elite residential groups, some of which had been occupied for centuries; over 40 of these might have been occupied during *Yax Pasah's* reign. While some might have been the establishments of members of the royal lineage, this settlement pattern more strongly suggests the presence of what Sanders (1989) has called multiple *maximal lineages,* each of which had its own hereditary high-ranking families supported by the labor of lesser kinspeople. According to his view, the elite occupants of these residences were leaders of their corporate kinship groups, which might have numbered in the hundreds or even thousands of people, and managers of their collective resources.

In some ancient civilizations such as Old Kingdom Egypt, all important people were officials of the royal household. Their authority was delegated by the king, and technically they possessed no personal wealth of any significance and no natural political constituencies of their own. We argue that Copán's political organization differed radically from this pattern and more closely approximates the kinship model outlined above: great noble families, supported by their commoner kin, constituted potent political factions with their own lands and other forms of wealth, and with their own authority not delegated by the kings.

Earlier we referred to Elliot Abrams' (1984b, 1994) studies of Maya construction and monument carving, and his investigations of the labor costs of residences are also germane to the issue of sociopolitical differentiation. Abrams quantified the construction costs for 46 residences on all social levels, and Gonlin (1993) later used his methods to estimate how much labor was expended on residential facilities at small, rural sites. Abrams calculates that a residential-type building of royal scale would have required about 24,700 person-days of labor. Complex elite residences such as the House of the Bacabs in Group 9N-8 absorbed on the order of 7,500 to 11,000 person-days of labor. Small commoner residences, according to Abrams and Gonlin, fall into the 19 to 154 person-day range.

Obviously Copán society was strongly hierarchical as measured by the amounts of labor that social groups of different kinds were able to mobilize. While commoner houses were easily built with the labor and materials at the disposal of the small household group, elites and kings were able to tap much larger labor pools and specialized materials, not only for houses, but also for shrines and other specialized structures, as well as complex sculptural programs. Even so, Abrams found that costs were far lower than expected and did not indicate oppressive demands by elites, a point to which we will return shortly. If the royal level of construction is excluded, the sample of residences examined by Abrams and Gonlin falls into a reasonable continuum (Figure 12-1).

Artifacts and Burials

Artifact assemblages recovered from households of different ranks also show less variation than we originally expected (Webster, Gonlin, and Sheets, 1997). Certainly elite rank sites are richer in the range of associated artifacts and also have more of some kinds of items, much as a well-to-do household today might have more television sets than a poor one. In general, household implements that have survived do not look much different at small rural sites than at urban core Type 4 groups such as 8N-11 or 9N-8. Common people, it seems, were not denied possession of most kinds of objects by sumptuary rules. Architecture therefore turns out to be a better measure of social differentiation and wealth at Copán than household possessions, as the Harvard project originally predicted.

Archaeologists frequently rely upon burials to detect differences in social status or wealth. Some very rich burials have been recovered at Copán, virtually

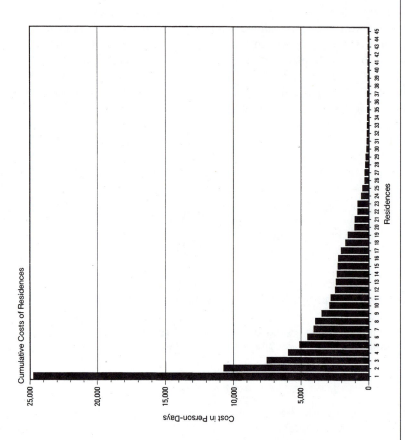

FIGURE 12-1 CONSTRUCTION COSTS OF 45 COPÁN RESIDENCES EXPRESSED AS PERSON–DAYS OF LABOR AS DETERMINED BY ELLIOTT ABRAMS.

all from the Main Group or the Los Cementerios zone of the royal household. Outside these royal precincts, the richest burial so far found, called "El Brujo" (the "Sorcerer") is from a 5th-century grave in the urban core Group 9N-8. Although we have excavated many burials dating to the 8th century from this and other elite groups, none is very impressive. The most obvious dimension of variation is grave form, which varies from simple pits to elaborate chambers built of cut-stone and roofed with large stone slabs (Diamanti, 1991). Even the latter, however, were not very costly to build.

Although no full analysis has yet been done of mortuary offerings associated with the hundreds of PAC II burials, we can say that (with the exception of El Brujo) most offerings were quite modest. Even in the chamber tombs a typical set of offerings consists of several ordinary pottery vessels. Moreover, costly items such as jade plaques or ear spools are sometimes found in very modest cist or pit graves. On the basis of current burial information it would be difficult to segregate an elite component of Copán society from a non-elite one, apart from the royal tombs themselves.

Diet and Health

A common archaeological assumption is that people of high status and wealth in stratified societies enjoyed a higher quality of life and enhanced well-being than less privileged people, including better diets and health, and less stress. One of our most unexpected research findings is Reed's discovery, reviewed in Chapter 9, that people of all social statuses had diets that were extremely high in maize, and that people of high rank seemed not to have been eating large amounts of high quality animal food. It remains to be seen whether this same pattern holds for people of royal rank. Nor, judging from both Storey's and Whittington's skeletal studies, did people who lived in impressive elite residences enjoy strikingly better levels of physical well-being or life expectancy than those from more modest households.

While none of these lines of evidence in itself is conclusive, we believe that taken together they strongly suggest that sociopolitical organization at Copán in the 8th century was predominantly kin-based, as opposed to highly stratified. If this interpretation is correct, Copán was probably always a polity characterized by strong internal factions that were competing against each other and the royal lineage, with obvious implications for the collapse of the polity that we will review in the next chapter. We must qualify this conclusion, however, by recognizing one final important point—Copán's sociopolitical organization was not static, and our conception of it will thus vary according to time period. Political arrangements at the time of the founder in the 5th century were no doubt profoundly different than those in *Yax Pasah's* time. We suspect that by the late 8th century two main changes were occurring. First, the polity became more stratified as nobles and royalty alike increasingly lived lives different from their subjects, recognized common elite interests, and intermarried. Second, nobles were increasingly competing with one another and with the royal dynasty. Both changes are intimately related to developments in the agrarian and political economy.

THE AGRARIAN ECONOMY

The basis for Copán's prosperity was local agricultural production underwritten by the domestic labor available to commoner households. As noted at the end of Chapter 7, an important but unresolved issue is how farmers got access to productive land. The answer to this question depends in large part on which of the above models of sociopolitical organization we use. In the stratified model, commoners would have had no "natural" rights to land not granted them by rulers. In the kinship model noble-kinspeople would have served as stewards for land corporately held by the maximal lineage (and of course there are other possibilities as well).

While a variety of crops was grown, we now have excellent empirical evidence that maize was by far the single most important staple, almost certainly heavily supplemented by beans. During *Yax Pasah's* time the floor of the valley and its adjacent uplands must have given the impression of a gigantic patchwork of cornfields among which were interspersed the houses, orchards, and dooryard gardens of farming families. Most people spent their lives in a yearly round of agricultural work, just, as their ancestors always had.

This much is quite clear, but our settlement surveys, demographic reconstructions, and agricultural simulation turned up a very puzzling pattern: the population, especially in the 8th century, was not distributed rationally in terms of agricultural production. Far too many people lived in the Copán pocket, where overall densities were in excess of 900 people per sq km. They could not conceivably have supported themselves by food production on the local landscape, much of which by this time was already heavily degraded. This conclusion is independently substantiated by Wingard's simulation, according to which at least half of all the food required by the whole population must have been produced outside the Copán pocket by the early 8th century.

The obvious solution is that food grown in other parts of the main valley and in the tributary valleys subsidized growing shortfalls in the Copán pocket. Certainly grain could have been hauled from as far away as Río Amarillo. Such a scenario, however, raises another serious question—where did the labor come from for such surplus production? Because of the simplicity of Maya agricultural technology and the lack of nonhuman sources of labor, farming families could only produce very small surpluses in excess of their domestic needs. By midway through *Yax Pasch's* reign, if the settlement distributions are correctly reconstructed, only about 5,300 people lived outside the Copán pocket. Such a small number of farmers (only 24% of all the inhabitants of the valley) could not possibly have produced over half of the food necessary for the population as a whole. In some way, Copán pocket labor must have subsidized outlying agricultural production.

People walk considerable distances to their fields today, and much land in the Sesesmil Valley or the El Jaral or Santa Rita pockets, was close enough so that people living in the Copán pocket in Classic times could have cultivated fields there. The most distant alluvial pocket, however, Río Amarillo, is about 15 to 20 km (or about a 3- to 4-hour walk) from the Main Group—too far for an easy round trip in a single day. One possibility is that some people spent part of the agricultural season actually living in distant parts of the valley not just in field-huts, but in more substantial farmsteads, then returned to their principal residences with their harvested crops.

While Freter questions the artifactual evidence for intermittent occupation, Webster and Gonlin believe that some sites, such as site 7D-3-1 (described in Chapter 7), might have been used in this manner. If so, we have "double-counted" some sites in our calculations; such an error would shift our population figures closer to Wingard's, which we feel are more reasonable anyway. Situational use of outlying sites as secondary or seasonal residences might also explain why so few burials are found in them—people who died at places far from their homes were brought back to the Copán pocket to be buried or otherwise disposed of.

But if intermittent rural occupation did occur, the question still remains: Why did people choose to live so far from where they had to carry out their all-important agricultural tasks? Part of the answer is probably sheer inertia in the settlement system—most people from early times traditionally lived in the Copán pocket and continued to do so for complex social and cultural reasons. A more important factor, however, was probably political. Farmers are quite rational about the ways they expend their labor, and Copán's elites probably meddled with peoples' decisions about where to live for their own reasons. In short, we think farmers were purposely inhibited from distributing themselves more rationally on the landscape, an inference supported by the later decentralization of population after A.D. 900, when elites were losing their power.

THE POLITICAL ECONOMY

This is a convenient point to turn our attention to the *political economy,* by which we mean the control or management of significant components of the economy by elites, who thus facilitated the acquisition, maintenance, and augmentation of their high positions, prestige, wealth, power, and authority. We know virtually nothing from Classic Maya inscriptions or art about such matters, and they are extremely difficult to reconstruct from archaeological data alone.

From the point of view of Copán's political economy, the single most important thing we would like to know is how individuals or groups asserted rights over basic resources, particularly land and labor. If the kinship model is correct in its essentials, then land, the most important resource, might have been held by corporate kin groups, whose high ranking members served as managers or stewards of it (Sanders, 1992). In return, they were supported by contributions of food and labor from the domestic economies of their producer-kinspeople. If the more stratified model applies, elites claimed to be proprietors of all productive resources, and in return for their use extracted goods and services from unattached commoner-clients. We already saw that the two proposed models of political organization have quite different implications for how elites claimed access to basic resources and how they could influence commoner claims to the agricultural landscape.

No matter which of these models is correct, we see very little evidence that Copán elites effectively managed agricultural production at the grass-roots level. Farming families knew perfectly well how to apply their labor to grow crops and could make most of the tools and facilities necessary for agricultural tasks.

More specifically, Copán's kings and elites seem largely to have ignored the agricultural infrastructure. They conspicuously failed to sponsor drainage of swamps, terracing of hillsides, or other agroengineering projects designed to increase, or at least stabilize, agricultural production. On the other hand, of course, they might well have tried to guarantee the prosperity of the realm through rituals, which to Maya sensibilities might have seemed to be equally pragmatic and efficacious management strategies.

Elites probably did have to manage access to land and other necessary resources. As population increased, more and more people had to work harder on more marginal parts of the landscape, where the security of their household economies was increasingly diminished. Whichever model of sociopolitical organization we prefer, elites by the 8th century probably had to manage the potential social discord and competition thus generated (more about this in the Chapter 13).

We must also consider another possibility—that as productive land became more limited and hence valuable, parts of it that had previously been held corporately became privatized. As we saw in Chapter 1, a striking pattern of the modern political economy of the Copán Valley is the concentration of high quality land in the hands of a few families. Under increasingly competitive conditions, ancient elite managers of corporate lands might have sought to establish more personal rights over the most valuable parts of the landscape—especially the irrigable zones of the valley floor in the Copán pocket. Control over such lands would strengthen their political leverage and augment their status and wealth. Kinspeople were increasingly transformed into economic clients. Here we see a process of emergent economic stratification, and we believe, based on our data, that something like this probably happened in 8th-century Copán.

If prized lands did gravitate into the control of privileged people, they might have been put to two main uses. By granting access to such lands to clients, elite patrons could have garnered both greater wealth and political support. Alternatively, they could have been devoted to the cultivation of nonsubsistence commercial crops, such as cacao, or more likely tobacco (for which the Copán Valley has been famed at least since the 18th century). Export of such products would have increased elite wealth, but at the same time decreased subsistence production when the kingdom could least afford it.

We have no direct evidence for such increased economic stratification, but kings and elites clearly had two major economic concerns. The first was extraction of enough food from farmers to provision their own households and support their ritual and political agendas, including the construction of buildings and monuments. This could have been accomplished either by asserting rights to products of the land directly, or rights to labor. Whichever strategy was used, most farming households would not have been hard-pressed to produce the necessary surpluses, because the proportion of nonfood producers in the society was so low. Most families could probably easily grow a surplus of 10% or so above their domestic needs, and as long as good land was available, probably did not feel overly burdened by the need to do so. Nor was the requirement to turn over part of their production necessarily couched in oppressive or even demanding terms. As long as things were going well, farmers might have considered their contributions to elites as reasonable support of valued leaders and senior kinspeople, who in turn looked out for the interests of common folk. But, of course, by the 8th century sociopolitical conditions were becoming increasingly worse, a theme we return to in the next chapter.

The second obvious preoccupation of elite people was to mobilize the labor necessary to build and maintain their elaborate household facilities. On the royal level, labor also had to be expended on many other kinds of construction projects, including ancestral temples, ball courts, altars, and stelae. Generations of Maya archaeologists, viewing site cores dominated by monumental architectural complexes, have imagined ceaseless construction activity and heavy, perhaps even oppressive, demands for labor. However intuitively convincing this impression is, few have ever tested it.

Fortunately, Abrams's studies of the energetics of construction, plus our own population reconstructions, provide the means to simulate the potential output of large buildings at Copán. Abrams focused on residences, but later Webster and Kirker (1995) applied his measures to the construction of large temple architecture at Copán. They discovered that, however impressive buildings on the scale of Structure 26 (the Temple of the Hieroglyphic Stairway) might appear, they really did not absorb very much labor. In fact, given the size of the population, construction labor was actually underutilized in the 8th century. Copán's kings were able to project psychological impressions of power and prestige while not paying too high a political price by making excessive demands on their subjects. To sum up, it is difficult to know exactly how Maya elites and commoners interacted in economic terms. Two things seem certain, however. First, the flow of material goods and labor tended to be from the bottom up. Second, elite demands for food or labor were small enough not to seriously stress the producing population as long as the resource base remained sound.

TERRITORIAL EXTENT AND INFLUENCE OF THE COPÁN POLITY

We are accustomed to thinking about political systems in terms of well-defined territorial boundaries. Such a spatial concept of sovereignty makes sense up to a point for the Classic Maya. Ruling dynasties such as Copán's clearly exerted influence over populations in their immediate hinterlands and thus had what might be thought of as core territorial domains on which their prosperity and security depended. We doubt, however, that kings thought of their realms in terms of lines on a map as we think of nation-states today. Rather, polities probably consisted more broadly of core populations as well as distant centers that might be expected to conform to the influence and authority of a particular ruler in the capital or central place. Such conformity likely varied according to the historical connections among royal and noble families and the specific political circumstances of the moment. More so than in our modern political systems, those of the Maya were defined by the nature of elite relationships that extended far beyond royal capitals and core territorial domains.

Maya archaeologists are currently divided in their conceptions of the maximal size and political organization of major Maya kingdoms. On the one hand, we have long known that royal dynasties were established at impressive regal-ritual centers and dominated core hinterlands where their supporting populations lived—what has been called the *city-state* model (Webster, 1997). Some huge centers such as Tikal have long been thought to have exerted strong influence, or even direct political control, over smaller nearby centers such as Uaxactun.

More recently, our increasingly sophisticated understanding of Classic Maya inscriptions indicates that some polities such as those centered on Tikal, Calakmul, Dos Pilas, and Caracol, engaged in what seem to be wars of conquest in which they and their allies or proxies sought to displace or dominate royal dynasties at distant centers (Martin and Grube, 1995). We also know that major political events at some centers were presided over by emissaries from other places, who apparently served in some sense as patrons of them. Some rulers, furthermore, are referred to as "possessed" by other, presumably more powerful ones. This "big-polity" perspective emphasizes the formation of grand alliances and the exercise of power for the sake of territorial aggrandizement, tribute, and other material and strategic goals. In some cases, such as the Dos Pilas kingdom (Houston, 1993), conquest clearly resulted in large, short-lived regional polities with multiple royal centers.

According to Joyce Marcus (1992a, 1992b, 1993) based on her interpretations of its iconography and inscriptions, Copán early on achieved regional state status between A.D. 500 and 600, dominating a territory of about 10,000 sq km on the southeastern Maya frontier. Quiriguá, Pusilhá, and other smaller centers were Copán's political dependents. That Copán's royal dynasty had obvious ritual and political relations with Quiriguá, and perhaps a hand in the founding of the Quiriguá dynasty in the 5th century, is the strongest element in this reconstruction. The final episode in the eventual decline of the Copán regional state presumably occurred when Quiriguá's ruler captured and sacrificed *18 Rabbit* in A.D. 738.

Our own surveys and demographic reconstructions lead us to another conclusion. With as few as 6,000 people as late as A.D. 600, we believe Copán would have been demographically too weak to extend effective political dominance over other centers at great distances. Even later, at its demographic peak of 20,000 to 30,000 people in the 8th century, Copán was still far smaller than previously thought, and there is no clear evidence for external warfare or territorial expansion. Moreover, it is unclear just what advantages Copán would have gained by controlling such a huge territory. There is no doubt that Copán's core territory—the region directly under the sway of its royal dynasty—centered on that portion of the river drainage in Honduras (some 400 to 500 sq km), and that the bulk of the supporting population lived within a day's walk of the Main Group. Direct political control possibly extended into some of the downstream parts of the valley in Guatemala, but independent surveys there suggest only very small Late Classic populations (Murdy, 1991). We think that throughout its history the Copán polity, comparatively isolated on the southeastern Maya frontier, was always a local rather than regional power.

Foreign Relations

Copán did, of course, have relationships with other Maya and non-Maya centers, although assessing the nature of these interactions is complicated by the over-whelmingly ritual and religious, rather than historical, content of its inscriptions. Evidence of indirect cultural influences from the great central Mexican metropolis of Teotihuacán was associated with the dynastic founder and continued to the 8th century (Stuart, 1994). During the latter period, however, Teotihuacán itself was in decline, and Central Mexican symbols on monuments and buildings probably reflect traditional themes of royal presentation and claims of ancestral connections rather than any kind of interaction between Copán and Central Mexico.

Closer to home, Copán's ties with Quiriguá are clear in the epigraphic record. Ruler 12, who presided over the rapid expansion of the kingdom in the 7th century, might have been related to the Quiriguá dynasty, but this connection did not prevent the violent rupture of relations signaled by the death of *18 Rabbit* in A.D. 738. Whatever the nature and cause of this crisis, *Yax Pasah* is recorded as carrying out rituals there in A.D. 810. At that time he was apparently interacting with an independent dynasty and polity. Copán is also mentioned in the inscriptions at Pusilhá, in southern Belize (Schele and Mathews, 1998, p. 346).

Exchange of spouses among kingdoms played an important role in Maya politics and formed part of the basis for political alliances. The only such recorded exchange we know about at Copán involves *Yax Pasah's* mother, who was a royal woman from Palenque. That she should be recruited from such a distant center 450 km away to the northwest suggests that *Yax Pasah's* father was more concerned with acquiring a wife from a prestigious dynasty than cementing a locally advantageous political or military alliance.

Elsewhere in the Maya Lowlands incidents of warfare are conspicuous in epigraphic records. Despite the military posturing of *Yax Pasah* and the more general war and sacrifice symbolism in much of Copán's iconography, there are no clear signs of external war, apart from the *18 Rabbit* incident, which is itself ambiguous. Our surveys found no formal fortifications, nor did our many excavations turn up convincing evidence of the kinds of violent destruction that might be expected if there were war with foreign enemies (more about this in the Chapter 13). Examination of hundreds of skeletons by Storey and Whittington showed no patterns of war-related trauma. Possibly because of its relative isolation, Copán seems to have escaped the escalating cycles of interpolity violence that plagued some other Late Classic Maya kingdoms.

Long Distance Exchange

Many archaeologists have assumed that Copán's position along a river (albeit un-navigable) must have made it an important force in long distance trade and exchange. More specifically, Copán has long been perceived as a kind of "gateway" polity in the transmission of objects and raw materials between the Maya and non-Maya worlds—exchanges that were accompanied by powerful cultural influences reflecting its prestige on the southeastern periphery.

Having excavated hundreds of archaeological sites in the Copán Valley, we are struck with the paucity of durable, imported objects in 8th-century contexts. The obvious exception is obsidian, which as we have already seen was widely used by people of all ranks. We do find the occasional artifact of jade, imported shell, pottery, or other exotic materials (especially in tombs), and since the Carnegie excavations we have known that gold objects were imported from as far away as Colombia or Panama (Stromsvik, 1941). Such items are few and far between, however, even in the impressive elite residences of the urban core. While admitting our inability to judge exchanges of perishable materials, long distance trade does not seem to have been central to Copán's prosperity or economic organization.

Nor is it easy to assess Copán's influence on distant regions, especially as more complete archaeological evidence accumulates. For example, it was long believed that Copador polychrome pottery was manufactured at Copán and exported to other centers. Our extensive tests have revealed no Copador production sites, however, and the distribution of this ware outside the Copán Valley is spotty at best. It is very rare even at Quiriguá and the wider Motagua Valley, and 8th-century polities throughout much of central Honduras have almost no Copáder pottery of any kind (Schortman and Urban, 1994; Hirth, 1988).

On a more general level, ceramic affiliations also point out Copán's distinctiveness. Despite its undoubted participation in the larger tradition of Late Classic Maya civilization, our residential excavations in 8th-century contexts turned up very few imported vessels from the Maya Lowlands proper. More common are polychromes from central Honduras, and overall the Copán ceramic tradition retains its similarities with the highlands of El Salvador and Guatemala.

All things considered, our projects at Copán and others on the southeast periphery have failed to support the assumption that Copán was a major factor in interregional economic exchanges. Schortman and Urban (1994) acknowledge that Copán might have had pre-eminent cultural prestige and thus exerted powerful noneconomic influences on distant polities. While it is true that ball courts, ritual objects, items of elite dress, carved stone stelae, and Maya elements on polychrome vessels in places like central Honduras might have derived from Maya influences, it is by no means sure that these emanated from Copán (Hirth, 1988). We agree with Schortman and Urban that other polities on the southeast periphery were not passive recipients of Copán's exports or influences and certainly were not under any sort of economic or political domination.

Our recent regional research, then, suggests that Copán never dominated any large territory, effectively subjugated other centers, or even managed to play a dominant "international" role in economic or cultural terms.

SUMMARY

The last 20 years of archaeological research provide us with a much better perspective on the mature Late Classic Copán polity than ever before. What emerges is the picture of a ruling center that is not particularly urban and a kingdom not nearly so populous, extensive, and powerful as some archaeologists once believed. The power of Copán's kings was not commensurate with the hypertrophied symbolism of monumental architecture and royal monuments and inscriptions. Although details of social relations and economy are still unclear, overall organization was probably fairly simple and heavily based on kinship, with, perhaps, increasing stratification by the time of *Yax Pasah*. Finally, the agricultural infrastructure was rendered unstable by rapid population growth and the heavy concentration of settlement in the Copán pocket.

Despite his numerous subjects and the splendor of his royal establishment, *Yax Pasah* might have felt some misgivings as he looked out over the Copán pocket from his lofty perch on the Acropolis. The many great noble households in the urban core were a reminder that he could no longer dominate political events as his royal ancestors had. Farmers complained more frequently about the insecurities of their lives, and it was harder to extract cheerful cooperation from them for royal projects and to keep them from defecting to distant parts of the valley. *Yax Pasah's* nobles were increasingly fractious as eroded soil from the hillsides invaded their compounds. Some people even murmured that perhaps the king's all important influence over the royal ancestors and gods who guaranteed cosmic balance and prosperity was not what it had been. Perhaps things were not going so well after all.

CHAPTER 13
The Collapse of the Copán Kingdom

INTRODUCTION

Few issues have been as central to Mesoamerican archaeology or as prominent in the popular imagination as the collapse of Classic Maya civilization. Much of our own research at Copán has been directly designed to investigate the collapse process, and nowhere else is the decline of a Classic Maya kingdom so well understood.

Copán figured importantly in forming early scholarly and public impressions of a dramatic and widespread ancient catastrophe. During his visit to the Main Group in 1839, John Lloyd Stephens (1949, p. 81) remarked, in the romantic style of his times, that

> ". . . architecture, sculpture, and painting, all the arts which embellish life, had flourished in this overgrown forest; orators, warriors, and statesmen, beauty, ambition, and glory, had lived and passed away, and none knew that such things had been, or could tell of their past existence. . . . The city was desolate. No remnant of this race hangs around the ruins, with traditions handed down from father to son, and from generation to generation. It lay before us like a shattered bark in the midst of the ocean, her masts gone, her name effaced, her crew perished, and none to tell whence she came. . . . All was mystery, dark, impenetrable mystery . . ."

Three centuries earlier, the first bishop of Yucatán, Diego de Landa, marveled at the abundance of ruins he observed on the landscape and correctly surmised that they were built by the ancestors of the living Maya (Tozzer, 1941). Such abandoned places raised no questions in Landa's mind of some ancient, mysterious, overall cultural collapse, because the Spaniards encountered thriving and populous polities during their exploration and conquest of Yucatán. For them Maya civilization was very much alive.

As the Spanish began to explore regions of the Maya Lowlands further to the south, however, it became evident that the forested landscapes of the central and southern parts of the Yucatán Peninsula—a region of about 100,000 sq km—had once been heavily occupied as well. As a result of his visit to long-deserted Copán in 1576, Diego Garciea de Palacio formed the opinion that the buildings and monuments there were made by the same people responsible for the ruins in Yucatán, far to the northwest. Gradually it became obvious that there had once been a great tradition of Lowland Maya civilization much more extensive than its historical remnants in Yucatán, and that something dramatic had led to widespread cultural decline and depopulation.

Of course, no early visitors to the great, forest-enshrouded ruins could tell when these places had been abandoned. Stephens assumed, correctly as it turned out, that inscriptions on Maya monuments at Copán and elsewhere contained historical information, and it was these inscriptions that eventually provided the first chronological insights.

By the beginning of this century it was clear that very few of the Long Count dates so often associated with Classic Maya monuments referred to times later than the 9th great cycle in the Maya calendar—or the 9th century A.D. in terms of our own.[1] The sudden decline of one of the principal symbolic hallmarks of Classic civilization, coming as it did after a 500-year period of widespread use, served as a potent barometer of the collapse process. The Maya seemed to have abandoned large construction projects about the same time at many centers.

Until the 1960s archaeologists lacked a sophisticated understanding of the sociopolitical context of this decline. Since then we have learned that most Long Count dates appear on royal monuments such as Copán's Altar Q and commemorate important events in the lives of rulers, or occasionally lesser nobles. Cessation of dated monuments, then, marks the end of dynastic rule, and/or a major shift in symbolic expression of such rule. The latest monuments at various abandoned centers showed that the overall collapse process took place over roughly 150 years, from about A.D. 750 to 900 (although a few Long Count inscriptions were somewhat later). However sudden the collapse process might have been at particular polities, it was quite protracted in time if our perspective is the whole central and southern portions of the Maya Lowlands.

Because dated monuments occur most frequently at Classic Maya regal-ritual cities, early perspectives heavily emphasized the collapse of the central organizational apparatus of Maya society. Archaeologists knew, however, that something more drastic than an elite collapse had occurred. The landscapes around Tikal, Palenque, and Copán were effectively deserted in Stephens's time, and 16th-century historical accounts revealed the same pattern centuries earlier. In 1524 and 1525 Hernán Cortés, the conqueror of the Aztecs, marched with a small army across the base of the Peninsula, through territory we know to be filled with abandoned centers. Cortés encountered a wilderness of forest, only a handful of large settlements, and so few people that his army was frequently lost and starving. At least by Cortés's time, then, there were very few people where once there had been millions, and natural vegetation had reclaimed a landscape once cleared and densely settled by farmers.

Considering all this evidence, one answer to the question so often heard by archaeologists—"Why did Maya civilization collapse?"—is that it didn't. The Maya whom Landa knew had kings and lords supported by farmers who built palaces for nobles and temples for their gods. The 16th-century Maya wrote

---

[1] The Long Count was a count of elapsed days, arranged in successive cycles somewhat like our centuries, from a beginning point in 3114 B.C.

hieroglyphic books, utilized complex calendars, played the ball game, and traded and fought with one another. In other words, a variant of Maya civilization survived in northern Yucatán that *Yax Pasah* would have found reasonably familiar.

Even after dismissing the notion of some overall collapse, however, two things must still be explained. First, what happened to the central political systems and the Great Tradition of the Classic Maya between A.D. 750 and 900? Second, where did all the people go that had supported the royal centers?

EXPLANATIONS OF THE CLASSIC MAYA COLLAPSE

Since Stephens's time archaeologists have advanced many explanations for the Classic collapse, including drought, earthquakes, hurricanes, diseases of humans or crops, internal rebellion, foreign invasion, internecine warfare, disruption of trade routes, environmental degradation, and ideological fatigue (see Webster, Evans, and Sanders, 1993, pp. 515–516; or Culbert, 1988, for recent reviews). Broadly speaking, all these explanations fall into two general categories. *Elite collapse causes* (e.g., rebellion, warfare, invasion) are most useful in answering the first question posed above: Why did the royal or noble components of Maya society and its distinctive Great Tradition of inscriptions, architecture, and art disappear? *Total system causes* such as disease or environmental degradation, by contrast, have implications as well for the second question—what larger processes of overall systemic failure and demographic decline affected all parts of ancient Maya systems?

Archaeologists agree that no single "prime-mover" explanation can explain such a complex and widespread process as the Maya collapse, and that a constellation of interactive causes contributed to the breakdown of Classic Maya civilization. Even so, some causes might be much more important than others. For example, extended drought and attendant crop failure might have triggered internal warfare and loss of faith in the ideological basis of Classic kingship. The collapse process also was far from uniform, so it is also apparent that we need to understand the detailed culture histories of the many individual Classic Maya polities before a comprehensive explanation of the Maya collapse process is possible.

Of the two most obtrusive effects of the Classic collapse—cessation of Long Count dates and depopulation—the first has long been the better understood and, by its very nature, seemed to indicate some sort of reasonably abrupt catastrophe at any particular royal center. Because there was no convenient way until recently to date demographic decline, archaeologists long assumed that it was closely correlated with the disappearance of royal dynasties. As we saw in Chapter 3, we thought until 1983 that the Copán Valley was effectively deserted within 50 to 100 years of the royal collapse (i.e, by A.D. 850–900).

As a result of the many large-scale projects carried out throughout the Maya Lowlands since the 1960s, and particularly the proliferation of regional settlement research, we now have a much better grasp of the complexities of the collapse.

Demographic reconstructions suggest that around many centers population decline was not so rapid or complete as earlier envisioned. Bey, Hanson, and Ringle (1997), on the basis of their recent work in northern Yucatán, document the gradual abandonment of Classic sites there and identify "post-monumental" phases of occupation. Elsewhere, particularly at small centers such as Lamanai (Pendergast, 1985, 1986) in Belize, even the central political institutions seemed comparatively unaffected, and polities continued to thrive long after Tikal, Palenque, and Copán had been abandoned. Finally, where decline did occur, different sets of causes clearly affected different polities. Particularly violent forms of warfare were associated with the collapse of the once-thriving Dos Pilas kingdom in the Petexbatun region of the southwestern Lowlands (Inomata, 1995; Houston, 1993). As we shall see shortly, at Copán the decline was more gradual and seemingly much less violent.

What happened to many Classic Maya polities in the 8th and 9th centuries is now known to be so variable that some archaeologists prefer not to use the term "collapse" at all because of its implications of a universal and sudden catastrophe. Nonetheless, something dramatic did eventually undermine many polities, no matter what the exact pattern in each case.

THE CLASSIC COLLAPSE AT COPÁN

Throughout much of the Maya Lowlands explanations for the decline of particular polities are hampered by insufficient information concerning both the culture-historical patterns of the local collapse process and its ecological setting—it is not clear exactly *what* must be explained. For example, at Palenque where *Yax Pasah's* mother was born, we possess an intricate understanding of the history of the royal dynasty but have virtually no associated settlement or landscape studies. By contrast, our comprehensive and detailed reconstruction of the collapse process at Copán derives from four main lines of evidence reviewed in preceding chapters: (1) dynastic history, (2) intensive, representative excavations of sites of all ranks, (3) effective chronological control over settlement and demographic history, and (4) reconstruction of land-use patterns. To these we must add the ancillary studies of diet, erosion, and paleopathology.

Any particular kind of archaeological inference tends to be weak, but for Copán we possess so many independent lines of mutually reinforcing research that combining them produces a very convincing picture of the collapse. This process is now seen to involve three distinct stages—the fall of the royal dynasty, the elite decline, and the eventual political decentralization and depopulation of the valley. We will first review the evidence and then discuss how it fits a larger set of explanations.

Yax Pasah in Trouble: The Collapse of the Dynasty

We saw in Chapter 12 that the reign of *Yax Pasah,* for all its accomplishments, was probably not a tranquil one. He came to the throne in A.D. 763 after the comparatively short reigns of the two successors of the mighty, but ingloriously departed, *18 Rabbit*. Because details of kinship are often unrecorded on monument inscriptions at Copán we are not sure who his father was—only that he was probably not the son of the preceding ruler *Smoke Shell*. This, plus the fact that *Yax Pasah's* mother was a royal woman from Palenque, may have rendered him something of an outsider in the arena of Copán politics. If, as seems likely, kin relationships were essential in gaining and maintaining power at Copán, *Yax Pasah* could not expect much help from his prestigious but distant maternal relatives and might well have lacked strong dynastic connections closer to home. Furthermore, if Barbara and William Fash correctly interpret the role of the *popol nah,* or council house, he also inherited a royal office in which there was less latitude for unilateral decisions than enjoyed by earlier rulers.

Yax Pasah appears to have carried on in grand royal style during the first half of his long reign, judging by the ambitious building projects he sponsored. Later, however, monumental construction at the Main Group was much reduced and by about A.D. 780 dated monuments at outlying elite residences show that the household establishments of lesser lords in the urban core and Copán pocket had become much larger and more elaborate than ever before. Both the fall-off in royal construction and increased building efforts by non-royal persons suggest the growing weakness of the royal dynasty.

While some nobles, such as the "scribal" lord of Group 9N-8, took care to celebrate their connections to the royal court, one might also interpret the increased elite interest in large, ornate buildings in terms of status rivalry among noble factions, each jockeying for position in a generally deteriorating political climate. Following the logic of Rene Viel (in press), some of these elite establishments might have been occupied by families descended from earlier kings, and the carved throne found at Group 8N-11 in Las Sepulturas conveys cosmological and celestial imagery of an extremely exalted kind.

Although *Yax Pasah* certainly completed some extremely impressive construction projects, his insecurities are probably reflected in his penchant for depicting himself on them as a great warrior, even though no specific conquests or wars can certainty be attributed to him on the basis of his inscriptions. We suspect that *Yax Pasah* devoted much of his time to a precarious political game, carefully playing off one elite faction against another, but unfortunately there are no historical records that clearly substantiate this idea.

In A.D. 810 he traveled to Quiriguá, where he undertook "scattering" rituals. Inscriptions from about this time in *Yax Pasah's* reign refer to other very exalted nobles, most importantly *Personage A* and *Yax Kam Lay,* the latter possibly a brother of the ruler. The overall impression is one of rather diffuse royal authority (Schele and Freidel, 1990, pp. 331–334). *Yax Pasah* died in A.D. 820, but we do not know if he was ever buried in the grand vaulted tomb beneath Temple 18. He was the final effective ruler of the 400-year-old dynasty, and one of his last monuments may even formally commemorate the end of that dynasty (Schele and Freidel, 1993, pp. 342–343; Stuart, 1993).

Some epigraphers (Grube and Schele, 1987; Schele and Mathews, 1998, p. 321) believe that there were later attempts to revive royal rule, possibly involving one *U Kit Tok,* whose name is mentioned on the very late and unfinished Main Group Altar L, which probably dates to A.D. 822. According to their reconstruction, this individual would be the last (17th) ruler. The final construction projects in the Main Group were probably finished shortly after A.D. 800, and thereafter neither *Yax Pasah* nor any other claimant to the throne was able to initiate new ones. If we follow the terminology of Bey, Hanson, and Ringle cited above, Copán enters a "postmonumental," or Terminal Classic, phase sometime shortly after A.D. 800.

Some violence was aimed at old royal facilities. Tulane University archaeologists have discovered that parts of the royal residence at Group 10L-2 were deliberately burned sometime in the mid-9th century, and that the group was subsequently abandoned (Andrews and Fash, 1992). This reconstruction is in excellent agreement with our 63 hydration dates from that group, which fall between A.D. 272 and 897 (Webster, Freter, and Rue, 1993).

The Carnegie projects found occupational debris apparently postdating the royal collapse, so people still used the great buildings (Longyear, 1952, p. 19). Intermittent small rituals were carried out there, especially around the old royal monuments. These rituals involved deposition of, among other things, imported ceramics definitive of the Ejar subcomplex, such as the Plumbate sherds from Tombs 10 and 1-40 and even pottery from as far away as Costa Rica (Longyear, 1952, p. 34). Despite such activity, the Main Group was defunct as a dynastic center.

Although we now appreciate nuances of the collapse of the Copán dynasty much better than ever before, thanks to the work of archaeologists, art historians, and epigraphers at the Main Group, the general dynastic picture confirms what was long believed: There was a comparatively abrupt royal debacle in the early 9th century consistent with internal political upheaval.

The Decline of the Subroyal Elites

Maya elites formed the connective political tissues of Classic society, articulating the vast mass of commoners with the royal dynasty. The Harvard project, and later our own excavations, provided evidence not only of the nature of these elites, but also how they were affected by the collapse. Most important, new data showed that contrary to earlier expectations Copán's elites did not suddenly lose power or abandon their residences when the dynasty fell.

We already reviewed the evidence that by the late 8th century Copán's elites were politically and symbolically assertive, and that they controlled resources not delegated by the kings. We might thus reasonably predict that the fate of at least some nonroyal families did not closely parallel the apparent abrupt demise of the central dynasty, and this is just what the hydration dates show. Twenty Type 3 and 4 sites now have associated, multiple obsidian hydration dates (Table 13-1): At 10 sites, including the royal residence 10L-2, the latest dates fall before or within a decade after A.D. 900 as expected according to original conceptions of the Copán collapse. In the other 10 cases, however,

TABLE 13-1
MINIMAL OCCUPATION SPANS OF TYPE 3 AND 4 SITES*

Early-ending Occupations		Late-ending Occupations	
Site # and Site Type	Dates	Site # and Site Type	Dates
11E-2 (3)	A.D. 768–866	6A-4-1 (3)	A.D. 1007–1212
12F-3 (3)	A.D. 770–909	8N-11 (4)	A.D. 524–1115
7M-16 (3)	A.D. 832–902	9I-1 (4)	A.D. 823-1045
7M-4 (3)	A.D. 469–786	9J-5 (4)	A.D. 722–927
14F-1 (4)	A.D. 678–849	50-1 (3)	A.D. 731–979
10L-16 (4)	A.D. 299–866	9N-8 (4)	890 B.C.–A.D. 1172
10L-2 (4)**	A.D. 272–897	10L-18 (4)	A.D. 724–984
10E-6 (4)	A.D. 759–901	8L-10 (3)	A.D. 703–960
10F-1 (3)	A.D. 731–901	8L-12 (3)	A.D. 740–935
9M-101 (4)	A.D. 792–819	9M-22 A,B	A.D. 464–1120

* Raw hydration dates without error ranges.
** Royal residence.

dates extend much longer—well into the 10th century and as late as the 13th century.

Of all these groups, 9N-8, with 476 associated hydration dates, is by far the best-known chronologically. Two hundred and twenty-two of these obsidian events, or 47% of the total, occurred later than A.D. 822—the date of the last inscription on Altar L. Obviously people still made and discarded obsidian at some elite rank sites long after the fall of the royal dynasty and long after the whole valley was believed to be depopulated according to the original collapse scenario.

How can we know, however, that the people still residing in or around these sites were still in any sense elites and not just squatters using long-abandoned structures? There are several kinds of evidence that help resolve this issue. First, a detailed study of the construction phasing at Group 9M-22A by James Sheehy (1991) suggests considerable activity after the time of the royal collapse, and specifically that the most impressively decorated building of the whole complex was probably built in the mid-9th century. Similarly, Randolph Widmer recovered a cache of obsidian blades sealed beneath a bench in Group 8N-11 (Webster et al., 1998). The latest of seven dates from this cache is A.D. 914, so construction plausibly extended well into the 10th century. No such late constructions appear to be very monumental, however, suggesting reduced ability to recruit labor.

We also know that rooms in many elite structures were generally well-maintained and cleaned until shortly before their collapse. At Group 8N-11 the vaulted roof and walls of two such buildings did not collapse before the mid-11th or even mid-12th century, judging from dated obsidian artifacts sealed beneath the collapsed wall (Webster et al., 1998).

Much more important is a series of finds made by Widmer during his excavations of Structure 110B in Group 9N-8 (Figure 13-1). The beam and mortar roof of this building collapsed suddenly, burying a whole workshop assemblage in its primary context in the northernmost two rooms (see Webster, Evans, and Sanders, 1993, pp. 282–287 for an extended discussion). Among the products of the workshop, recovered in several stages of production, were flower-shaped chest ornaments made from imported marine shell. These are undoubtedly elite items and, in fact, are depicted on figures carved on a hieroglyphic bench excavated at the same elite group. Dates from three obsidian blades associated with this assemblage show that the collapse of the roof probably occurred during the mid-late 10th century (A.D. 955, 980, 988). Some elite artisans, probably directly attached to the lord of 9N-8, clearly carried on their normal activities here for about a century and a half after the dynastic collapse.

Late ritual behavior at the Main Group also supports the survival of post-dynastic hierarchical organization. Some people kept the valley involved in widespread exchange. They had access to distant trading partners and valued imported goods that they deposited near Main Group monuments or tombs that were still of ideological significance to them—perhaps associated with

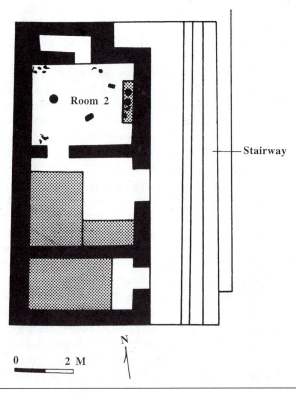

FIGURE 13-1   PLAN OF STRUCTURE 110B, GROUP 9N-8, SHOWING THE WORKSHOP AREA IN ROOM 2 EXCAVATED BY RALPH WIDMER. STIPPLED AREAS ARE RAISED FLOORS OR BENCHES. MANY ARTIFACTS WERE PRESERVED IN THEIR ORIGINAL POSITIONS ON THE FLOOR OF ROOM 2 BY THE COLLAPSE OF THE BEAM AND MORTAR ROOF OF THE BUILDING, POSSIBLY DURING AN EARTHQUAKE THAT OCCURRED IN THE MID-10TH CENTURY A.D.

ancestors. It is much more plausible that local Copán Maya rather than intrusive foreigners carried out such rituals. This whole pattern suggests to us the continued presence of people with pretentions to social rank and with effective external contacts. Retention of principles of ranking and differential social prestige, however, does not necessarily mean that there was any effective political hierarchy still present in the Copán region and this was particularly true after about A.D. 1000.

Some archaeologists working with ethnohistoric records from Postclasic period highland Guatemalan Maya kingdoms believe that Copán long remained a potent political place to which highland princes traveled to procure legitimation for their own rule. Copán, even as an abandoned center, could have played this symbolic political role, and visits by foreigners might explain some of the exotic objects found in ritural contexts.

In summary, our research reveals that although some elite residences were certainly abandoned at or shortly after the time of the dynastic collapse, others were occupied for generations thereafter by people who still continued to engage in characteristically elite activities. By about A.D. 1000, however, the elite tradition at Copán was effectively finished, in the sense that people who still lived in impressive compounds probably no longer enjoyed elite prerogatives.

General Population Decline and Decentralization

Over the long run something very dramatic happened to the whole population of the Copán polity, not just the king and nobles. Now that we have been able to reasonably quantify the rate of population loss, however, it no longers seems appropriate to use the word "catastrophic" to characterize it. In fact, the idea that the valley was never suddenly and wholly abandoned is not a new one. John Longyear (1952, pp. 71–72) thought that long after the Main Group was abandoned, many people still lived in the hills under local chiefs.

The general pattern of decline is shown by our simulations of population from settlement data discussed in Chapter 11. According to the simulation between A.D. 800 and 1200 the overall mean annual rate of decline was just about 1%—not much different from the rate of growth after about A.D. 600. Some combination of declining fertility increased mortality, and outmigration caused such population loss.

To put all of this in somewhat more human terms, imagine being born into a small Copán community of 100 people at about A.D. 1000. If you were fortunate enough to live to the age of 60, there would be 56 people left given this annual attrition rate of 1%. At the end of your life you would certainly know that your community was much reduced in size, but might not perceive this as very disorienting or even threatening. Nor would the mechanisms of loss be very dramatic— a few more deaths than births each year, or an occasional neighboring family moving away in search of new opportunities elsewhere. Certainly you would know that your community was not thriving or prospering, and some of the causes would be evident—poorer yields from the fields, more bickering and ill feeling among neighbors and perhaps feuds with more distant families that the diminished authority of local leaders could not settle.

Of course demographic decline and stress were not uniform processes. Overall population remained quite high for several generations after the collapse of the royal dynasty (until about A.D. 900), and significantly it is during this time that we detect a continued elite presence. After A.D. 900 the decline was much more precipitous, and people increasingly were able to leave the Copán pocket, where they had formerly been inconveniently concentrated. This decentralization of population probably reflects heightened political decentralization as well as the waning of the authority of traditional lords in their Copán pocket residences. Colonization of other parts of the valley, however, does not necessarily imply defection from any sort of hierarchical structure, as Longyear anticipated. Some outlying sites such as Llano Grande probably grew in population and scale as migrants coalesced around new leaders, a process most obvious at Piedras Negras.

After A.D. 1050 the dispersal is most pronounced, despite the fact that almost half of the people still lived in the Copán pocket. That so many people remained there reflects the importance this part of the valley had in subsistence terms. Despite deforestation and erosion, the valley floor of the pocket, and especially the irrigable sections of it, remained the prime resource zones as Wingard has argued. This brings us back to another prediction of Wingard's model: There always were sufficiently stable and productive parts of the landscape to support some thousands of people, yet still the population was essentially gone by A.D. 1250. We will address this puzzling fact shortly.

CERAMIC MARKERS OF THE COPÁN DEMOGRAPHIC DECLINE   The much-debated issue of the late duration of Coner-type ceramics is central to our perceptions of the royal collapse and its demographic aftermath. It might well be possible in the future to usefully subdivide post-A.D. 900 ceramic assemblages into two or more new phases based on detection of fine-grained changes in form, decoration, and paste. For example, Freter has observed that assemblages with late dates have Coner-like ceramics that are more crudely made, coarsely tempered, and poorly-fired compared to earlier assemblages. This is just what we would expect if deforestation made fuel more scarce, and if there were post-dynastic changes in the household economies of potters.

It is also possible that a few "foreign" people who used complete, nonlocal ceramic assemblages (i.e., using no or very few Coner or Coner-like types) settled in the Copán Valley as the indigenous population declined. If it could be shown that their numbers were impressive, it would strengthen the idea of an invasion. Residential sites might also be detected in which some Ejar imported wares were used in combination with Coner forms (it is highly likely that such sites exist).

Neither of the latter possibilities is relevant, however, to the late duration of Coner-type ceramics (and the almost complete absence of Ejar wares) in the sites we have excavated and dated and would not seriously change our general conclusions about Copán culture history. Put simply, there are many sites occupied long after A.D. 850–900 that have Coner forms as presently defined and that lack diagnostic Ejar or other non-Coner Postclassic forms. The individual buried in Site 99A-18-2 in the 14th century probably came from a local household that still used ceramic assemblages that a farmer of *Yax Pasah's* time would have found reasonably familiar, but sadly impoverished in fine wares. No one made poly-chrome pottery anymore, although a handful of venerable painted vessels made long before was cherished by the last few people in the valley.

According to Ricardo Agurcia (1998, p. 354) remains of ". . . a small Post-classic village . . ." lying to the southwest of the Acropolis have recently been detected by William Fash and his students. While details of the ceramic assem-blages recovered from this locale are as yet unavailable, these finds seem consis-tent with our own reconstruction of Copán's post-dynastic population history.

EXPLAINING THE COPÁN COLLAPSE

For Copán, the overall pattern of what must be explained is pretty clear. We now know, or strongly suspect, the following:

1. After A.D. 400 the population of the environmentally-circumscribed Copán Valley began to increase, and between A.D. 600 and 750 it doubled approximately every 70 years—a very respectable rate of sustained growth for a preindustrial population.
2. This growing population depended heavily on a single staple crop—maize, had an extremely conservative agricultural technology, and could not effectively import large subsidies of food energy from outside the Copán Valley.
3. Population was at first heavily concentrated on or adjacent to the most stable and productive, but spatially limited, agricultural land—the alluvial soils of the Copán pocket. By early in the 6th century the carrying capacity of this environmental zone was exceeded, and farmers began to colonize less productive and more fragile parts of the landscape—particularly foothill zones—initiating a downward spiral of increasing labor input for less return of food energy.
4. Residential sites that were founded late and situated in marginal agricultural zones had attenuated occupations.
5. By at least the mid-8th century there was widespread deforestation and erosion in the Copán pocket, coinciding with the population peak of the polity.
6. Population densities, according to the settlement projection, reached the respectable overall level of 55 people per sq km and 370 to 453 people per sq km for the most productive sections of the valley. This population was not distributed as expected with respect to its productive landscape.
7. There are no indications of spatially extensive agroengineering innovations such as terracing or drained fields that might have helped stabilize productivity.
8. By the 8th and 9th centuries all elements of the Copán population were plausibly af-flicted with high levels of infant and adolescent mortality, and many individuals survived severe, repeated stresses. Pathological indicators on bones and teeth are consistent with poor nutrition.
9. The royal dynasty collapsed abruptly about A.D. 820–822, and the royal household was deliberately destroyed shortly thereafter. Copán nobles were extremely as-sertive during the last reigns.
10. Although the Main Group ceased to function as a royal center, some elite house-holds survived and continued to function for another two centuries
11. Demographic growth peaked at A.D. 750–800 and remained reasonably stable until A.D. 900. At about that time people began to heavily colonize outlying sections of the valley, and the population started a long, steady decline until the 13th century.

We believe that one fundamental process—human-induced environmental degradation—most powerfully explains the syndrome of political collapse and demographic decline of the Copán kingdom.

At this point we return full circle to Livi-Bacci's comments on the long-term, adaptive relationships between people and their agricultural resources in circumscribed environments (1997, pp. 12–13). At Copán, to slightly rephrase his imaginary example, *"... demographic growth in a fixed environment (and, it must be added, given a fixed level of technology) [led] to the cultivation of progressively less fertile lands with ever greater inputs of labor, while returns per unit of land or labor eventually diminish[ed]"* (Livi-Bacci, 1997, p. 81). In short, the ultimate cause of the decline of Copán was a complex Malthusian feedback process (Malthus, 1976) of population growth, with consequent population stress and pressure on limited resources, especially land, in the absence of significant innovation.

This is scarcely a new insight. Human-induced ecological stress is one of the oldest hypotheses advanced to account for the collapse of Classic Maya civilization, and archaeologists long ago singled it out as the most important explanation for the Copán collapse (e.g, Fash, 1983a). Our research for the first time adequately documents the process with multiple lines of evidence and allows us to evaluate it in general quantitative terms.

Historical demographers know that under conditions of resource limitation there are recurring subsistence crises, followed shortly by pronounced increases in mortality (Livi-Bacci, 1997, p. 85). The coarse chronological reconstruction of events made possible by archaeology, even using hydration dates, masks such undoubted short-term crises. What from our perspective seems a rather uniform process of decline was probably experienced by Copán farmers as a succession of increasingly frequent crop failures, followed by seasons of hunger, physical debilitation, and death or departure of family members.

The population reconstructions in Chapter 11 are too coarse-grained to show these periodic crises that probably affected Copán's people each decade or generation, especially during poor years when yields were substandard. A dramatic modern example of the latter occurred in October of 1998 as we were writing this book. Excessive rainfall in Honduras from Hurricane Mitch caused severe flooding and landslides that killed thousands of people and destroyed crops and homes. Although few lives were lost at Copán, the floor of the valley, including parts of the Las Sepulturas urban enclave, was flooded (possibly a modern example of the erosion event reviewed in Chaper 8). Hundreds of people were homeless and lost all of their possessions, including their stores of food.

This particular tragedy was, of course, caused by factors beyond human control, but its effects at Copán were aggravated by deforestation and other anthropogenic alterations to the landscape. Today, fortunately, Copán's population is linked to larger national and international systems that provide external resources and relief efforts to prevent the worst effects of disease and starvation. Imagine, by contrast, the effects of such a catastrophe in ancient times when Copán was comparatively self-contained in basic economic terms, and especially after about A.D. 700, when population was high, deforestation reached its peak, and political relationships were increasingly fragile.

Such episodic catastrophes aside, the overall events and processes we have documented represent a classic "boom and bust" population cycle from which the Copán polity never recovered. One difficulty for those who earlier advocated anthropogenic ecological degradation as a prime cause of the collapse of Classic Maya polities was the inferred suddenness of demographic decline. We now know that the Copán polity gradually disintegrated, both politically and demographically, over several hundred years. This history of protracted *total system decline* is much more congruent with ecological causes than political ones alone.

An Interacting Set of Causes

Having identified the overarching cause of total system decline, it is now possible to place a series of related, subsidiary causes into their proper perspective. In addition to disease and increased mortality related to poor diet, the ecological explanation incorporates the following effective causes.

ELITE DEMANDS   We saw in Chapter 12 that elite demands on the Copán producing population, whether for food energy or labor, would probably not have produced significant stress. By the 8th century, however, even small surplus production beyond the needs of producing households might have become burdensome. So too were demands for labor by kings and elites who were increasingly seen as ineffective in guaranteeing the well-being of their commoner-kin. If parts of the valley were appropriated for commercial agriculture, production shortfalls would have been exacerbated, and, of course, the apparent policy of keeping people settled in the Copán pocket increased local environmental destruction and decreased the efficiency of agricultural labor.

What can happen when ordinary people experience extreme anxiety is illustrated by an anecdote from our own experience at Copán. One year there was widespread crop failure due to insufficient rain. An employee of the Instituto, along with her husband, cultivated a cornfield in the hills far from where they lived, traveling to attend to it every few days. Just before harvest time they visited their field, only to find that it had been entirely stripped of corn. This family, fortunately, was buffered by nonagricultural employment and a system of food importation from other parts of Honduras. Ancient Copán farmers were not so lucky. Many probably resorted to the kind of antisocial behavior recounted in our anecdote, which we could probably never detect archaeologically.

Ironically, such competition and social disruption might have strengthened political elites for a while. Mayanists have always had a difficult time in specifying exactly what managerial functions elites had with respect to the subsistence economies of their kingdoms, apart from extracting surpluses and labor from producers.

A feature of intensification processes such as those that occurred in the Copán Valley is what Wood (1998) has called "variance in well-being." By well-being he means ". . . any aspect of individual health or physical condition that is either positively associated with the probability of childbirth, or negatively associated with the risk of death" (Wood, 1998, p. 104). Variance becomes greater as populations depend on increasingly marginal resources for their subsistence. To Wood's concept we would add a sociocultural dimension of well-being: Some Maya farmers increasingly saw their general household well-being undermined vis-à-vis that of others or they were relegated to more substandard parts of the agricultural landscape. Conceived of in either way, variance in well-being is potentially very disruptive to sociopolitical systems because it can cause competition and discontent.

As the Copán subsistence base deteriorated, competition was intensified among people both within and between lineages. We believe that commoners increasingly turned to their high-ranking kinspeople to manage internal competition, both within and among lineage factions. As population increased and fields deteriorated, the issues of who had access to which parts of the landscape and how inequalities of production should be redistributed were essential to household well-being, but of course, were also subject to destructive and self-serving elite agendas.

The self-interests of lineage factions probably began to cause competition in the political system during *Yax Pasah's* time and intensified after the royal collapse. Ultimately such internal competition was destructive to the whole political system. This brings us to the role of conflict.

Conflict, Violence, and the Copán Collapse

Some of our colleagues have recently raised the possibility that warfare contributed to the downfall of the Copán kingdom, in particular because of the apparent deliberate destruction of the royal residence at Group 10L-2. They believe that this incident, along with other proposed instances of burning or destruction, show that much of central Copán was sacked by enemies from outside the polity. This is a legitimate issue because we know that other Lowland Maya polities were largely destroyed by warfare. An important, if poorly understood issue, is how (or if) Copán related to the large Classic Maya coalitions, centered primarily on Tikal and Calakmul, that were apparently involved in military confrontations for generations during the Late Classic period. According to some epigraphers, Quiriguá had affiliations with Calakmul at the time of the ill-fated expedition of *18 Rabbit,* which might have been undertaken to bring that errant center back into the Tikal political orbit (Schele and Mathews, 1998). This incident, of course, is too early to tell us anything directly about the collapse but if properly understood, it does underscore Copán's wider interactions in Maya geopolitics.

In evaluating the issue of conflict, we should emphasize what most Copán researchers agree about. First, the last kings were losing control of a polity burdened by overpopulation, declining agricultural productivity, and increasingly powerful and assertive nobles. Second, the royal collapse was abrupt, and plausibly associated with internal violence; forms of internal factional competition are increasingly evident in the Maya Lowlands (e.g., Pohl and Pohl, 1994), and it is a reasonable hypothesis that they were responsible for some of the destructive episodes detected.

In our opinion the archaeological evidence for Copán's conquest by external enemies, however, is poor. War is admittedly difficult to detect in the archaeological record. Published sources on other regions of the southeast periphery present little evidence for it. Just who Copán's external enemies might have been is uncertain, and there were no nearby polities as centralized and powerful as Copán itself. The old enemy Quiriguá does not seem to be a good candidate, because *Yax Pasah* was participating in rituals there in A.D. 810.

Even weak invaders might have disrupted an already disintegrating political system, but if they did so, they left behind few clear archaeological traces. As we saw in Chapter 9, the many burials examined by Storey and Whittington show no obvious patterns of trauma suggesting widespread violence, nor, as at some of the centers in the Petexbatun region, are there fortifications.

Most important, most buildings seem to have been gradually abandoned. Longyear notes that Carnegie archaeologists found buildings in the Main Group well preserved, that the contents of rooms had been largely removed, and that abandonment was ". . . quiet and orderly . . ." (Longyear, 1952, p. 71).

The authors of this book have collectively been closely involved in the intensive excavation of approximately 150 buildings in groups of all subroyal social ranks in the urban core and 27 more in rural zones. Of these only about five appear to have been violently destroyed. Fash (1989) discovered that façade sculpture on the "House of the Bacabs" at Group 9N-8 was purposely defaced by burning, but the building's lintel was not deliberately burned to cause its collapse as at Group 10L-2. The nearby Structure 9N-81 (probably a young men's house) did burn down, but this might well have been an accidental fire in a thatched-roof building and probably occurred after about A.D. 900.

Fully excavated buildings both in the Copán urban core and in rural sites usually have few artifacts on their floors—abruptly destroyed buildings usually have many. Excavations by Inomata (1995) at Aguateca and Sheets (1992) at Ceren provide good examples of the kinds of archaeological residues we could expect in residences suddenly abandoned and/or destroyed by enemy attack, but we know of no comparable examples at Copán, apart from a handful of isolated contents such as Widmer's workshop rooms. All this evidence, along with the lack of evidence for destruction in the hundreds of test excavations completed by Freter, suggests that internal conflict disrupted the royal dynasty, destroying parts of the Main Group, Group 10L-2 (and possibly other as yet unexcavated sites) in the process, but that such violence was limited and sporadic rather than systematic.

Obvious weaponry is not encountered very often in Copán artifact assemblages, although it is depicted in royal art. Interestingly, we found what seems to be spear points at two of the extensively excavated small rural sites that long postdate the royal collapse. Judging from Reed's dietary analysis (which includes some late burials), these weapons were probably not often used for killing large mammals such as deer. Quite possibly as political fragmentation and decentralization occurred in the Copán Valley, local feuding became common.

Outmigration

In addition to increased mortality, people probably defected from the Copán system by simply leaving it. Remember that Wingard's agricultural simulation predicts that the valley could always have supported some thousands of people, whereas the settlement data show almost complete abandonment. Obviously one cannot explain such abandonment in strictly ecological terms. We think that unstable local political conditions and the attraction of other polities elsewhere in Mesoamerica made outmigration an attractive alternative to many residents of the Postclassic Copán Valley. We could probably never detect the gradual departure of a few thousand people over several generations with available archaeological methods.

Kingship and the Classic Maya Collapse

Classic Maya polities were strongly theocentric, and the collapse of Classic society in the 8th and 9th centuries was partly a failure of a particular kind of kingship. Maya rulers, like those of many other ancient civilizations, were thought to be ritually responsible for the order of the cosmos as a whole and more important, for the well-being and prosperity of their subjects. Such conceptions no doubt formed the foundation of the institution of kingship from very early times. During the evolution of royal institutions, ruling lines probably arrogated to themselves responsibilities for maintenance of cosmic order that had earlier been more widely distributed among lineage heads or other leaders, thus excluding them from dominant social power.

Despite some regional fits and starts that caused abandonment of early centers, Maya polities, royal capitals, dynasties, and their attendant Great Tradition elements spread widely until the 8th century, a process accompanied by rapidly growing regional populations (Culbert and Rice, 1990). During this period Maya kings no doubt seemed to their subjects to be able to deliver order and prosperity consistently enough to justify their pretentions to privilege and divine influence. Although there might have been situational deviations from order and balance, over the long run things worked pretty well. As Mann (1976, p. 23) puts it, "Powerful ideologies are at least highly plausible in the conditions of the time, and they are genuinely adhered to."

After about A.D. 650, however, there are many signs of strain in Maya polities, including increasingly frequent and violent warfare between centers, more internal status rivalry, and, in some places, sure signs of environmental deterioration. At Copán neither kings nor elites were able to manage in any effective sense the problems caused by too many people and too many competing factions, all trying to make a living from a deteriorating landscape.

The institution of kingship was the first casualty of this situation, while some lesser elite establishments, as we have seen, survived the royal debacle. This pattern of political collapse is extremely suggestive. We believe elites outlasted kings at Copán for three reasons. We already reviewed the first: in times of internal upheaval and competition elite leadership and managerial functions became more crucial than before for the survival of corporate social groups. In addition, however, some elites were not related to the royal dynasty, or at least were sufficiently distanced from it to avoid implication in royal failures. Finally, elites had long before relinquished most of their own original ritual responsibilities to maintain the order and prosperity of the cosmos and polity.

In the end, the royal strategy backfired. As order and prosperity deteriorated at Copán, kings became the scapegoats for nobles and commoners alike, culpable both ideologically, and perhaps in other ways, for the polity's misfortunes. Ultimately, divine kingship at Copán floundered on the paradox of the assumption of divine kingship everywhere: that the moral order is identical with the natural order. Identification of the moral order with kings essentially *personalized* the deterioration of polities. The question was not "What is the matter?", but rather "Who is the matter?" (Sahlins, 1970, p. 215).

Permanence and universality mediated by divine kings at Copán, and probably elsewhere in the Maya Lowlands, were consistently disturbed from the beginning, and ultimately undermined at the end, by the expedient ambitions of kings and nobles, and more fundamentally, by inevitable alterations of the agrarian landscape undertaken by countless historically faceless people. Kings had sometimes failed before, but always kingship had remained. At the end, kingship itself was rejected. The conditions of royal time had changed. Perhaps, in their continued impoverishment and anxiety, ordinary Maya looked for a while to their lesser lords for the order and prosperity formerly guaranteed by kings, but nobles were equally helpless, and in the long run, lost their own privileges.

All this, of course, does not mean that Copán collapsed for ideological reasons, but rather that destructive ecological processes triggered ritual and political responses inconsistent with the ideological postulates of royal rule.

Under our old understanding of the Maya collapse at Copán, it was easy to explain why no kings or elites ever reconstituted any kind of new, centralized political system—after A.D. 900 we thought there were no people left in the valley. Given our more recent reconstructions we must address this question, however, because the populations necessary to support a complex political hierarchy were present until quite late. According to our estimates, some 150 to 200 years after the royal collapse there were as many people in the valley as there had been when the Copán dynasty first established itself in the 5th century. Why were ambitious individuals or familes never able to re-establish kingship? Why did even the remaining nonroyal lords eventually lose all semblance of privilege and political power?

We cannot answer these questions for certain. Our own guess is that a traditional system of royal legitimacy was permanently undermined by the recurring crises of the collapse and stifled by nobles scrambling to retain some semblance of their former rank. Those nobles who managed to hold on to power for a few generations, however, proved to be ineffective managers of the human and natural resources of the valley, and themselves eventually disappeared.

SUMMARY

David Stuart (1993) recently observed that the whole Late Classic period at Copán and other Maya polities might be regarded as a protracted collapse process. By this he means that behind the glittering façade of temples, buildings, and monuments there lay fundamental and potentially destructive weaknesses. At

Copán we have amply documented such weaknesses, which as the Late Classic system matured eventually manifested themselves in unmanageable ways.

Kings and nobles disappeared, and in the end the last to go were the rural farmers, who were also the first to arrive in the valley 2,000 or 3,000 years before. A few farmers cultivated their fields and harvested crops until the 13th and 14th centuries as Longyear originally envisioned, but they soon departed, leaving the great forests to reclaim a largely deserted landscape.

In conclusion, we must emphasize that our evidence and interpretations about what happened at Copán do not necessarily mean that exactly the same set of causes was responsible for the decline of other Classic Maya polities. Each polity was in important ways unique in its ecological setting, its larger social environment, and its culture history. To understand the Classic Maya collapse comprehensively, we must reconstruct what happened at many other Maya polities in as much detail as we have done at Copán.

CHAPTER 14

Epilogue

We have come a long way since Stephens and Catherwood first explored the ruins of Copán in 1839. As they surveyed the fallen and overgrown monuments (Figure 14-1) Stephens and Catherwood made two very basic assumptions. They thought that the inscriptions carved on the monuments recorded the deeds of kings, warriors, and other powerful people (i.e., history), and they imagined that Copán was part of a great Maya civilization, similar to those of the Near East and Egypt in the Old World.

Archaeological research over the last century, and more specifically since 1975, has documented in great detail Copán's culture history. We now have a firm grasp of the dynastic sequence and can associate individual rulers with specific events and buildings. Equally sophisticated is our larger understanding of Copán's origins, its basic institutions, and the processes by which the kingdom grew and declined. Copán was clearly, as Stephens anticipated, part of the much larger cultural phenomenon we call Classic Maya civilization. What we know

FIGURE 14-1 COLLAPSED STELA AT THE ABANDONED SITE OF COPÁN AS SHOWN IN A LITHOGRAPH MADE FROM A 1839 DRAWING BY FREDERICK CATHERWOOD.

about Copán has important implications for understanding the Maya more generally, and within a wider comparative perspective, all ancient complex societies.

Archaeologists interested in basic issues of cultural adaptation and evolution, as we are, often make very broad generalizations about the nature and processes of culture change. Just like other scientists, we aspire to ascertain fundamental and widely applicable principles about how the world—in our case how the human biological, social, and cultural world—works. What we often forget in these efforts is the degree to which our task is an empirical one, informed from the ground up (no archaeological pun intended) by what we know about specific regional sequences of ancient human behavior, culture change, and evolution. Such knowledge is laboriously acquired through years, and sometimes decades, of intense and varied archaeological research.

The tradition of Copán research summarized and interpreted in the preceding chapters is an excellent example of such an archaeological endeavor. It is now fair to say that nowhere else in the Maya Lowlands, and perhaps nowhere else in all of Mesoamerica, do we have such an effective grasp of the development and decline of a major preColumbian kingdom from a regional perspective. Nor is this information only preserved in the records, collections, and publications of archaeologists. Few other great centers provide the general public with a comparable opportunity to view a wealth of restored buildings, sculpture, or well-displayed artifacts.

We have been able to find out so much about Copán partly because of the conjunction of a favorable set of circumstances. Gordon Willey began the Harvard project in 1975, about the time that our understanding of Maya inscriptions and iconography was rapidly maturing. Copán's unusually large corpus of well-preserved and accessible art and writing rapidly yielded highly detailed information concerning kings, nobles, rituals, and political events, all comprehensible within a framework of monument dates. By the same time there had emerged a strong awareness among archaeologists that settlement, landscape, and household research were needed to supplement information from the spectacular centers that had long preoccupied Maya archaeologists.

Work has continued at the Copán Main Group, but the Harvard, PAC I, and PAC II projects all initiated increasingly ambitious research efforts aimed at understanding the ecology of land use and landscape modification, settlement distribution, household size and character, and demographic history for the polity as a whole. Such studies continue today.

Archaeology had also become heavily problem-oriented. Groundwork concerning Copán's culture history was laid by previous generations of archaeologists, especially before World War II. Much of that work was basically descriptive and exploratory, and necessarily so. By the mid-1970s, however, archaeologists realized that they had to formulate and systematically investigate particular questions stimulated by this exploratory phase. We have reviewed interpretations related to many specific research questions. Do large-scale excavations support the results of test pitting? How many people lived in the Copán Valley at any given time? What did people eat? Is the dynastic sequence recorded in glyphs and art consistent with architectural stratigraphy? We can now give reasonable answers to these and many other questions.

None of this, of course, would have been possible without the unusually generous funding made available by the Honduran government and other private and institutional sources. Copious support over many years has enabled Copán researchers to overcome perhaps the largest single methodological problem archaeologists face anywhere—*scale* of research. Interpretations of the archaeological record are always limited by what we don't know. At Copán, tunneling, mapping and survey, test excavations, extensive lateral exposures, studies of epigraphy and art, biological assays of skeletons, chronometric dating, and architectural analysis and restoration (and the list could go on) have all been carried out on a massive scale.

Equally important is the *variety* of Copán research. Another major problem faced by archaeologists is that any particular line of evidence tends to be weak or suspect. Thus developing independent lines of inquiry bearing on the same question is essential. We reviewed many examples of such convergence in the preceding chapters. Recovery of a wide range of botanical and faunal remains tells us what foods were available to the ancient Maya, but not how much each might have contributed to the Maya diet. Isotopic analysis of human bone independently helps resolve this question. Reconstruction of ancient populations is always problematical, but when simulations from settlement data and from agricultural models closely agree, we can be pretty confident that our order-of-magnitude figures are reasonably correct. Both the radiocarbon and obsidian hydration methods of dating are prone to errors, but when they mutually reinforce each other we can be more certain of their chronological implications.

All this variety, of course, depends upon a wide range of skills and knowledge that no individual solely possesses, therefore problem-oriented archaeology necessitates the co-operation of many specialists. Sometimes the personnel of a particular project possess such variable skills. For example, Freter is an expert in obsidian hydration dating, so we did not have to ask an independent lab to conduct this study in the course of our settlement research. On the other hand, some analyses, such as AMS radiocarbon dating or the preparation of sediment cores, are usually done by highly trained people in their own laboratories, and their services are frequently contracted and paid for as consultants.

More commonly, teams of people with specialized skills are directly attached to specific research efforts. During the PAC I phase Claude Baudez recruited geographers, botanists, geologists, and geomorphologists to complement the skills of his archaeological personnel. Proper interpretation of inscriptions and art requires specialized training, so epigraphers and art historians have all contributed their expertise as well. Some nonarchaeologists organize their own projects, such as the Austrian architects Hasso Hohmann and Anegrete Vogrin, who have provided us with highly detailed images and analyses of the Main Group and the urban core.

Of course there is a downside to all this diversity, especially where, as at Copán, there has been no central institution organizing all the work (as there was, for example, during the University of Pennsylvania excavations at Tikal between 1956–1970). Teams of different people have varying assumptions and think that certain issues are important, and recover and interpret segments of the Copán's archaeological record accordingly. What results is an archaeological version of the old parable about several blind people who, each feeling different parts of an elephant, give idiosyncratic descriptions of the whole animal. Groups of archaeologists, or even individuals, tend to formulate their larger conceptions of Copán through the peepholes of their own proclivities and experiences, and these different perspectives often create, at least for a time, a certain amount of confusion, misunderstanding, and even outright bickering. Such discord can be beneficial in the long run. We might never have devised and carried out our concordance experiment reviewed in Chapter 10 if so many colleagues had not voiced skepticism about the utility of obsidian hydration dating at Copán.

Much still remains to be discovered, especially, as we saw in Chapter 12, unresolved questions about the sociopolitical organization of the kingdom. We predict, however, that Copán holds comparatively few major surprises for us. If we have done our work well, future research will increasingly refine the basic outlines of what we already know.

So where do we go from here? Certainly more excavations are needed, both in the Main Group and the larger regional hinterland. Equally important, however, is the much more laborious and time-consuming laboratory analysis of the millions of artifacts—stone tools, ceramics, fragments of plants and animals, sculptural elements, and a host of others-that have been collected over the years. Here, more perhaps than beneath the ground, lurk new and unexpected discoveries.

Long before Gordon Willey began his work at Copán in 1975, he wrote that "Archaeology is the imaginative recapture of the past within the hard boundaries of the evidence. . . . " (Willey, 1966, p. 3). His comment is even more appropriate today, when according to the rhetoric of some archaeologists, objective knowledge of the past is impossible. Instead, they say, we impose (and should be free to impose) any conceptions we like on the material remains we recover. For each of us the past is a highly subjective mirror that reflects back our individual biases, cultural assumptions, and philosophical or political agendas. More broadly, our scientific accounts of the past are "meta-narratives" of Western culture, no different and no more reliable than non-scientific or non-Western narratives of other kinds.

We strongly reject this view of archaeology. We are all, as Willey asserted, constrained by hard evidence. Sometimes this evidence, to be sure, is so limited or ambiguous that numerous and at times, conflicting interpretations may be honorably held by individual archaeologists. And certainly individuals do have their own conscious or unconscious personal and cultural biases and they do sometimes misuse information about the past for their own purposes. Ultimately, however, the reality of what is "out there" in the archaeological record simply cannot be forced to accord with our fondest wishes or theories. Perhaps the best measure of this reality is the experience of being wrong. As it turns out, many of the cherished ideas and assumptions with which we began our work at Copán turned out to be wrong. We were wrong about how much human energy went into the construction of major buildings. We were wrong about how many people lived in the valley, and we were wrong about how the polity declined, both politically and demographically. Being wrong can be good. As an archaeologist, if nothing you uncover changes your mind, then you're in trouble.

Thoughtful scientists, of course, shy away from assertions of absolute truth. Rather, they ". . . are satisfied to consider as true that which appears most probable on the basis of the available evidence, or that which is consistent with more, or more compelling, facts than competing hypotheses" (Mayr, 1988, p. 26). According to the best current evidence, labor investment in Copán's buildings was much less than we originally thought, the population was smaller, and the decline of the kingdom was unexpectedly protracted. These discoveries are only a small part of the payoff of the last quarter century of research.

Students commonly ask "What is the relevance of archaeology for people today?" For those of us who have long worked at Copán one fundamental answer is painfully obvious. In a real sense modern history is recapitulating that of ancient times, albeit much faster. At Copán, and in Honduras as a whole, population growth, deforestation, and erosion are causing severe environmental destruction. Between 1964 and 1989 a total of almost 26% of all the forests in Honduras were lost (Stonich and DeWalt, 1996). Today resources in Honduras are used with little thought to their sustainability, just as they were in the past, and the rate of population growth far outstrips that of ancient Copán. Political problems associated with such growth and destruction are already apparent, and will probably get worse. And, of course, such processes now occur on a worldwide scale.

Perhaps the single most important message that Copán has for us is that we humans, for all of our great cultural accomplishments, are parts of nature, and in the long run we are most threatened not by what nature does to us, but by what we do to ourselves.

REFERENCES CITED

Abrams, E.M.

1984a   *Systems of Labor Organization in Late Classic Copán, Honduras: The Energetics of Construction.* Unpublished Ph.D. dissertation, Department of Anthropology, The The Pennsylvania State University, University Park.

1984b   Replicative experimentation at Copán, Honduras: Implications for ancient economic specialization. *Journal of New World Archaeology* 6: 39–48.

1987   Economic specialization and construction personnel in Classic period Copán, Honduras. *American Antiquity* 52:485–499.

1994   *How the Maya Built their World.* University of Texas Press, Austin.

Abrams, E.M. and A. Freter

1996   A Late Classic lime-plaster kiln from the Maya centre of Copán, Honduras. *Antiquity* 70:423–428.

Abrams, E.M., A. Freter, D. Rue, and J. Wingard

1996   The role of deforestation in the collapse of the Late Classic Copán State. In *Tropical Deforestation: The Human Dimension,* edited by L. Sponsel, T. Headland, and R. Bailey, pp. 55–75. Columbia University Press, New York.

Abrams, E.M. and D. Rue

1988   The causes and consequences of deforestation among the prehistoric Maya. *Human Ecology* 14:377–395.

Agurcia, R.

1998   Copán: art, science, and dynasty. In *Maya,* edited by P. Schmidt, M. Garza, and E. Nalda, pp. 336–354. Rizzoli, New York.

Andrews, E.W. V, and B. Fash

1992   Continuity and change in a royal Maya residential complex at Copán. *Ancient Mesoamerica* 3:63–87.

Andrews, E.W. V, and N. Hammond

1990   Redefinition of the Swasey Phase at Cuello, Belize. *American Antiquity* 55:570–584.

Ashmore, W.

1991   Site-planning principles and concepts of directionality among the ancient Maya. *Latin American Antiquity* 2:199–226.

1992   Deciphering Maya architectural plans. In *New Theories on the Ancient Maya,* edited by E. Danien and R. Sharer, pp. 173–184. University Museum, University of Pennsylvania, Philadelphia.

Aveni, A.
1977   Concepts of positional astronomy employed in ancient Meso-american architecture. In *Native American Astronomy,* edited by A. Aveni, pp. 3–19. University of Texas Press, Austin.

Baudez, C.F., editor
1983   *Introduccíon a la arqueología de Copán, Honduras, tomos 1–3.* Secretaría del Estado en el Despacho de Cultura y Turismo, Tegucigalpa.

Baudez, C.F.
1994   *Maya Sculpture of Copán.* University of Oklahoma Press, Norman.

Baudez, I.S.
1983   Agricultura y agricultores en el regien de Copán. In *Introduccíon a la arqueología de Copán,* edited by C.F. Baudez, pp. 195–228. Secretaría del Estado en el Despacho de Cultura y Turismo, Tegucigalpa.

Bey, G. III, C. Hanson, and W.M. Ringle
1997   Classic to postclassic at Ek Balam, Yucatan: architectural and ceramic evidence for defining the transition. *Latin American Antiquity* 8:237–254.

Black, S.L.
1990   *Field Methods and Methodologies in Lowland Maya Archaeology.* Unpublished Ph.D. dissertation, Department of Anthropology, Harvard University, Cambridge.

Braswell, G.E.
1992   Obsidian-hydration dating, the Coner phase, and revisionist chronology at Copán, Honduras. *Latin American Antiquity* 3:130–147.

Bricker, H. and V. Bricker
1999   Astronomical orientation of the Skyband Bench at Copán. Manuscript.

Campbell, K.L. and J.W. Wood
1988   Fertility in traditional societies. In *Natural Human Fertility: Social and Biological Determinants.,* edited by T. Diggory, M. Potts, and S. Teper, pp. 39–69. Macmillan Press, London.

Carr, H.S.
1996   Precolumbian Maya exploitation and management of deer populations. In *The Managed Mosaic,* edited by S. Fedick, pp. 251–261. University of Utah Press, Salt Lake City.

Cheek, C. and M. Spink
1986   Excavaciones en el grupo 3, estructura 223 (operacion VII). In *Excavaciones en el área urbana de Copán, Vol.1,* edited by W.T. Sanders, pp. 37–91. Secretaría del Estado en el Despacho de Cultura y Turismo, Tegucigalpa.

Culbert, T.P.
1988   The collapse of Classic Maya civilization. In *The Collapse of Ancient States and Civilizations,* edited by N. Yoffee, and G. Cowgill, pp. 69–101. University of Arizona Press, Tucson.

Culbert, T.P., L.J. Kosakowsky, R. Fry, and W.A. Haviland
1990   The population of Tikal, Guatemala. In *Precolumbian Population History in the Maya Lowlands,* edited by T.P. Culbert and D.S. Rice, pp. 103–122. University of New Mexico Press, Albuquerque.

Culbert, T.P. and D.S. Rice, editors
1990   *Precolumbian Population History in the Maya Lowlands,* University of New Mexico Press, Albuquerque.

Curtis, J.H., D. Hodell, and M. Brenner
1996   Climate variability on the Yucatan Peninsula (Mexico) during the past 3500 years, and implications for Maya cultural evolution. *Quaternary Research* 46:37–47.

Diamanti, M.
1991   *Domestic Organization at Copán: Reconstruction of Maya Elite Households through Ethnographic Analogy.* Unpublished Ph.D. dissertation, Department of Anthropology, The Pennsylvania State University, University Park.

Fash, B., W.L. Fash, Jr., S. Lane, R. Laríos, L. Schele, J. Stomper, and D. Stuart
1992   Investigations of a Classic Maya council house at Copán, Honduras. *Journal of Field Archaeology* 19:419–442.

Fash, W.L., Jr.
1983a   *Maya State Formation: A Case Study and its Implications.* Unpublished Ph.D. dissertation, Department of Anthropology, Harvard University, Cambridge.

1983b   Reconocimiento y excavaciones en el valle. In *Introduccíon a la arqueología de Copán,* edited by C.F. Baudez, pp. 229–470. Secretaría del Estado en el Despacho de Cultura y Turismo, Tegucigalpa.

1989   The sculptural faéade of structure 9N-82: Content, form, and significance. In *The House of the Bacabs,* edited by D. Webster, pp. 41–72. Studies in Precolumbian Art and Archaeology 92, Dumbarton Oaks, Washington, D.C.

1991   *Scribes, Warriors and Kings.* Thames and Hudson Inc., New York.

Fash, W.L., Jr. and K. Long
1983   Mapa arqueologio del Valle de Copán. In *Introduccíon a la arqueología de Copán,* edited by C.F. Baudez, pp. 5–48 (map supplement volume). Secretaría del Estado en el Despacho de Cultura y Turismo, Tegucigalpa.

Fash, W.L., Jr. and D. Stuart
1991   Dynastic history and cultural evolution at Copán, Honduras. In *Classic Maya Political History,* edited by T.P. Culbert, pp. 147–179. Cambridge University Press, New York.

Fash, W.L., Jr., R.V. Williamson, R. Larios, and J. Palka
1992   The hieroglyphic stairway and its ancestors. *Ancient Mesoamerica* 3:105–115.

Fedick, S., editor
1996   *The Managed Mosaic.* University of Utah Press, Salt Lake City.

Feldman, L.
1994   Appendix E: The mollusks of Copán. In *Ceramics and Artifacts
            from Excavations in the Copán Residential Zone,* edited by G.R.
            Willey, R.M. Leventhal, A. Demarest, and W.L. Fash, Jr.,
            pp. 477–479. Papers of the Peabody Museum of Archaeology and
            Ethnology, Vol. 80. Harvard University, Cambridge.

Flannery, K.
1998   The ground plans of archaic states. In *Archaic States,* edited by
            G.M. Feinman and J. Marcus, pp. 15–57. SAR Press, Santa Fe.

Flannery, K., editor
1982   *Maya Subsistence: Studies in Memory of Dennis E. Puleston.* Aca-
            demic Press, New York.

Fox, R.
1977   *Urban Anthropology.* Prentice Hall, Englewood Cliffs.

Freter, A.
1988   *The Classic Maya Collapse at Copán, Honduras: A Regional Set-
            tlement Perspective.* Unpublished Ph.D. dissertation, Department
            of Anthropology, The Pennsylvania State University, Univer-
            sity Park.

1992   Chronological research at Copán, Honduras: Methods and impli-
            cations. *Ancient Mesoamerica* 3:117–133.

1994   The Classic Maya collapse at Copán, Honduras: An analysis of
            Maya rural settlement trends. In *Archaeological Views from the
            Countryside,* edited by G.Schwartz and S. Falconer, pp. 160–176.
            Smithsonian Institution Press, Washington, D.C.

1996   Rural utilitarian ceramic production in the Late Classic period
            Copán Maya state. In *Arqueologia Mesoamericana: Homenaje a
            William T. Sanders,* edited by A. Guadalupe, J. Parsons, R. Sant-
            ley, and M. Serra, pp. 209–230. Instituto Nacional de Antropolo-
            gia e Historia, Mexico.

1997   The question of time: the impact of chronology on Copán pre-
            historic settlement demography. In *Integrating Archaeological
            Demography,* edited by R. Paine, pp. 21–42. Occasional Papers
            Series, Vol. 24, Center for Archaeological Investigations,
            Southern Illinois University, Carbondale.

Friedman, I. and R. Smith
1960   A new method using obsidian hydration dating: part 1. *American
            Antiquity* 25:476:522.

Gerry, J.
1993   *Diet and Status among the Classic Maya: An Isotopic Perspective.*
            Unpublished Ph.D. dissertation, Department of Anthropology,
            Harvard University, Cambridge.

Gerstle, A.
1988   *Maya-Lenca Ethnic Relations in Late Classic Period Copán, Hon-
            duras.* Unpublished Ph.D. dissertation, Department of Anthro-
            pology, University of California, Santa Barbara.

Gonlin, N.

1993   *Rural Household Archaeology at Copán, Honduras.* Unpublished
            Ph.D. dissertation, Department of Anthropology, The Pennsylva-
            nia State University, University Park.

1994   Rural household diversity in Late Classic Copán, Honduras.
            In *Archaeological Views from the Countryside,* edited by
            G. Schwartz and S. Falconer, pp. 177–197. Smithsonian Institu-
            tion Press, Washington, D.C.

1996   Methodological Analysis of the Copán Testing Program. In *Arque-
            ologia Mesoamericana: Homenaje a William T. Sanders,* edited by
            A. Guadalupe, J. Parsons, R. Santley, and M. Serra, pp. 231–252.
            Instituto Nacional de Antropologia e Historia, Mexico.

Gordon, G.B.

1896a   *Prehistoric Ruins of Copán, Honduras: A Preliminary Report of
            the Explorations by the Museum, 1891-1896.* Memoirs of the
            Peabody Museum of Archaeology and Ethnology, Vol. 1.

1896b   *Caverns of Copán, Honduras.* Memoirs of the Peabody Museum
            of Archaeology and Ethnology, Vol. 1.

Grube, N.

1990   A reference to Water-Lily Jaguar on Caracol stela 16. *Copán
            Notes 68,* Copán Mosaics Project and the Instituto Hondureño de
            Antropología e Historia, Honduras.

Grube, N. and L. Schele

1987   U Cit Tok', the last king of Copán. *Copán Notes 21,* Copán Mo-
            saics Project and the Instituto Hondureño de Antropología e His-
            toria, Honduras.

Hajual, J.

1982   Two kinds of preindustrial household formation systems. *Popula-
            tion and Development Review* 8:449–494.

Harbottle, G., H. Neff, and R. Bishop

1994   Appendix C. The sources of Copán Valley obsidian. In *Ceramics
            and Artifacts from Excavations in the Copán Residential Zone,* ed-
            ited by G.R. Willey, R.M. Leventhal, A. Demarest, and W.L.
            Fash, Jr., pp. 445–459. Papers of the Peabody Museum of Archae-
            ology and Ethnology, Vol. 80. Harvard University, Cambridge.

Harrison, D. and B.L. Turner III, editors

1978   *Pre-Hispanic Maya Agriculture.* University of New Mexico Press,
            Albuquerque.

Haviland, W.

1985   *Excavations in Small Residential Groups of Tikal: Groups 4F-1
            and 4F-2. Tikal Report 19.* University Museum, University of
            Pennsylvania, Philadelphia.

Hendon, J.A.

1987   *The Uses of Maya Structures: A Study of Architecture and Arti-
            fact Distribution at Sepulturas, Copán, Honduras.* Unpublished
            Ph.D. dissertation, Department of Anthropology, Harvard Uni-
            versity, Cambridge.

Hirth, K.
1988   Beyond the Maya frontier: Cultural interaction and syncretism along the central Honduran corridor. In *The Southeast Classic Maya Zone,* edited by E. Boone and G.R. Willey, pp. 297–334. Dumbarton Oaks, Washington, D.C.
1998   The distributional approach: A new way to identify marketplace exchange in the archaeological record. *Current Anthropology* 39:451–476.

Hirth, K. and R. Santley
1992   Household studies in western Mesoamerica. In *Prehispanic Domestic Units in Western Mesoamerica,* edited by R.S. Santley and K. Hirth, pp. 3–20. CRC Press, Inc., Boca Raton.

Hodell, D., J.H. Curtis, and M. Brenner
1995   Possible role of climate in the collapse of Classic Maya civilization. *Nature* 375:790–793.

Hohmann, H.
1995   *Die Architekture der Sepulturas-Region von Copán in Honduras.* Academic Publishers, Graz, Austria.

Hohmann, H. and A. Vogrin
1982   *Die Architekture von Copán.* Akademische Druck-u, Verlagsanstalt, Graz, Austria.

Houston, S.
1993   *Hieroglyphics and History at Dos Pilas: Dynastic Politics of the Classic Maya.* University of Texas Press, Austin.

Houston, S., editor
1998   *Classic Maya Architecture: Form, Function, and Meaning.* Dumbarton Oaks, Washington, D.C.

Inomata, T.
1995   *Archaeological Investigations at the Fortified Center of Aguateca, El Peten, Guatemala: Implications for the Study of the Classic Maya Collapse.* Unpublished Ph.D. dissertation, Department of Anthropology, Vanderbilt University, Nashville.

Johnston, K. and N. Gonlin
1998   What do houses mean? Approaches to the analysis of Classic Maya commoner residences. In *Function and Meaning in Classic Maya Architecture,* edited by S. Houston, pp. 141–187. Dumbarton Oaks, Washington, D.C.

Kirch, P.
1990   The evolution of sociopolitical complexity in prehistoric Hawai'i: an assessment of the archaeological evidence. *Journal of World Prehistory* 4:311–345.

Lentz, D.
1991   Maya diets of the rich and poor: Paleoethnobotanical evidence from Copán. *Latin American Antiquity* 2:269–287.

Leventhal, R.M.
1979   *Settlement Patterns at Copán, Honduras.* Unpublished Ph.D. dissertation, Department of Anthropology, Harvard University, Cambridge.

Livi-Bacci, M.
1997   *A Concise History of World Population.* Blackwell Publishers Ltd., Oxford.

Longyear, J.
1952   *Copán Ceramics: A Study of Southeastern Maya Pottery.* Carnegie Institution of Washington Publication 597, Washington, D.C.

Mallory, J.K.
1984   *The Place of Obsidian in the Economy of Copán, Honduras.* Unpublished Ph.D. dissertation, Deptartment of Anthropology, The Pennsylvania State University, University Park.

Malthus, T.
1976   *An Essay on the Principle of Population.* Norton, New York [original 1798].

Mann, M.
1976   *The Sources of Social Power.* Cambridge University Press, London.

Marcus, J.
1992a   Political fluctuations in Mesoamerica. *National Geographic Research and Exploration* 8:392–411.

1992b   *Mesoamerican Writing Systems.* Princeton University Press, Princeton.

1993   Ancient Maya political organization. In *Lowland Maya Civilization in the Eighth Century A.D.,* edited by J. Sabloff, and S.J. Henderson, pp. 111–184. Dumbarton Oaks, Washington D.C.

Martin, S. and N. Grube
1995   Maya superstates. *Archaeology* 48:41–46.

Maudslay, A.P.
1889–1902   *Biologia Centrali-Americana: Archaeology.* Dulau and Co., London.

Mayr, E.
1988   *The Growth of Biological Thought.* Harvard University Press, Cambridge.

McAnany, P.
1995   *Living with the Ancestors.* University of Texas Press, Austin.

Meighan, C.W. and P.I. Vanderhoeven, editors
1978   *Obsidian Dates II: A Compendium of the Obsidian Hydration Determinations Made at the UCLA Obsidian Hydration Laboratory.* Monograph Number VI Insitute of Archaeology, University of California., Los Angeles.

Merriwether, A., D.M. Reed, and R.E. Ferrell
1997   Ancient and contemporary mitochondrial DNA variation in the Maya. In *Bones of the Maya,* edited by S.L. Whittington and

D.M. Reed, pp. 208–217. Smithsonian Institution Press, Washington, D.C.

Michels, J.
1982   *MOHLAB Technical Report No. 7: The Hydration Rate for Ixtepeque Obsidian at Archaeological Sites in the Department of Chiquimula, Guatemala.* Department of Anthropology, The Pennsylvania State University, University Park.
1986   Obsidian hydration dating. *Endeavor, New Series,* 10:97–100.

Morley, S.G.
1920   *The Inscriptions at Copán.* The Carnegie Institution of Washington, Washington, D.C.

Murdy, C.
1991   Investigaciones arqueologicas el el Valle del Río Camotan, Departamento de Chiquimula, Guatemala, 1989–1990. Report submitted to the Instituto de Antropología e Historia, Guatemala City.

Narrol, R.
1962   Floor area and settlement population. *American Antiquity* 27:587–589.

Netting, R.
1989   Smallholders, householders, freeholders: why the farm works well worldwide. In *The Household Economy: Reconsidering the Domestic Mode of Production,* edited by R. Wilk, pp. 221–244. Westview Press, Boulder.

Nichols, D.
1996   An overview of regional settlement pattern survey in Mesoamerica: 1960-1995. In *Arqueologia Mesoamericana: Homenaje a William T. Sanders,* edited by A. Guadalupe, J. Parsons, R. Santley, and M. Serra, pp. 59–96. Instituto Nacional de Antropologia e Historia, Mexico.

Olson, G.
1975   *Study of the Soils in Valle de Naco (near San Pedro Sula) and La Canteada (near Copán), Honduras: Implications to the Maya Mounds and Other Ruins.* Cornell Agronomy Mimeo 75–19. Cornell University, Ithaca.

Paine, R.
1996   *Model Life Table Fitting by Maximal Likelihood Estimation: A Procedure to Reconstruct Paleodemographic Characteristics in Archaeological Demography.* Unpublished Ph.D. dissertation, Department of Anthropology, The Pennsylvania State University, University Park.

Paine, R. and A. Freter
1996   Environmental degradation and the Classic Maya collapse at Copán, Honduras, (A.D. 600–1250). *Ancient Mesoamerica* 7:37–48.

Paine, R., A. Freter, and D. Webster
1996   A mathematical projection of population growth in the Copán Valley, Honduras, A.D. 400–800. *Latin American Antiquity* 7:51–60.

Pendergast, D.

1985   Lamanai, Belize: An updated view. In *The Lowland Maya Post-classic,* edited by A. Chase and P. Rice, pp. 91–103. University of Texas Press, Austin.

1986   Stability through change: Lamanai, Belize, from the ninth to the seventeenth century. In *Late Lowland Maya Civilization,* edited by J. Sabloff and E.W. Andrews V, pp. 223–250. University of New Mexico Press, Albuquerque.

Pohl, M.

1994   Appendix D. Late Classic Maya fauna from settlement in the Copán Valley, Honduras: Assertion of social status through animal consumption. In *Ceramics and Artifacts from Excavations in the Copán Residential Zone,* edited by G.R. Willey, R.M. Leventhal, A. Demarest, and W.L. Fash, Jr., pp. 459–476. Papers of the Peabody Museum of Archaeology and Ethnology, Vol. 80. Harvard University, Cambridge.

Pohl, M.D. and J. Pohl

1994   Cycles of conflict: political factionalism in the Maya Lowlands. In *Factional Competition and Political Development in the New World,* edited by E. Brumfiel and J. Fox, pp. 138–157. Cambridge University Press, Cambridge.

Pohl, M., Pope, K., Jones, J., Jacob, J., Piperno, D., deFrance, S., Lentz, D., Gifford, J., Danforth, M., & Josserand, J.K.

1996   Early agriculture in the Maya lowlands. *Latin American Antiquity,* 7(4), 355–372.

Popenoe, W.

1919   The useful plants of Copán. *American Anthropologist* 21:125–138.

Redfield, R., & Villa Rojas, A.

1934   *Chan kom: A Maya Village.* Carnegie Institution of Washiongton Publication No. 488. Washington, D.C.: Carnegie Institution.

Reed, D.M.

1994   Ancient Maya diet at Copán, Honduras, as determined through analysis of stable carbon and nitrogen isotopes. In *Paleonutrition: The Diet and Health of Prehistoric Americans,* edited by K.D. Sobolik, pp. 210–221. Occasional Papers Series, Vol. 22. Center for Archaeological Investigations, Southern Illinois University, Carbondale.

1997   Commoner diet at Copán: Insights from stable isotopes and porotic hyperostosis. In *Bones of the Maya,* edited by S.L. Whittington and D.M. Reed, pp. 157–170. Smithsonian Institution Press, Washington, D.C.

1998   *Ancient Maya Diet at Copán, Honduras.* Unpublished Ph.D. dissertation, Department of Anthropology, The Pennsylvania State University, University Park.

Rue, D.

1986   *A Palynological Analysis of Prehispanic Human Impact in the Copán Valley, Honduras.* Unpublished Ph.D. dissertation,

Department of Anthropology, The Pennsylvania State University, University Park.

1987   Early agriculture and early Postclassic Maya occupation at Copán, Honduras. *Nature* 326:285–286.

Rue, D., A. Freter, and D. Ballinger

1989   The caverns of Copán revisited: Preclassic sites in the Sesesmil river valley, Copán, Honduras. *Journal of Field Archaeology* 16:395–404.

Sahlins, M.

1970   Poor man, rich man, big-man, chief. In *Cultures of the Pacific,* edited by T. Harding and B. Wallace, pp. 203–215. The Free Press, New York.

Sanders, W.T., editor

1986–90   *Excavaciones en el área urbana de Copán Volumes 1–3* Secretaría del Estado en el Despacho de Cultura y Turismo, Tegucigalpa.

1989   Household, lineage, and state at eighth-century Copán, Honduras. In *The House of the Bacabs,* edited by D. Webster, pp. 89–105. Studies in Precolumbian Art and Archaeology 92, Dumbarton Oaks, Washington, D.C.

1992   Ranking and stratification in prehispanic Mesoamerica. In *Mesoamerican Elites,* edited by D.Z. Chase and A.F. Chase, pp. 278–291. University of Oklahoma Press, Norman.

Sanders, W.T. and D. Webster

1988   The Mesoamerican urban tradition. *American Anthropologist* 90:521–46.

Santley, R., and Hirth, K.

1983   *Prehispanice domestic units in western Mesoamerica: Studies of the Household, Compound, and Residence.* Ann Arbor: CRC Press.

Schele, L. and D. Freidel

1990   *A Forest of Kings.* William Morrow and Co., New York.

Schele, L. and P. Mathews

1998   *The Code of Kings.* Scribner, New York.

Schele, L. and M. Miller

1986   *The Blood of Kings.* Kimbell Art Museum, Fort Worth.

Schortman, E. and P. Urban

1994   Living on the edge: Core/periphery relations in ancient southeastern Mesoamerica. *Ancient Mesoamerica* 35:401–430.

Sharer, R., L. Traxler, and J.C. Miller

1991   The Copán corte: A window on the architectural history of a Maya City. *Expedition* 33:46–54.

Sharer, R., J.C. Miller, and L. Traxler

1992   Evolution of Classic period architecture in the eastern acropolis, Copán: A progress report. *Ancient Mesoamerica* 3:145–159.

Sheehy, J.

1991   Structure and change in a late classic Maya domestic group at Copán, Honduras. *Ancient Mesoamerica* 2:1–19.

Sheets, P.
1992   *The Ceren Site: A Prehistoric Village Buried by Volcanic Ash in Central America.* Harcourt College Publishers, Fort Worth.

Smith, A.L.
1950   *Uaxactun, Guatemala: Excavations of 1931–37.* Carnegie Institution of Washington, Publication 588, Washington, D.C.

Spink, M.
1983   *Metates as Socioeconomic Indicators during the Classic Period at Copán.* Unpublishesd Ph.D. dissertation, Department of Anthropology, The Pennsylvania State University, University Park.

Stephens, J.L.
1949   *Incidents of Travel in Central America, Chiapas, and Yucatán.* Rutgers University Press, New Brunswick [original 1841].

Stomper, J.A.
1996   *The Popol Nah.* Unpublished Ph.D. dissertation, Department of Anthropology, Yale University.

Stonich, S. and B. DeWalt
1996   The political ecology of deforestation in Honduras. In *Tropical Deforestation,* edited by L. Sponsel, T. Headland, and R. Bailey, pp. 187–215. Columbia University Press, New York.

Storey, R.
1992   The children of Copán. *Ancient Mesoamerica* 3:161–168.
1997   Individual frailty, children of privilege, and stress in Late Classic Copán. In *Bones of the Maya,* edited by S.L. Whittington and D.M. Reed, pp. 116–126. Smithsonian Institution Press, Washington, D.C.

Stromsvik, G.
1941   *Sub-stela Caches and Stela Foundations at Copán and Quiriguá.* Carnegie Institution, Contributions to American Anthropology and History, 7:63–96.
1942   *The Ball Courts at Copán, with notes on Courts at La Union, Quirigua, San Pedro Pinula, and Ascucion Mita.* Carnegie Institution of Washington, Contributions to American Anthropology and History, 11:183–214.

Stuart, D.
1992   Hieroglyphics and archaeology at Copán. *Ancient Mesoamerica* 3:169–184.
1993   Historical inscriptions and the Maya collapse. In *Lowland Maya Civilization in the eighth century A.D.,* edited by J. Sabloff and J.S. Henderson, pp. 321–354. Dumbarton Oaks, Washington D.C.
1994   The texts of temple 26: The presentation of history at a Maya dynastic shrine. Paper presented at the Advanced Seminar on the Archaeology of Copán, Honduras. School of American Research, Santa Fe.
1995   *A Study of Maya Inscriptions.* Unpublished Ph.D. dissertation, Department of Anthropology, Vanderbilt University, Nashville.

1998   The arrival of strangers. *Precolumbian Art Research Institute Newsletter* 15:10–12.

Stuart, G.

1997   The royal crypts of Copán. *National Geographic Magazine* 192:61–93.

Thompson, E.H.

1886   Archaeological research in Yucatan. *Proceedings of the American Antiquarian Society* 4:248–254.

Tozzer, A.

1941   Land's Relacíon de las cosas de Yucatán. Papers of the Peabody Museum of American Archaeology and Ethnology, Vol. XVIII, Cambridge.

Traxler, L.

1998   The royal courts of Copán. Paper presented at the Conference on the Royal Courts of the Ancient Maya, Yale University, Nov. 8.

Trik, A.

1939   *Temple XXII at Copán.* Contributions to American Anthropology and History, Vol. 5(27), Washington, D.C.

Turner II, B.L., W. Johnson, G. Mahood, F. Wiseman, and J. Poole

1983   Habitat y agricultura en la región de Copán. In *Introduccíon a la arqueología de Copán,* edited by C.F. Baudez, pp. 35–142. Secretaría del Estado en el Despacho de Cultura e Turismo, Tegucigalpa.

van Rossum, P.

1998   The Copán population simulation: methodology. Manuscript on file at the Department of Anthropology, The Pennsylvania State University, University Park.

Viel, R.

1983   Evolución de la cerámica en Copán: resultados preliminares. In *Introducción a la arqueología de Copán,* edited by C.F. Baudez, C.F., pp. 471–550. Secretaría del Estado en el Dispacho de Cultura e Tursimo, Tegucigalpa.

1993a   Copán Valley. In *Pottery of prehistoric Honduras,* edited by J.S. Henderson and M. Beaudry-Corbett, pp. 12–19. Institute of Archaeology Monograph 35, University of California, Los Angeles.

1993b   Evolución *de la cerámica de Copán, Honduras,* Instituto Hondureno de Antropología e Historia,Tegucigalpa.

in press   The pectorals of Altar Q and Structure 11: an interpretation of the political organization at Copán, Honduras. *Latin American Antiquity.*

Vlcek, D. and W.L. Fash, Jr.

1986   Survey in the outlying areas of the Copán region and the Copán-Quiriguá connection. In *The Southeast Maya Periphery,* edited by P. Urban and S. Schortman, pp. 102–113. University of Texas Press, Austin.

Vogrin, A.
1979   Zur astronomischen ausrichtung der Stela 1 in Copán. *Mexicon*
              1:29–30.
Wauchope, R.
1934   *House Mounds of Uaxactun, Guatemala.* Carnegie Institution of
              Washington Publication. 436, Washington, D.C.
Webster, D.
1985   Recent settlement survey in the Copán Valley, Honduras. *Journal
              of New World Archaeology.* 5:39–51.
1997   City-states of the Maya. In *The Archaeology of City-States:
              Cross-Cultural Approaches,* edited by D. Nichols, D. and
              T. Charleton, pp. 135–154. Smithsonian Institution Press, Wash-
              ington, D.C.
1998   Status rivalry warfare: some Maya-Polynesian comparisons. In
              Archaic States, edited by G. Feinman and J. Marcus, pp. 311–
              352. School of American Research, Santa Fe.
1999   The Archaeology of Copán, Honduras. *Journal ofAnthropological
              Research* 7:1–53.
Webster, D., editor
1989   *The House of the Bacabs.* Studies in Precolumbian Art and Ar-
              chaeology 92, Dumbarton Oaks, Washington, D.C.
Webster, D., S.T. Evans, and W.T. Sanders
1993   *Out of the Past.* Mayfield Publishers, Mountainview.
Webster, D., B. Fash, R. Widmer, and S. Zeleznik
1998   The skyband house: Investigations of a Classic Maya elite resi-
              dential complex at Copán, Honduras. *Journal of Field Archaeol-
              ogy* 25:319–343.
Webster, D. and A. Freter
1990a   Settlement history and the Classic collapse at Copán: A refined
              chronological perspective. *Latin American Antiquity* 1:66–85.
1990b   The demography of Late Classic Copán. In *Precolumbian Popula-
              tion History in the Maya Lowlands,* edited by T.P. Culbert
              and D.S. Rice, D.S., pp. 37–62. University of New Mexico Press,
              Albuquerque.
Webster, D., A. Freter, and D. Rue
1993   The obsidian hydration dating project at Copán: A regional ap-
              proach and why it works. *Latin American Antiquity* 4:303–324.
Webster, D., A. Freter, and R. Storey
1997   Analysis of Copán Obsidian Hydration and ^{14}C Concordance Ex-
              periments. Final Report Submitted to the Foundation for the Ad-
              vancement of Mesoamerican Studies Inc., Crystal River, Fl.
Webster, D. and N. Gonlin
1988   Household remains of the humblest Maya. *Journal of Field Ar-
              chaeology* 15:169–190.
Webster, D., N. Gonlin, and P. Sheets
1997   Copán and Ceren: Two perspectives on ancient Mesoamerican
              households. *Ancient Mesoamerica* 8:43–61.

Webster, D. and J. Kirker
1995   Too many Maya, too few buildings: Investigating construction potential at Copán, Honduras. *Journal of Anthropological Research* 51:363–387.

Webster, D., W.T. Sanders, and P. van Rossum
1992   A simulation of Copán population history. *Ancient Mesoamerica* 3:185–198.

Webster, D., A. Traverse, D. Rue, and W.T. Sanders
1997   Vegetational and Settlement History at Copán, Honduras. Final Report to the Human Dimensions Program, National Oceanic and Atmospheric Association, U.S. Department of Commerce (Grant # GC94-838), Silver Spring, Md.

Whittington, S.L.
1989   *Characteristics of Demography and Disease in Low-Status Maya from Classic Period Copán, Honduras.* Unpublished Ph.D. dissertation, Department of Anthropology, The Pennsylvania State University, University Park.

1990   The Ostuman Archaeological Project. Report submitted to the National Science Foundation.

1991   Detection of significant demographic differences between subpopulations of prehispanic Maya from Copán, Honduras. *American Journal of Physical Anthropology* 85:167–184.

1992   Enamel hypoplasia in the low status Maya population of prehistoric Copán, Honduras. *Journal of Paleopathology* 2:185–205.

Whittington, S.L. and D.M. Reed
1997   Commoner diet at Copán: insights from stable isotopes and porotic hyperostosis. In *Bones of the Maya,* edited by S.L. Whittington and D.M. Reed, pp. 157–170. Smithsonian Institution Press, Washington, D.C.

Whittington, S.L. and D.M. Reed, editors
1997   *Bones of the Maya.* Smithsonian Institution Press, Washington, D.C.

Willey, G.R.
1966   *An Introduction to American Archaeology,* Vol. 1. Prentice-Hall, Inc., Englewood Cliffs.

Willey, G.R., R. Bullard, J. Glass, and J.C. Gifford
1965   *Prehistoric Maya Settlements in the Belize Valley.* Papers of the Peabody Museum of Archaeology and Ethnology, Vol. 54. Harvard University, Cambridge.

Willey, G.R. and R.M. Leventhal
1979   Prehistoric settlement at Copán. In *Maya Archaeology and Ethnohistory,* edited by N. Hammond, pp. 57–102. University of Texas Press, Austin.

Willey, G.R., R.M. Leventhal, A. Demarest, and W.L. Fash, Jr.
1994   *Ceramics and Artifacts from Excavations in the Copán Residential Zone.* Papers of the Peabody Museum of Archaeology and Ethnology, Vol. 80. Harvard University, Cambridge.

Wingard, J.
1992   *The Role of Soils in the Development and Collapse of Classic Maya Civilization at Copán, Honduras.* Unpublished Ph.D. dissertation, Department of Anthropology, The Pennsylvania State University, University Park.
1996   Interactions between demographic processes and soil resources in the Copán Valley, Honduras. In *The Managed Mosaic,* edited by S. Fedick, pp. 207–235. University of Utah Press, Salt Lake City.

Wisdom, C.
1940   *The Chorti Indians of Guatemala.* University of Chicago Press, Chicago.

Wolf, E.
1966   *Peasants.* Englewood Cliffs, Prentice-Hall.

Wood, J.W.
1998   A theory of preindustrial population dynamics. *Current Anthropology* 391:99–135.

Wood, J.W., G.R. Milner, H.C. Harpending, and K.M. Weiss
1992   The osteological paradox: problems of inferring prehistoric health from skeletal samples. *Current Anthropology* 33:343–370.

CREDITS

Figure 1-3:   courtesy of Dover Publications

Plate 1-1:   project photo byJean-Pierre Courau—courtesy of Mayfield Publishing Co.

Figure 1-4:   courtesy of the *Journal of Archaeological Research*

Figures 3-1
and 3-2:   courtesy of the *Journal of Archaeological Research*

Figure 3-3:   courtesy Mayfield Publishing Co.

Figure 4-2:   reprinted with the permission of the Trustees of Boston University and the *Journal of Field Archaeology*

Figure 4-3:   drawing and reconstruction by Barbara Fash

Figure 4-4:   reconstruction by Hasso Hohmann from original drawings by Barbara Fash, courtesy of Hasso Hohmann

Figure 4-5:   courtesy of Hasso Hohmann

Figure 4-6:   original drawing by Barbara Fash, modified by David Webster

Figure 4-7:   drawing by Barbara Fash—reprinted with the permission of the Trustees of Boston University and the *Journal of Field Archaeology*

Figure 6-1:   modified from Freter 1996, p. 212, Figure 2

Figure 6-2:   modified from Freter, 1996, p. 224, Figure 7

Figure 6-3:   from Abrams and Freter 1996, p. 426, Figure 4—courtesy of *Antiquity*

Figure 7-2:   courtesy of *Ancient Mesoamerica*

Figure 7-4:   courtesy of *Ancient Mesoamerica*

Figure 7-5:   drawing by Timothy Murtha

Figure 8a,b: David Rue

Plate 9-1:   photo by Randolph Widmer

Figure 9-1:   drawing and caption courtesy of David Reed

Figure 10-2:   Timothy Murtha

Figure 10-3:   Timothy Murtha

Figure 11-2:   Timothy Murtha

Figure 11-3:   modified from Freter, 1992, p. 126, Figure 3

Figure 11-4:   modified from Freter, 1992, p. 127, Figure 4

Figure 11-5:   modified from Freter, 1992, p. 129, Figure 6

Figure 11-5:   data courtesy of John Wingard

Figure 12-1:   courtesy of Elliot Abrams

Figure 14-1:   courtesy of Dover Publications

INDEX

Acbi phase, 25, 84, 85, 105, 109, 110, 124, 128, 132, 163
Acbi/Coner transition, 110, 112, 127, 132, 144, 151, 161
Accession dates, 26
Accelerator Mass Spectrometer. *See* AMS
Acropolis, 3, 6, 25, 27, 28, 30, 40, 45, 175, 176, 178, 193, 205
Adobe, 7, 11, 24, 25
Aerial photographs, 10, 62, 67, 69, 70
Age at death tables, 126, 127
Agrarian economy, 186–187
Aggregate sites, 69, 78, 81, 109
Agriculture, 12–19, 64–67, 131, 153–174
See also Swidden agriculture
Agricultural history, 153–174
Aguada Petapilla, 39, 115
Agua Dulce, 45
Aguateca, 209
Alluvium, 15, 169, 170, 171, 172, 205
Altar, 1, 5, 17, 22, 23, 27, 56, 178, 189
L, 200, 201
Q, 6, 7, 25, 28, 196
Altar de Sacrificios, 61
Ambrose thermal cells, 141
AMS, 110, 147–151
Ancestors, 51
Ancient diets. *See* Diet
Anemia, 127, 128
Animal bones, 82, 129, 131–132
Archaeobotanical remains, 130–131
See also Flora
Archaeological survey. *See* Survey
Archaeomagnetic dating, 53, 139, 144, 146
Art, 56
Artifacts, 50–51, 183, 185
See also Ceramics; Chert; Chipped stone; Grinding stones; Manos; Metates; Obsidian
Astronomy, 8, 53
Atomic absorption spectroscopy, 90
Ax-event, 27
Aztec, 58, 196

Bajareque, 101
See also Wattle and daub
Ball court, 1, 3, 25, 27, 189, 192
A, 30
B, 32
Basal platforms, 11, 100, 101

Basalt, 17
Basin of Mexico, 11, 24, 59
Bat, 24
Beans, 16, 65, 130–132, 135, 186
Becan, 61
Belize, 16, 18, 25, 61, 64, 117, 191, 198
Bench, 54–56, 101, 107–108, 178, 201–202
Bioanthropology, 123–135
See also Diet, Paleodemography, Paleopathology
Bishop of Yucatán. *See* Diego de Landa
Bolon-K'awil, 24
Bolsa, 14
See also Copán pocket, El Jaral pocket, Río Amarillo East pocket, Río Amarillo West pocket, Santa Rita pocket
Bonampak, 9
Bone chemistry, 11, 40, 131–134
See also Isotope studies
Bone collagen, 40
Bosque. *See* El Bosque
Burgh, Robert, 30
Burials, 3, 9, 22, 38, 50–51, 57, 79, 82, 94, 98, 105, 109, 123–135, 142, 148–150, 181, 183, 185, 187, 209
See also Skeletons; Tombs
Buried platforms, 83, 109, 112, 155
Butz' Chan, 26

Cacao, 16, 130–131, 188
Calakmul, 3, 190, 208
Caracol, 3, 25, 190
Carbon, 110
Carbon-14 dating. *See* Radiocarbon dating
Caries, 127
Carnegie Institution of Washington projects, 30, 200, 209
Carrying capacity, 205
Cartography, 32
Catherwood, Frederick, 5, 29, 66, 101, 113, 213
See also Stephens, John Lloyd
Cattle, 66
Cauac Sky, 27
Causeway, 7, 45
Cave sites, 30, 69
Carrizalito, 87
Celts, 82–83, 88, 107
Cementerios. *See* Los Cementerios
Cemetery, 51, 123